American English

Personal Best

Student's Book

B2
Upper Intermediate

Series Editor
Jim Scrivener

Author
Luiz Otávio Barros

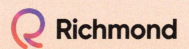

CONTENTS

		LANGUAGE			SKILLS	
		GRAMMAR	**PRONUNCIATION**	**VOCABULARY**		
1	**Your unique style**	■ present forms; *like, as if,* and *as though* ■ narrative tenses	■ *as* ■ stress in narrative tenses	■ body language and communication ■ compound adjectives ■ expectations	**LISTENING** ■ identifying attitude ■ consonant-consonant reduction	**WRITING** ■ making a narrative interesting ■ time linkers **PERSONAL BEST** ■ a blog post about an unexpected event
1A	Communication and you p4					
1B	The cool factor p6					
1C	Great expectations p8					
1D	My bad purchase! p10					
2	**Culture vultures**	■ question patterns ■ using linkers (1)	■ intonation in tag questions ■ sentence stress	■ adjective suffixes ■ phrasal verbs (1)	**READING** ■ skimming and scanning ■ clauses with *what*	**SPEAKING** ■ making recommendations ■ describing a movie **PERSONAL BEST** ■ recommending and deciding what to see
2A	But is it art? p12					
2B	Dear Juliet … p14					
2C	It's music to my ears! p16					
2D	It's definitely worth seeing p18					
1 and **2**	**REVIEW and PRACTICE** p20					
3	**A sense of place**	■ advice, expectation, and obligation ■ phrasal verbs	■ *supposed, ought,* and *allowed* ■ linking in phrasal verbs	■ urban places and problems ■ easily confused words	**LISTENING** ■ identifying advice ■ intonation in negative questions	**WRITING** ■ writing a persuasive article ■ contrasting expectations with reality **PERSONAL BEST** ■ a text persuading someone to move to a new city
3A	You're not supposed to do that here! p22					
3B	My special place p24					
3C	To go, or not to go p26					
3D	A fantastic place to live p28					
4	**Mind and behavior**	■ subject-verb agreement ■ perfect and past forms	■ *of* ■ sentence stress in perfect forms	■ personality and behavior ■ word families	**READING** ■ identifying attitude ■ conditionals for advice and suggestions	**SPEAKING** ■ responding to arguments ■ describing memorable experiences **PERSONAL BEST** ■ talking about a memorable experience
4A	It really annoys me … p30					
4B	How to get along p32					
4C	I see you've been busy! p34					
4D	Road rage p36					
3 and **4**	**REVIEW and PRACTICE** p38					
5	**Our planet**	■ *so* and *such; so much/many, so little/few* ■ future predictions	■ sentence stress with *so* and *such* ■ *will have*	■ the environment ■ moods ■ adjective prefixes	**LISTENING** ■ identifying cause and effect ■ linking consonants and vowels	**WRITING** ■ writing an opinion essay ■ formal linkers **PERSONAL BEST** ■ an essay using topic sentences and formal linkers
5A	Going green p40					
5B	Weather effects p42					
5C	In the year 2100 … p44					
5D	Let me persuade you … p46					
6	**Habits and change**	■ the habitual past ■ *be used to* and *get used to*	■ *use* and *used* ■ sentence stress with *be used to* and *get used to*	■ expressions with *time* ■ expressions with prepositions	**READING** ■ understanding non-literal meaning ■ contradicting	**SPEAKING** ■ challenging assumptions ■ solving problems **PERSONAL BEST** ■ solving a family problem
6A	My best decade p48					
6B	Healthy living: myths and facts p50					
6C	My generation and me p52					
6D	A suitable roommate p54					
5 and **6**	**REVIEW and PRACTICE** p56					

2   Language App with unit-by-unit grammar and vocabulary games

CONTENTS

		LANGUAGE			SKILLS	
		GRAMMAR	PRONUNCIATION	VOCABULARY		

7 Lifelong learning

- 7A Unique college programs p58
- 7B Successful learning p60
- 7C If I remember correctly … p62
- 7D It's never too late to learn! p64

GRAMMAR
- relative clauses; reduced and comment clauses
- present and future real conditions

PRONUNCIATION
- comment clauses
- sentence stress in conditional sentences

VOCABULARY
- collocations with *attend*, *get*, *make*, and *submit*
- ability
- mind and memory

LISTENING
- identifying sequence
- reduced forms

WRITING
- writing a set of guidelines
- linkers to add ideas

PERSONAL BEST
- a blog post on something you've learned or would like to learn

8 The changing media

- 8A TV in the 21st Century p66
- 8B Digital media for you p68
- 8C Binge-watching p70
- 8D Ads to drive you crazy p72

GRAMMAR
- using linkers (2)
- -ing forms and infinitives

PRONUNCIATION
- emphatic stress
- *to*

VOCABULARY
- the media
- expressions with *at*, *for*, *in*, and *on*

READING
- inferring meaning using related words
- generalizing

SPEAKING
- expressing annoyance and indifference
- clarifying and reacting

PERSONAL BEST
- talking about annoying things on TV

7 and 8 REVIEW and PRACTICE p74

9 The power of design

- 9A Steps to a better life p76
- 9B Good or bad design? p78
- 9C Extreme designs p80
- 9D Accessible spaces p82

GRAMMAR
- position of adverbs
- passives and causative *have*

PRONUNCIATION
- syllable stress with adverbs of degree
- stress in passive and causative *have* sentences

VOCABULARY
- collocations with *have* and *take*
- colors
- dimensions and weight

LISTENING
- understanding key points
- silent *h*

WRITING
- writing a magazine article
- articles *a*, *an*, *the*, and zero (–)

PERSONAL BEST
- an article about improving your city or neighborhood

10 The business world

- 10A Careers on the rise p84
- 10B Starting your own business p86
- 10C Job interview tips p88
- 10D Two job offers p90

GRAMMAR
- quantifiers
- comparison

PRONUNCIATION
- (a) few and (a) little
- sentence stress with *the … the* comparisons

VOCABULARY
- trends and business
- word pairs: *sooner or later*, *ups and downs*, *side by side*

READING
- understanding text development
- complex negative sentences

SPEAKING
- discussing pros and cons
- being supportive

PERSONAL BEST
- talking about things that upset you and offering support

9 and 10 REVIEW and PRACTICE p92

11 Fact and fiction

- 11A It can't have been real! p94
- 11B Fake news p96
- 11C The science of sleep p98
- 11D I first met Julia … p100

GRAMMAR
- present and past modals of deduction
- reported speech patterns

PRONUNCIATION
- reduction of past modals
- /t/ and /d/

VOCABULARY
- science
- opposite adjectives
- sleep

LISTENING
- identifying conclusions
- the "flap" in American English

WRITING
- writing a personal recommendation
- order of adjectives

PERSONAL BEST
- a recommendation using adjectives of opinion and fact

12 New discoveries

- 12A Must-have apps p102
- 12B A robot revolution? p104
- 12C Changes and regrets p106
- 12D Fads and trends p108

GRAMMAR
- present and future unreal conditions
- past unreal conditions

PRONUNCIATION
- consonant-vowel linking
- stress in conditional sentences

VOCABULARY
- phrasal verbs (2)
- collocations with *come*, *do*, *go*, and *make*

READING
- predicting
- adverbs and intended meaning

SPEAKING
- talking about future trends
- keeping a conversation going

PERSONAL BEST
- having an extended conversation about fads and trends

11 and 12 REVIEW and PRACTICE p110

Grammar practice p112   Vocabulary practice p136   Communication practice p158   Irregular verbs p175

Language App with unit-by-unit grammar and vocabulary games

3

UNIT 1

Your unique style

LANGUAGE present forms; *like*, *as if*, and *as though* ■ body language and communication

1A Communication and you

1 A Complete the quiz. Choose a, b, or c for each question.

What's your communication style?

1 If you try to hide something from someone, …
   a your voice changes.
   b you don't make eye contact.
   c your body language changes.

2 When you're angry, you tend to …
   a raise your voice.
   b imagine a response in your head.
   c physically show you're angry, e.g., slam the door.

3 If you want to get someone's attention, you …
   a say his/her name.
   b look at the person.
   c tap him/her on the shoulder.

B Discuss your answers in pairs. Did you choose mostly *a*, *b*, or *c* answers?

Go to Vocabulary practice: body language and communication, page 136

2 Check your answers to the quiz in exercise 1A. What type of communicator are you?

a answers: **audio communicators**	**b** answers: **visual communicators**	**c** answers: **kinesthetic communicators**
Audio communicators mainly interact with the world using their ears, and enjoy listening to people. They often notice small changes in people's voices, so they can tell immediately if someone sounds sad or worried. They often say things like, "I hear what you're saying," "How does that sound?," or "Sounds good!"	Visual communicators primarily interact with the world using their eyes. They understand ideas through images, and when they try to remember information, they feel as if a little movie is running in their heads. They often nod and say things like, "I see what you mean," "As I see it … ," or "It looks (like rain)." They can lose focus if other speakers talk too much.	Kinesthetic communicators interact with the world mostly using their body and intuition. They're attracted to people and situations that feel familiar. They like to learn by using their hands and moving as though they're acting in a play. They often need more words to communicate their message than visual and audio communicators. They say things like, "I know how you feel."

3 A Choose the correct options and check your answers in exercise 2. Which sentence refers to <u>right now</u>?
   1 Audio communicators *interact / are interacting* with the world using their ears.
   2 Visual communicators *understand / are understanding* ideas through images.
   3 When they try to remember information, they feel as if a little movie *runs / is running* in their heads.
   4 Kinesthetic communicators *need / are needing* more words to communicate their message.

B <u>Underline</u> *sound*, *look*, and *feel* in exercise 2. Complete the rules with *noun*, *adjective*, or *clause*. Then read the Grammar box.
   1 Use *sound/look/feel* + _____ .
   2 Use *sound/look/feel like* + _____ .
   3 Use *sound/look/feel as if/though* + _____ .

present forms; *like*, *as if*, and *as though* ■ body language and communication   **LANGUAGE 1A**

Grammar — present forms; *like*, *as if*, and *as though*

Simple present with action or state verbs:
The sun (always) **sets** in the west.
I **think** I **know** the answer.
It definitely **sounds**/**looks**/**feels** weird.

Present continuous with action verbs:
Look outside. The sun**'s setting** (right now).
I**'m thinking** of going to London
She**'s** always **criticizing** me!

Sense verbs with adjectives, nouns, and clauses:
It **looks** strange. (adjective)
It **sounds like** a nightmare! (noun)
It **feels as if** I've been here before. (clause)
It **sounds as though** you need help. (clause)

Look! We can also use *like* before a clause, but only in informal speech:
It looks **like** Mary's not coming to the party. (= informal conversation)
As though is a little more formal than **as if**:
It sounds **as if**/**as though** John's health is improving. (= neutral/formal speech and writing)

Go to Grammar practice: present forms; *like, as if,* and *as though,* page 112

4 A ▶1.3 **Pronunciation:** *as* Listen to the sentences. Notice how *as* is pronounced.
1 It sounds as if you're working really hard.
2 This coat looks as if it's never been cleaned!
3 It feels as though we've lived here for ages.
4 It looks as though he'll be late.

B ▶1.3 Listen again and repeat. Then practice saying the sentences in pairs.

5 A Fill in the blanks with the correct form of *sound*, *look*, or *feel*, adding *like*, *as if*, or *as though* where necessary. Then choose the correct verb forms.

👂 Six things a **good listener** might say

Good listeners are authentic in their desire to hear what the other person has to say. Before rushing to give advice, they often say things like:

1 You l_____ worried. What's on your mind? *Do you need / Are you needing* some help?
2 It s_____ you've had an exhausting day. *You work / You're working* too hard these days!
3 Wow! Your class s_____ a nightmare. *Do you want / Are you wanting* to talk about it?
4 You l_____ you could use a friend. *Does something bother / Is something bothering* you?
5 Hmm … You l_____ you're not sure what to do. *Do you think / Are you thinking* of dropping out of college?
6 Your boss s_____ awful! I mean, he *never listens / is never listening* to you.

B Choose two sentences in exercise 5A to start conversations. Your partner will give his/her own response.

Go to Communication practice: Both students, page 170

6 A Complete the sentences below about prompts 1–4 on the right.
1 I just received an e-mail telling me _____ .
2 Tomorrow's weather _____ .
3 Did you hear the news about _____ ?
4 You won't believe it, but Lucy _____ .

B Discuss the sentences in exercise 6A in pairs. Respond using sense verbs and ask follow-up questions.
A *I just received an e-mail telling me I won some money.*
B *It sounds like a trick to me. Are you planning to reply?*

1

2

3 **BREAKING NEWS:**
GOVERNOR RESIGNS

4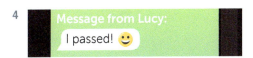

Personal Best   Think of a good communicator you know. List five things he/she does or says.   5

1 SKILLS LISTENING   identifying attitude ▪ consonant-consonant reduction ▪ compound adjectives

1B The cool factor

1 A Have you ever thought about what makes someone "cool"? Discuss the question in pairs.

B In pairs, discuss which words in the box you would use to describe the people in the pictures. In your opinion, are any of these people cool?

> open-minded   world-famous   good-looking   forward-thinking

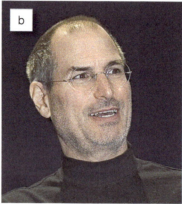

Go to Vocabulary practice: compound adjectives, page 137

Skill identifying attitude

You can often identify a speaker's attitude by listening to how certain or fixed his/her opinions are. Some clues include:
- words or expressions showing more or less certainty:
  Definitely not! I have no doubt that … , I tend to think … , In a way, I think …
- modal verbs or adverbs expressing probability:
  It might be … , This is probably the most important …
- tone of voice and style:
  A rising, louder tone may show the speaker feels strongly. A moderate tone and "filler" words like *uh, I mean* or *you know* may show uncertainty.

2 ▶ 1.5 Read the Skill box. Then watch or listen to the first part of a webshow called *Talking Zone*. What is Albany's attitude toward being cool? Choose the correct answer.
  a She tries very hard to be cool all the time.
  b She sometimes tries to be cool.
  c She never thinks about being cool and doesn't try.

identifying attitude ■ consonant-consonant reduction ■ compound adjectives   **LISTENING**   **SKILLS**   **1B**

3 A ▶ 1.5   Watch or listen again. Check (✓) the things the speakers say about being cool.

1 Cool people are just people who act very naturally. ☐
2 It's easy to act cool. ☐
3 It's important to care about being cool. ☐
4 You should tell people when you think they're cool. ☐
5 You can't plan to be cool since the definition keeps changing. ☐

Cathy

Tom

Sara

B What do you remember from the video so far? Use the Skill box to help you. Complete the blanks.

1 _____, I think cool is just being yourself.
2 _____, most people care about that kind of thing.
3 I have _____ that you're the ones who really deserve the award.
4 I _____ think it's because I'm 'warm'.

4 Discuss the questions in pairs.

1 Which statements in exercise 3A do you agree with?
2 Has your own definition of "cool" changed since high school? In what way?

5 Look at the pictures. Tell your partner which one best matches your personal definition of "cool."

a

b

c

6 ▶ 1.6   Watch or listen to the second part of the show. What is Albany's most important advice?

7 ▶ 1.6   Watch or listen again. Are the sentences true (T) or false (F)?

1 Albany isn't surprised that she has two million viewers. _____
2 She acts as if she knows her viewers and talks directly to them. _____
3 Albany only promotes products she identifies with. _____
4 Albany thinks you can succeed quickly. _____

Listening builder   consonant-consonant reduction

In fast speech, similar sounds can merge between words so that you only hear one sound. This can sometimes make the words harder to understand.
Same sound: *Do you expec**t t**o be home early?*
Different sounds: *Not in my wildes**t d**reams!*

8 A ▶ 1.7   Read the Listening builder. Then listen to the sentences from the video. Cross out the sounds you don't hear in the underlined words.

1 She's <u>been nominated</u> for a "Cool Tube" award.
2 Did you <u>expect to</u> be so successful?
3 I <u>just create</u> videos about my everyday life.
4 I <u>hoped that</u> my friends and coworkers would watch them.
5 It <u>might be</u> that my videos are natural and unrehearsed.
6 Sounds like a dream job and leads me to my <u>next question</u>.

B ▶ 1.7   Listen again and repeat each sentence.

9 In pairs, discuss these questions.

1 Do you follow any YouTubers? What do they talk about?
2 Would you ever start your own channel? What would it be about?

Personal Best   Describe someone you think is cool and explain why.

7

1 LANGUAGE   narrative tenses ■ expectations

1C Great expectations

1 A Match the two parts to make complete sentences.

1 If you don't succeed at first,
2 You never get a second chance
3 If you want to avoid disappointment,
4 It is impossible to live without

a lower your expectations.
b failing at something.
c try again until you do.
d to make a good first impression.

B In pairs, discuss whether or not you agree with the statements, and give a reason.

Go to Vocabulary practice: expectations, page 137

2 A Read the comments on a forum about people's disappointing experiences. Who feels more negative about his/her experience?

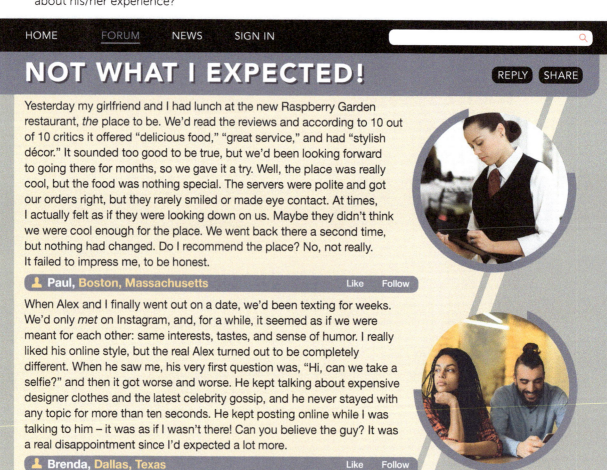

HOME   FORUM   NEWS   SIGN IN

NOT WHAT I EXPECTED!   REPLY SHARE

Yesterday my girlfriend and I had lunch at the new Raspberry Garden restaurant, *the* place to be. We'd read the reviews and according to 10 out of 10 critics it offered "delicious food," "great service," and had "stylish décor." It sounded too good to be true, but we'd been looking forward to going there for months, so we gave it a try. Well, the place was really cool, but the food was nothing special. The servers were polite and got our orders right, but they rarely smiled or made eye contact. At times, I actually felt as if they were looking down on us. Maybe they didn't think we were cool enough for the place. We went back there a second time, but nothing had changed. Do I recommend the place? No, not really. It failed to impress me, to be honest.

👤 **Paul,** Boston, Massachusetts   Like   Follow

When Alex and I finally went out on a date, we'd been texting for weeks. We'd only *met* on Instagram, and, for a while, it seemed as if we were meant for each other: same interests, tastes, and sense of humor. I really liked his online style, but the real Alex turned out to be completely different. When he saw me, his very first question was, "Hi, can we take a selfie?" and then it got worse and worse. He kept talking about expensive designer clothes and the latest celebrity gossip, and he never stayed with any topic for more than ten seconds. He kept posting online while I was talking to him – it was as if I wasn't there! Can you believe the guy? It was a real disappointment since I'd expected a lot more.

👤 **Brenda,** Dallas, Texas   Like   Follow

B Read the text again. Order the events for each story.

Story 1:
a ☐ Paul and his girlfriend went to the restaurant.
b ☐ They ate at the restaurant for a second time.
c ☐ They read the restaurant reviews.

Story 2:
a ☐ They met face to face.
b ☐ Brenda and Alex spent weeks texting each other.
c ☐ Brenda was surprised by Alex's behavior.

3 Choose the correct options to complete the sentences. Check your answers in the text in exercise 2A.

1 We *looked / 'd been looking* forward to going there for months, so we gave it a try.
2 At times, I actually felt as if they *were looking / had looked* down on us.
3 We went back there a second time, but nothing *had changed / had been changing*.
4 When Alex and I finally went out on a date, we *texted / 'd been texting* for weeks.
5 He kept posting online while I *was talking / had talked* to him.

narrative tenses ■ expectations   LANGUAGE   1C

4   In pairs, match sentences 1–5 in exercise 3 with timelines a–c below. What are the tenses in a–c called? Then read the Grammar box.

a A **was in progress at the same time as** B.
b A **happened before** B.
c A **was in progress before** B.

   **Grammar**   narrative tenses

Simple past:
I **parked** the car and **walked** into the restaurant.
I **wrote** to her every day for several months.
We **didn't enjoy** our vacation much.

Past continuous:
The phone rang while I **was taking** a shower.
She spent ages talking to her friend while we **were waiting** for our food.

Past perfect:
The place we went to looked familiar. It felt as if I**'d been** there before.
When I arrived, they **had** already **started**.

Past perfect continuous:
I was tired because I**'d been working** hard.
It **had been snowing** for days.

Look! The past continuous and past perfect continuous usually aren't used with state verbs:
I**'d had** my car for five years when I sold it. NOT ~~I'd been having~~

Go to Grammar practice: narrative tenses, page 113

5   ▶ 1.11   **Pronunciation:** stress in narrative tenses Listen to the sentences. Circle the stressed word in each underlined phrase.
   1 I was feeling a bit nervous before the interview.
   2 I had never done anything like skiing before.
   3 I'd been saving money for a trip for months.
   4 I fell when I was walking home from work.
   5 It felt as if we'd known each other for a long time.

6   Read the second part of Brenda's story and complete the sentences with the correct tense of the verbs in parentheses. Have you ever changed your mind about someone you met online?

At the end of our disastrous date, I ¹_____ (not think) Alex and I would ever see each other again. I mean, clearly we didn't really know each other at all, although we ²_____ (spend) months texting each other. But he called me and said he ³_____ (think) a lot about me since that day and wanted to see me again, so I decided to give him a second chance. As it turns out, we ⁴_____ (have) much better chemistry when we met again. We ⁵_____ (talk) about lots of different things, and, surprisingly, he was a lot more interesting than he ⁶_____ (seem) on our first date. Lesson learned: everyone deserves a second chance.

Go to Communication practice: Student A page 158, Student B page 164

7   Tell your partner about a person, place, or event that surprised you. Use the prompts to help you, and different narrative tenses.

   What was the situation?   Had you been looking forward to it?   What happened?
   Had you ever had a similar experience before?   Did the person/place/event turn out to be better/worse than you thought?   What did you learn from the experience?

tive tenses, write a paragraph about something funny or embarrassing that happened to you.

9

1 SKILLS WRITING making a narrative interesting ■ time linkers

1D My bad purchase!

1 In pairs, talk about a bad purchase you made, for example, an item of clothing, a piece of furniture, or a gadget. Think about something:
1 you bought, but couldn't really afford.
2 you thought was cool, but didn't really need.
3 you paid a lot of money for and quickly got tired of.

2 Read the blog post about Donald and his dog, Buster. In what ways was Buster a good purchase and a bad purchase? What do you think happened next?

| Home | About | Blog | Contact |

What was I thinking?

Posted 3.45pm

1 I still remember my 30th birthday. It seems like only yesterday. I'd been invited to my sister's place for lunch, and I was walking by a pet shop, when I saw the cutest little dog watching me from the window. **In the beginning**, I wasn't sure as I was very busy at work. Then I looked at him and started to wonder if a pet might fit my lifestyle. After all, I often take a walk in the park after work. As soon as he saw me, he gave me a look that seemed to say, "Please take me home!" We should never have made eye contact.

2 After lunch, I walked back to the pet shop, and, **before long**, that little dog, which felt like a tiny black and white teddy bear, was in my arms. "He's affectionate and full of energy," the salesclerk assured me. I'd been thinking of giving myself a birthday gift for weeks, so one hour later, I was on my way home with a smile on my face, a six-month-old puppy, and a hole in my bank account. I had no idea what the next few months would be like.

3 For a while, it felt as if Buster – I named him after a cartoon character that I love – made my life complete. It was nice to come home to a friendly face after a long, stressful day and have some company. I didn't mind the torn sofa or the missing remote controls. [1]My apartment looked like a disaster area, but I kept telling myself, [2]"Don't worry! That's what puppies do." I hoped Buster would start to behave, and [3]I would soon find out if my hope was realistic.

4 Unfortunately, Buster seemed to get worse with every passing day. He ran around the apartment, jumping on and off the furniture, like a mad frog, and barking for no reason. I'd never seen anything like it! **As time went on**, Buster developed other strange habits, such as moving food from his bowl to the floor before eating it, or pulling off my socks and hiding them – every single day. I failed at every attempt to train him. **Eventually**, I told myself, "Enough is enough!" I knew what I had to do.

5 In despair, I Skyped my brother, Barry. He lives on a small farm with his wife, kids, and two dogs, so I asked him how he'd feel about having a third one. He finally agreed, and **in a matter of hours**, Buster was gone. I still miss him, but it looks as if he's adapted well to his new home. As for me, I swear I'll never buy another pet again. Well, maybe a goldfish.

Donald F. Brattleboro, Vermont

 Share   Like   Comment

making a narrative interesting ▪ _time linkers_ **WRITING** | **SKILLS** | **1D**

3 Read the story again. In which paragraph (1–5) does Donald:

a talk about the "honeymoon" phase? ____

b give the background to the story? ____

c solve the problem? ____

d realize that he'd made a mistake? ____

e talk about buying the dog? ____

4 Read the blog post again. Find examples of simple past, past continuous, past perfect, and past perfect continuous verbs.

> **🔧 Skill** | **making a narrative interesting**
>
> **When writing a narrative, make your story more interesting by including:**
> - predictions or comments about the future: _I had no idea what the next few months would be like._
> - interesting comparisons: _... that little dog, which felt like a tiny black and white teddy bear ..._
> - examples of direct speech: _"He's affectionate and full of energy," the salesclerk assured me._
> - a variety of narrative tenses, e.g., simple past, past continuous, past perfect, past perfect continuous.

5 A Read the Skill box. Match strategies 1–3 below with their purpose a–c. Which strategy is each <u>underlined</u> sentence in paragraph 3?

1 provide a comparison

2 make a prediction

3 use direct speech

a to give someone a "voice"

b to help the reader visualize your descriptions

c to create suspense for the next paragraph

B Find one more example of a comparison and one of direct speech in paragraph 4.

> **✦⬌✦ Text builder** | **time linkers**
>
> **We use time linkers like _at first_, _in no time_, and _after a while_ to say how much time has passed between different past actions:**
>
> **1 at the start**
> _At first_, Donald wasn't sure he should buy a dog.
>
> **2 after a short time**
> _He held Buster in his arms and, in no time, changed his mind._
>
> **3 some time later**
> _After a while_, Donald regretted his decision.

6 Read the Text builder. Which meaning (1, 2, or 3) do the **bold** linkers in the blog post have?

7 Read Donald's brother's message to a friend a few weeks later. Choose the correct time linkers.

> Last month, my brother Donald asked me if I could adopt his dog. I said yes, and ¹_before long / in the beginning_, he brought the dog over. ²_At first / After a while_, we were happy to welcome him, but ³_in the beginning / in no time_, Buster showed his true colors. He spent most of the day bullying the other dogs and destroying our living room, which Donald hadn't warned us about! ⁴_As time went on / At the start_, though, the dogs became best friends. Are we going to keep him? Yes! We've grown fond of him, I guess.

8 A PREPARE Choose an experience below that didn't turn out as you had expected. Make notes about the main events.

(something you bought) (a blind date) (a new restaurant) (a party) (a vacation)

B PRACTICE Write a blog post, using your notes to help you. Include different narrative tenses and time linkers. Use comparisons, predictions, and direct speech to make your story more interesting.

C PERSONAL BEST Exchange your blog post with your partner. Do your stories have anything in common?

Personal Best Write a one-paragraph summary of your partner's story in exercise 8. Give it a different ending.

UNIT 2 Culture vultures

LANGUAGE — question patterns ■ adjective suffixes

2A But is it art?

1 Discuss the questions in pairs.
   1 What pictures or posters do you have on your walls at home?
   2 Describe the pieces of art below. What do you think of them? Which is your favorite?

2 Read the text. In pairs, share one interesting fact you learned about each piece of art.

Raccoon (2015) by Artur Bordalo (Bordalo II)

Bordalo's *Trash Animals* series gives a whole new meaning to the word "garbage." Old tires, useless appliances, and discarded items combine to create larger-than-life colorful 3D murals like *Raccoon*. Born in Lisbon in 1987, Bordalo is helping the city's recycling effort and increasing social awareness. He is an environmentally conscious young artist.

The Kiss (1908) by Gustav Klimt

Austrian painter Klimt rebelled against the traditional art of the time, and while his subject matter was controversial, his works created considerable excitement in the art world. *The Kiss*, one of Klimt's most famous and memorable paintings, is known for its highly decorative style. In his "golden phase," Klimt used the effective technique of gold leafing (applying very thin sheets of gold) to make his paintings shine.

Fearless Girl (2017) by Kristen Visbal

Visbal's *Fearless Girl* strikes a confident pose in downtown New York. Placed in front of *Charging Bull* (sculpted by Arturo Di Modica), the girl seems to challenge the powerful bull, even though this was not Visbal's intention. Di Modica feels the new sculpture detracts from the bull as a symbol of prosperity and strength, instead making it look aggressive.

3 Look at the highlighted words in the text. What do they have in common? How are they different?

Go to Vocabulary practice: adjective suffixes, page 138

4 Find six more adjectives in the text with the suffixes *-al*, *-able*, *-ful*, *-ive*, *-less*, and *-ous*.

5 A ▶ 2.2 Listen to three conversations. Which piece of art in exercise 2 is each conversation about?
Conversation 1 _____   Conversation 2 _____   Conversation 3 _____

B ▶ 2.3 Choose the correct option to complete 1–6 below. Then listen and check.
1 You don't really like this painting, *do you / don't you*?
2 Do you know what *is the title / the title is*?
3 What a contrast! This is a bit surprising, *doesn't it / isn't it*?
4 *Isn't / Is not* the bull a symbol of strength?
5 Who *painted / did he paint* it?
6 Excuse me, could you tell me if a local artist *made / did make* this?

question patterns ▪ adjective suffixes **LANGUAGE** **2A**

6 Look at 1–6 in exercise 5B again and answer the questions below. Then read the Grammar box.

Which ones:

a ask about the subject of a sentence? _____

b include a tag question? _____ _____

c are negative questions? _____

d ask a question indirectly? _____ _____

📖 **Grammar** question patterns

wh- subject and object questions:
*Who **gave you** this present?*
*Who **did you give** the book to?*

Negative questions:
***Doesn't** the bus **come** every 20 minutes?*
*Why **didn't** you **call** me?*

Tag questions:
*You haven't heard from James, **have you**?*
*Ann wants to go out tonight, **doesn't she**?*

Indirect questions:
*Do you have any idea **where Tom is**?*
*Could you tell me **if the museum is** open today?*

Look! When forming questions, check the correct use (or not) of auxiliary verbs:
*Could you tell me **where the bus stops**?* NOT ~~where does the bus stop?~~
*You live upstairs, **don't you**?*

Go to Grammar practice: question patterns, page 114

7 A ▶2.5 **Pronunciation:** intonation in tag questions Listen to the questions. Does the intonation go up (↗) or down (↘) at the end of the questions?

1 The weather's awful today, isn't it?

2 This silk shirt's washable, isn't it?

3 These cheap umbrellas don't last long, do they?

4 John didn't call, did he?

B ▶2.5 Match the sentences in exercise 7A with functions a–b below. Listen again and repeat.

a real question _____ _____

b comment or conversation opener _____ _____

8 A ▶2.6 Complete the conversations with appropriate question forms. Use the verbs in parentheses. Then listen and check.

1 **A** **Street art**'s so cool, _____ it? (be) What kind of **art** _____ you _____ ? (like)

B I prefer more conventional art, actually.

2 **A** Do you have any idea what time **the movie** _____ tonight? (start)

B I think at eight. Why? Are you thinking of going?

3 **A** Your **leg's bleeding**! What _____ ? (happen)

B I fell while I was crossing the street. It's OK. It's not painful.

4 **A** _____ we _____ before? (not met) _____ you at **Meg's party** last month? (not be)

B No, but maybe my twin sister was there.

5 **A** You really _____ **dancing**, _____ you? (not enjoy)

B No, I don't. You're right. I look ridiculous on the dance floor.

B In pairs, practice the conversations. Then ask your partner new questions, changing the parts in **bold**. Your partner will give an appropriate answer.

Go to Communication practice: Student A page 158, Student B page 164

9 Ask which of these activities your partner enjoys. Then ask follow-up questions to comment on or ask about three of the activities, using the different question patterns.

| photography | going to the movies | reading novels | going to concerts | going to exhibits |

A *Do you like photography?*

B *Yeah, I love taking pictures of people on my cell phone.*

A *That's great, but shouldn't you be a little cautious? I mean, you need to ask permission, don't you?*

Personal Best Think of a painting, sculpture, or mural you've seen. Write six questions about it.

13

2 SKILLS

READING skimming and scanning ■ clauses with *what*

2B Dear Juliet …

1 What do you know about the story of *Romeo and Juliet?* Compare your answers in pairs.

2 Read the first paragraph of the article on page 15. Check (✔) the information you think the rest of the text will contain.

1 the story of *Romeo and Juliet* ☐
2 the history of the Juliet Club ☐
3 the history of Verona ☐
4 the life of Shakespeare ☐
5 who writes letters to Juliet ☐
6 who replies to the letters ☐

> **Skill** skimming and scanning
>
> **Skimming and scanning are reading techniques that help us find and understand information in a text quickly.**
> - Skimming gives us a general understanding of the main ideas in the text. Read the introduction and first sentence of each paragraph carefully, and then move your eyes quickly over the rest of the text, skimming it to find key words and ideas.
> - Scanning helps us find and understand specific information. Move your eyes quickly over the text, looking for key words or synonyms that correspond to the specific information that you are looking for. Read that part in detail to see if it contains the information. If not, continue scanning.

3 Read the Skill box. Then skim the article and check your answers to exercise 2.

4 Scan the article to answer the questions.

1 When was the first letter to Juliet received?
2 Who was the first person to reply to the letters?
3 When did the Juliet Club start replying to the letters?
4 Why was the Juliet Club created?
5 How many letters are received nowadays?
6 What is the nationality and age group of the people who write to Juliet most?
7 Are the messages to Juliet only written in English?
8 Do letter writers often use the Internet to write to Juliet?
9 How much are the people who reply to the letters paid?
10 Why do Giovanni Carabetta and Elena Marchi work for the Juliet Club?

5 Read the underlined sentences 1–4 in the article. What does the word *what* mean in each sentence?

> **Text builder** clauses with *what*
>
> **Clauses with *what* can be about the subject or the object of the sentence. *What* can refer to singular or plural things. Subject clauses with *what* are often at the start of a sentence. The verb is singular, not plural:**
> ***What people say* <u>is</u> *very important.* (= the things people say)
> ***What they do* <u>is</u> *even more important, though.* (= the things they do)
>
> **Object clauses with *what* are often at the end of a sentence:**
> *I just finished reading **what you wrote.*** (= the thing/things you wrote)
> *I like **what you wrote in the last sentence.*** (= the thing/things you wrote in the last sentence)

6 Read the Text builder. Look at sentences 1–4 in the article again. In which sentences is the clause with *what* the subject?

7 What does the word *what* refer to in the sentences below?

1 What I don't understand is why someone would write to a fictional character.
2 I don't think I'd enjoy reading what people write to Juliet. It's too personal!

8 Would you like to be a secretary for the Juliet Club? Why/Why not?

14

skimming and scanning ■ clauses with *what* **READING** **SKILLS** **2B**

Lovesick? Broken heart?
Write to Juliet

If you know the famous story of *Romeo and Juliet*, written by Shakespeare in the 16th century, you'll know that their home city is Verona, Italy. Verona is now also the home of the *Club di Giulietta* (the Juliet Club), a remarkable association that receives letters from all over the world addressed to Shakespeare's heroine. The writers, often in love, write to Juliet to seek advice or to unburden themselves. [1]And a group of committed volunteers, known as Juliet's secretaries, read what they write and reply to every single letter that arrives.

Probably as the result of George Cukor's 1936 film version of Shakespeare's tragedy, the first letter, addressed simply to "Juliet, Verona," arrived in the 1930s. The letter found its way to "Juliet's tomb," in a monastery just outside the city walls. The attendant there, a veteran who had picked up some English in the First World War, decided to reply. And he carried on replying as more letters arrived. After the Second World War, a local poet secretly took on the role of Juliet's secretary, but gave it up, apparently in embarrassment, when his identity became known. Finally, in the 1980s, the mayor of Verona decided to give the task to the *Club di Giulietta*, a group formed to promote initiatives linking their city to the famous play.

Sitting around a table strewn with handwritten letters, three of Juliet's "secretaries," Giovanna Tamassia, Elena Marchi, and Gioia Ambrosi, tell stories that are by turns touching and weird, thought-provoking, and heart-rending. "It's a great responsibility," says Tamassia, whose father Giulio is the club's president and a founder member. Ambrosi, a 25-year-old student, describes the correspondence as "a blog on humanity." "We get more than 5,000 letters a year," says Tamassia. "And then there are the thousands of notes that get left behind at Juliet's house and tomb."

She reckons about three-quarters of the messages are from women, and that the biggest single group is made up of American teenagers. On the wall of the arch leading to Juliet's house in the medieval centre of Verona, though, there are notes in every conceivable language. Some of the letters and professions of undying love are genuinely poetic: "For hope and love; for the one I loved most, my heart"; others less so: "I've got a stomach ache in the heart." When letters are serious, the secretaries can call on the services of a psychologist, and sometimes they need them.

Juliet's house also has a post box where letters can be left and four computer work stations where visitors may tap out a message to her. But surprisingly, perhaps, emails account for fewer than 10% of the messages that end up in her secretaries' offices. Of the letters, the vast majority are handwritten in pen and ink. And that is how they are always replied to. "[2]What people often write is: 'You are the only one who can understand me'," says Giovanni Carabetta, the club's archivist. Perhaps the most extraordinary aspect of this whole endeavor is that the secretaries do it for free. "Well, the council gives us the money for the stamps," explains Giulio Tamassia. "But it's not even enough to cover the postage. Right now, I'm having a battle with the council. [3]What we do brings all sorts of advantages for Verona, and I think it is time they stopped treating us like this. We're all working for nothing." Carabetta smiles. "Not for nothing, Giulio … for the pleasure of reading these wonderful letters."

And perhaps, in some cases, for other, more personal reasons. "It has helped me to believe again in feelings," says Marchi. "[4]But what counts is to have a heart that is alive, no? To be in touch with your feelings, however things go. It's not as if there is a guarantee as to the future." A sentiment with which the real – or rather, fictional – Juliet would have fervently agreed.

Adapted from theguardian.com

Personal Best Write a paragraph to Juliet with an imagined problem.

2 LANGUAGE using linkers (1) ■ phrasal verbs (1)

2C It's music to my ears!

1 A Read the questions. In pairs, explain the meaning of the phrasal verbs in **bold**.
1 Who's your favorite musician? Are there any musicians you really **look up to**?
2 Have you **come across** any new groups or albums lately that you really like?
3 Would you be able to **do without** music? How would you feel without it?
4 Have you ever tried to get tickets for a concert that had **sold out**? What was it?

B Discuss the questions with your partner.

Go to Vocabulary practice: phrasal verbs (1), page 139

2 A Read the text about Taylor Swift and Ed Sheeran. Complete the phrasal verbs 1–5.

The secret of success

Taylor Swift and Ed Sheeran have a very special friendship and often sing together. They may come from very different backgrounds, but both have had a similar path to success.

Swift, who grew up on a family farm in Pennsylvania, had two passions: writing and music. In spite of the fact that her writing talent was noticed very early (she won a national poetry contest and even wrote an unpublished novel), Swift really wanted to be a singer. How did she achieve her goal to become the Taylor Swift we know today?

To put it simply, Swift had determination. In 2004, she ¹**talked** her family _____ moving to Nashville so she could be part of the country music scene. (Despite having a grandmother who was a well-known opera singer, Swift preferred country music.) She wrote and performed non-stop and, before long, her concerts started to ²**sell** _____ the minute tickets went on sale. Those who know her say her secret is an ability to visualize her lyrics before she writes a song. Maybe all that writing as a child ³**paid** _____ in the end!

Superficially, Ed Sheeran could not have been more different. He was a shy child who stuttered when he spoke, so he would repeat the lyrics of an old Eminem album hundreds of times. In spite of his shyness, Sheeran moved to London at 16 in order to become a professional musician. In the beginning, it was hard to ⁴**figure** _____ how to make a living, and even though he was playing over 300 live shows a year, he often had to sleep on the Underground, the London subway system. Sheeran never ⁵**gave** _____ , though, and he released his first album in 2011. Two years later, everything changed when he went on a world tour supporting Taylor Swift. So what was his secret? According to Sheeran, he played music instead of video games when he was growing up.

Incredible tales like Swift's or Sheeran's are an inspiration to us all!

B Read the text again. What do the two success stories have in common?

3 A Match the two parts to make sentences from the text.
1 **In spite of** the fact that her writing talent was noticed very early,
2 She talked her family into moving to Nashville **so**
3 **Despite** having a grandmother who was a well-known opera singer,
4 **In spite of** his shyness,
5 Sheeran moved to London at 16 **in order to**
6 **Even though** he was playing over 300 live shows a year,

a Sheeran moved to London at 16.
b she could be part of the country music scene.
c he often had to sleep on the Underground.
d Swift really wanted to be a singer.
e become a professional musician.
f Swift preferred country music.

16

using linkers (1)   ■   phrasal verbs (1)   **LANGUAGE 2C**

B Look at the sentences in exercise 3A again and answer the questions. Then read the Grammar box.
1. Which of the linking words in **bold** express contrast and which express purpose?
2. Which one means the same as *although*?
3. Which one can be replaced by *to*?
4. Which three grammatical forms can follow *despite* and *in spite of*?

Grammar using linkers (1)

Expressing contrast:
Despite taking lessons/all the lessons, I still can't play the guitar.
In spite of the fact that I've taken lessons, I still can't play the guitar.
Even though/Although I listen to a lot of jazz, I prefer rock music.
I listen to a lot of jazz. *However*, I prefer rock music.

Expressing purpose:
I listen to music *In order to* feel more relaxed.
I listen to music *to* feel more relaxed.
I upgraded my phone *so* (*that*) I could stream music.

Look! We can also end a sentence with *though*:
I listen to a lot of jazz. I prefer rock music, *though*.

Go to Grammar practice: using linkers (1), page 115

4 A ▶ 2.10 **Pronunciation:** sentence stress Listen to the sentences. Circle the stressed words in the underlined phrases.
1. I haven't eaten <u>in spite of the fact that I'm hungry</u>.
2. My best friend came in the end <u>despite not feeling well</u>.
3. <u>Despite having had a bad day</u>, I had a great evening.
4. I called my parents <u>so that they wouldn't worry</u>.
5. We left in a rush <u>in order not to be late</u>.
6. It ended up being a great day <u>in spite of the weather</u>.

B ▶ 2.10 Listen again and repeat.

5 A Rewrite the sentences so they have the same meaning, using the words in parentheses.
1. I love rock, pop, and dance music, but I never listen to classical music. (however)
2. I'd travel for a whole day so I could see my favorite singer perform live. (in order to)
3. Despite being a good dancer, I never go to clubs. (although)
4. I wear headphones to listen to music on the subway. (so)
5. I don't have any CDs any longer. However, I still have some records. (though)
6. I love foreign music, but I can't understand the lyrics. (even though)
7. In spite of having bought tickets to the concert, I didn't go in the end. (the fact that)
8. Even though I don't have a good voice, singing makes me happy. (despite not)

B Are the sentences true for you? If not, change them so that they are true.

Go to Communication practice: Both students, page 170

6 Which different kinds of music do you prefer in the following situations? Why? Tell your partner.

- on a road trip with friends
- jogging in the park
- studying
- cleaning the house
- getting ready to go out
- commuting to work/college
- relaxing at home
- dancing at a party

Personal Best Write two advantages and two disadvantages of streaming music online.

17

2 SKILLS SPEAKING making recommendations ■ describing a movie

2D It's definitely worth seeing

1 A Look at the posters. Which movie looks the most interesting?

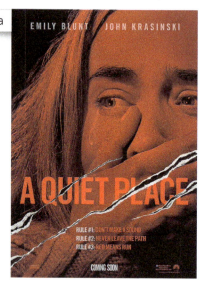
a

b

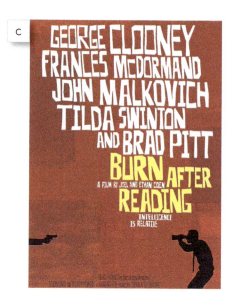
c

B In pairs, discuss which movie to see. Use some of the adjectives in the box.

cheerful   controversial   conventional   harmless   impressive   memorable   painless   powerful

A *What do you think this one's about?*
B *Let's see. I think …*

2 A ▶ 2.11 Watch or listen to the first part of *Talking Zone*. Fill in Ben and Abigail's missing words.

1	**Ben**	I'm not really big on _____ movies.
2	**Abigail**	Oh, if you like George Clooney, you're going to _____ it.
3	**Ben**	Good. I'm not in the mood for anything too _____ .
4	**Abigail**	It's both _____ and _____ at the same time. Oh and Brad Pitt is in it.
5	**Ben**	Look – here's one that's definitely worth _____ .
6	**Abigail**	I'm not really into _____ .
7	**Ben**	It's one of the _____ things I've seen in a long time.

B ▶ 2.11 Watch or listen again. Match sentences 1–7 in exercise 2A with the correct movies a–d. One sentence refers to two movies.

a *A Quiet Place* ____
b *Paranormal Activity* ____
c *Burn After Reading* ____ ____ ____
d *Mamma Mia! Here We Go Again* ____ ____ ____

Conversation builder — making recommendations

Making recommendations:
If you like comedies, you're going to love this one.
It's both entertaining and serious at the same time.
This documentary is definitely worth seeing.
It's one of the best things I've seen in a long time.

Responding to recommendations:
I'm not big on romances.
I'm (not) in the mood for a comedy.
I'm (not) crazy about/really into documentaries.
I (don't) feel like watching that movie today.

3 Read the Conversation builder. In pairs, recommend three movies you've seen recently. Choose sentences from the box to make recommendations and give responses.

making recommendations ■ describing a movie   **SPEAKING**   SKILLS **2D**

4 Make a list of four movies you'd like to see soon. In pairs, practice short dialogues, beginning with the recommendations in 1–4 below.
1 Let's see … . They say it's one of the … movies that's showing.
2 If you like … , you're going to love … . It's definitely worth seeing.
3 How about seeing … ? It's both … and … at the same time.
4 I'm in the mood for a … . The movie … is …

5 A Look at the poster and the pictures from the movie. Predict what *Brooklyn* will be about. When do you think the movie takes place?

B ▶ 2.12 Watch or listen to the second part of the show. Choose the correct answer. Abigail tells us that *Brooklyn* is about a young woman who leaves Ireland …
a and moves permanently to Brooklyn.
b and moves to Brooklyn, but returns to Ireland to live.
c and moves to Brooklyn, but we don't really know what happens after that.

Skill describing a movie

When we describe a movie, we need to give enough information for someone to decide whether he/she would like to see it.
• Say when the movie takes place: *It's set in …*
• Briefly describe the plot: *It tells the story of …*
• Mention the cast and scriptwriter: *… is in it, it was written by …*
• Give your overall impressions: *I think what I loved was …*

6 ▶ 2.12 Read the Skill box. Number the sentences in Abigail's description in the order you hear them. Then watch or listen again and check.
a ☐ But the whole cast is fantastic and the script is written by Nick Hornby.
b ☐ It got great reviews at the time, and was nominated for two or three Oscars.
c ☐ It's set in the 1950s.
d ☐ I don't want to spoil the ending, but I think what I loved was the message.
e ☐ I don't remember the actors' names, except for Saoirse Ronan, who plays the leading role.
f ☐ It tells the story of a young Irish woman who moves to New York, where she falls in love.

7 Cover exercise 6. Looking only at the Skill box, take turns recommending *Brooklyn* to your partner. Did you forget any important details?

8 Would you like to see *Brooklyn*? Why/Why not?

Go to Communication practice: Student A page 159, Student B page 165

9 A PREPARE Find a movie, concert, or show online that you'd really like to see or go to. Prepare a recommendation to convince your partner.

B PRACTICE Practice a conversation about the event. Were you able to decide whether to see or go to it together?

C PERSONAL BEST Choose a new activity and practice a similar conversation. Which time was your recommendation more convincing?

Personal Best Describe the last movie you saw. Give it 1–5 stars (1 = bad, 5 = great).

19

1 and 2 REVIEW and PRACTICE

Grammar

1 Cross (**X**) the sentence that is NOT correct.

1. a I know London quite well now.
   b I'm getting to know London quite well now.
   c I'm knowing London quite well now.
2. a I just went to bed when the phone rang.
   b I had just gone to bed when the phone rang.
   c I went to bed, and then the phone rang.
3. a Why did you laugh when she said her name?
   b Why you laughed when she said her name?
   c Why were you laughing when she said her name?
4. a Where can I get coffee?
   b Do you know where can I get coffee?
   c Do you know where I can get coffee?
5. a Even I've lived in Spain for a long time, I don't speak very good Spanish.
   b Despite living in Spain for a long time, I don't speak very good Spanish.
   c I've lived in Spain for a long time. I don't speak very good Spanish, though.
6. a I leave work early on Fridays so that I can pick up the kids from school.
   b I leave work early on Fridays to pick up the kids from school.
   c I leave work early on Fridays that I can pick up the kids from school.
7. a You've done this before, don't you?
   b Haven't you done this before?
   c You've done this before, haven't you?
8. a Hadn't you been pretty lonely before you met your boyfriend?
   b You'd been pretty lonely before you met your boyfriend, hadn't you?
   c You'd been being pretty lonely before you met your boyfriend, hadn't you?

2 Use the words in parentheses to complete the sentences so they mean the same as the first sentence.

1. I've saved a lot of money, but I still can't afford it.
   _____ a lot of money, I still can't afford it. (spite)
2. Although we only just met, I have the sensation that we've known each other for ages.
   Although we only just met, _____ we've known each other for ages. (feels)
3. What time does the post office close?
   _____ the post office closes? (could)
4. I go running every day so that I get in shape.
   I go running every day _____ get in shape. (order)
5. From what you are saying, I think you've had a good day.
   _____ you've had a good day. (sounds)
6. Is Buenos Aires the capital of Argentina?
   Buenos Aires _____ ? (isn't)

3 Choose the correct options to complete the interview.

Each week we talk to a graduate of our university ¹*in order to find / despite finding* out about his or her job and how he or she went from college into the world of work. This week we ²*spoke / had spoken* to Julia Gonzales, who graduated in 2016.

Hi Julia. Could you tell me what ³*your job title is / is your job title*?

I'm a junior fashion designer. I work for a company that ⁴*makes / is making* clothes for children.

And what ⁵*are you doing / do you do* on a typical day? It sounds ⁶*as / like* an interesting job.

It can be interesting. I travel a lot and I meet a lot of cool people. ⁷*Even though / However*, I ⁸*spend / spent* most of my day at my desk researching new ideas and reading and sending e-mails.

And how did you get your job? The fashion industry is very difficult to get into, ⁹*doesn't / isn't* it?

Yes, you're right. You have to work very hard to be successful in fashion. Most of my classmates from college didn't apply for jobs until after they ¹⁰*had graduated / were graduating*, but by then, I ¹¹*had been contacting / was contacting* companies for months. Luckily for me, ¹²*even though / despite* I didn't have much experience, one of those companies liked my designs and offered me a job.

Vocabulary

1 Circle the word or expression that is different. Explain why.

1. wink   nod   stare   gaze
2. open-minded   forward-thinking   well-educated   middle-aged
3. fail to impress   make a good impression   be a success   impress
4. shake hands   give someone a hug   kiss on the cheek   shrug your shoulders
5. accidental   cheerful   endless   breakable
6. dreadful   harmless   ridiculous   useless

20

REVIEW and PRACTICE 1 and 2

2 Match the words in the box with definitions 1–8.

> frown wave effective reasonable attractive
> far-reaching highly-respected record-breaking

1 have an influence on a lot of people or things _____
2 move your hand as a greeting _____
3 fair and sensible _____
4 admired by many people _____
5 beating the previous best performance _____
6 nice to look at _____
7 facial expression for disapproval _____
8 producing the intended or expected result _____

3 Complete the sentences with the words in the box.

> time-consuming raise your voice pay off impress
> get a second chance controversial turn down
> be a disappointment forward-thinking look up to

1 It's not because of the money that I want a good job. It's because I don't want to _____ to my parents.
2 As a teacher, you need to _____ sometimes or the children just won't listen!
3 I thought everyone would agree to my idea, but, actually, it seems to be quite _____ .
4 I spent two hours reorganizing my lecture notes yesterday. I know it's useful, but it's so _____ !
5 I'm really grateful to _____ because I thought my first interview went so badly!
6 It's important to have people in your life that you can _____ .
7 My girlfriend and I are very different. She's very _____ and is always planning ahead. I just think about today!
8 Christina spends a lot of money on her clothes because she likes to _____ people.
9 Don't _____ this job. It's perfect for you!
10 I know you're very tired, but I promise that all this exam preparation will _____ in the end!

4 Complete the story with the correct form of the words and expressions in the box.

> show up be a success memorable
> lower your expectations give shake hands
> ridiculous kiss make a good first impression

I had a job interview yesterday. I was desperate for it to [1]_____ . However, it started badly. I knew how important it was to [2]_____ , but I did something very silly as soon as I [3]_____ . Instead of [4]_____ like you should in a formal interview, I [5]_____ the interviewer a hug and [6]_____ her on the cheek! I felt [7]_____ ! Anyway, because the interview started badly, I [8]_____ , but by the end, it had gone quite well. And at least I was a [9]_____ candidate. Who could forget that introduction?

Personal Best

Lesson 1A
Name four things you do when greeting someone or saying good-bye.

Lesson 2A
Write four questions: a *wh-* question, a tag question, a negative question, and an indirect question.

Lesson 1A
Describe a situation using three different sense verbs.

Lesson 2A
Write four sentences that include an adjective with the suffix *-ous*, *-ful*, *-able*, or *-less*.

Lesson 1B
Describe someone you know using four different compound adjectives.

Lesson 2B
Write four sentences including a clause with *what* about things you believe very strongly.

Lesson 1C
Describe something that happened when you were a child. Use different narrative tenses.

Lesson 2C
Name four things you regularly do and explain why you do them.

Lesson 1C
Write two sentences describing a positive experience and two sentences about a negative one.

Lesson 2C
Describe three things that happened recently using phrasal verbs.

Lesson 1D
Describe a time you changed your mind about something using time linkers.

Lesson 2D
Recommend a movie, a book, and a TV program and explain why each one is good.

21

UNIT 3

A sense of place

LANGUAGE advice, expectation, and obligation ■ urban places and problems

3A You're not supposed to do that here!

1 Read the dictionary definition. Which customs, rules, or behavior might visitors to your city find different from their own?

> **"When in Rome, do as the Romans do."** (saying)
> When you are in a different country or unfamiliar situation, follow the customs, rules, and behavior of the people around you.

2 Read Ana and Piotr's stories about their trips to the U.S. Which local custom or rule didn't they know about? Are these the same or different where you are from?

Ana's story:

My boyfriend Raúl and I were on vacation in New York last year, and the first evening we were there, we went out for dinner at a nice restaurant, down by the harbor. The meal was delicious, and I wanted to leave a generous tip. I left a tip in cash – about 10%, which is more than I would leave at home in Madrid. But I was shocked when the waiter told me it wasn't enough. [1]He explained that in New York the tip ought to be 20%. He even told us that it was an important part of his salary! Raúl said quietly, "[2]You'd better give him 20% – [3]it's what you're supposed to do here." So I left the tip he wanted, and we left in a hurry. We really hadn't expected dinner to cost that much, and when we got to the taxi stand, we realized we didn't have any money left for a taxi back. It was all kind of embarrassing, but I learned a lesson about New York for my next trip.

Piotr's story:

I was on a business trip in the Washington D.C. area and was staying at a hotel in a fairly central business district. I arrived one rainy Monday morning. The sky was dark gray (I wondered if it was smog), and I was just about to cross the street to get to the hotel when a man in a suit said, "You can't cross here." I ignored him – it didn't seem dangerous. In fact, the traffic was moving slowly because of the congestion. But just as I stepped off the sidewalk he suddenly yelled, "Sir, stop! [4]You're not allowed to cross here." Imagine my surprise when he pulled out his police badge! I had no idea that the guy was a police officer, and I wasn't aware that in many U.S. cities [5]you have to cross the street at a crosswalk – jaywalking is forbidden. The officer gave me an $80 fine, which I was really annoyed about, as a colleague told me later that these rules are rarely enforced. Not a great start to my week!

3 Find words in the stories that match definitions 1–5.

1 a place to keep boats and ships   _____
2 a place where you can get a taxi   _____
3 a commercial area in a city   _____
4 a type of weather that affects cities _____
5 when roads are blocked by cars   _____

Go to Vocabulary practice: urban places and problems, page 140

advice, expectation, and obligation ■ urban places and problems

LANGUAGE **3A**

4 **A** Look at the underlined sentences 1–5 in the text on page 22. Which function does each sentence express? Write *A* (advice), *E* (expectation) or *O* (obligation).

1 ____   2 ____   3 ____   4 ____   5 ____

B Read the Grammar box and check.

📖 **Grammar** **advice, expectation, and obligation**

Advice:
You should/ought to take a pill for your headache.
I'd take a pill (if I were you).

Strong advice/warning:
You'd better buy your plane ticket right away.
You'd better not make noise!

Expectation:
You're supposed to leave the waiter a tip.

Personal obligation:
I should/ought to visit my grandparents this weekend.

External obligation/rules:
You can park over there.
You can't cross the street here.
You have to/must cross at the crosswalk.
You're allowed to vote at the age of 18.
You're not allowed to turn left here.

Look! We can use *prohibited* or *forbidden* to talk about rules in more formal or written English:
Driving while using your cell phone is strictly prohibited/forbidden.

Go to Grammar practice: advice, expectation, and obligation, page 116

5 **A** ▶3.3 **Pronunciation:** *supposed, ought,* and *allowed* Listen to three sentences from the text. Notice how the sounds in **bold** are pronounced.

1 You're not all**ow**ed to cross here.
2 In New York, the tip **ou**ght to be 20%.
3 It's what you're supp**o**sed to do here.

B ▶3.4 Listen and repeat the sentences.

1 You're **supposed** to take off your shoes.
2 I think you **ought** to apologize for being late.
3 You're not **allowed** to use your cell phone here.
4 You **ought** to get your mom some flowers.
5 I'm not **supposed** to study today. It's Saturday.
6 Are you **allowed** to drive so fast on this street?

6 **A** Complete the sentences with the modals or expressions in the box.

supposed   has   'd better   not allowed (x2)   have (x2)

In which countries might **someone say these things?**

1 You're _____ to buy chewing gum here. Selling or importing it is against the law.
2 You _____ to wear a bike helmet. The police will fine you for not wearing one.
3 At least 20% of music played on the radio _____ to be from this country. It's the law.
4 You _____ not give the waiter a tip. It can be considered bad manners.
5 By law, you _____ to have a license to watch TV.
6 I think we're _____ to get in line. Everyone else is lining up.
7 In this part of the country, the official language is French, so restaurants are _____ to have menus written only in English.

B ▶3.5 Guess the country for each sentence in exercise 6A. Listen and check.

Australia ____   Canada ____ ____   Japan ____   Singapore ____   the UK ____ ____

Go to Communication practice: Both students, page 171

7 How would you improve life in your city? What new customs or laws would you introduce? Discuss in pairs, and write a list of ten customs or laws that you decide together.

Personal Best Write ten real or imaginary rules or customs that the people living in your house should follow.

23

3 SKILLS LISTENING identifying advice ■ intonation in negative questions ■ easily confused words

3B My special place

1 A Choose the correct word. Then complete the questionnaire.

When I'm alone and I want to think …	Yes	No
1 I really *mind / matter* when the phone rings.	☐	☐
2 I *discuss / argue* with people who try to talk to me.	☐	☐
3 I *claim / pretend* not to be home.	☐	☐
4 I *choose / elect* a quiet place to go to.	☐	☐

B In pairs, compare your answers. If you answered "Yes" to item 4, where do you go?

Go to Vocabulary practice: easily confused words, page 141

2 A ▶ 3.8 Watch or listen to the first part of *Talking Zone*. What is a 'third place'? Why do we need one?

B ▶ 3.8 Listen to the three speakers. What are their 'special places'?

3 ▶ 3.8 Watch or listen again. Fill in the missing words in Tasha and David's advice.
1 These hideaways are _____ . According to _____ , we're all supposed to have one.
2 _____ really ought to have somewhere like that.
3 Many workplaces can be … stressful. _____ advise that we're really not supposed to live like this.
4 You _____ tell someone what their safe place should be.
5 It can be _____ . It doesn't even have to be a particularly quiet or peaceful place.
6 You _____ come and go whenever you want.

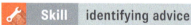 **Skill** identifying advice

When we give advice, it is often more polite to be indirect. It is easier to tell that someone is giving you advice if you listen for:
• a confident tone of voice showing the speaker is sure the advice is a good idea.
• words that mention people in authority: *Most doctors emphasize the need to exercise.*
• modal verbs and expressions: *You can't just expect to pass if you don't study.*
• sentences starting with general *you* that may also apply to you as an individual.
• other general statements: *Everyone should get eight hours' sleep a night.*

4 Read the Skill box. Look at the sentences in exercise 3 again. In pairs, identify the words that tell you that these sentences are giving advice.

identifying advice ■ intonation in negative questions ■ easily confused words **LISTENING**   **SKILLS**   **3B**

5 ▶ 3.9 Watch or listen to the second part of the show. Choose the correct answer.
David created the MyThirdPlace app when …
a he came back from a trip to London.
b he did some historical research.
c he moved to New York.

6 ▶ 3.9 Watch or listen again. Number the reasons for having the app in the order David mentions them. There is one extra.
a ☐ An app can match you to places based on your personality.
b ☐ There are fewer quiet places than in the past because of technology.
c ☐ It's cheaper to use an app than to visit possible safe places.
d ☐ You might move to a new city and not know where the quiet places are.

Listening builder | intonation in negative questions

When we hear a negative question, the intonation is an important clue to its meaning.
When we want to check information we think we know, the intonation rises:

Isn't Spruce Street the street after this one? ↗

However, when we give an opinion or make a comment, the intonation falls:

Wasn't that movie awful! ↗↘

7 A ▶ 3.10 Read the Listening builder. Then listen to the negative questions from the video. Does the intonation rise (R) or fall (F)?
1 And don't we all want to keep our special places to ourselves? _____
2 Wouldn't you want to be free of your boss or even … your mother-in-law? _____
3 Isn't it hard for an app to get to know us as individuals? _____

B ▶ 3.10 Listen again and repeat each question.

8 Fill in the blanks, and, in pairs, take turns asking the questions. Your partner will decide if you are checking *something* or giving an opinion, and will then respond.
1 Isn't learning _____ difficult?
2 Don't people around here ever _____ ?
3 Wouldn't you be mad if _____ ?

9 Look at the pictures. In pairs, discuss which one you would choose as your third place and explain why.

a

b
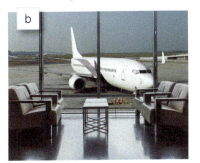

c

10 In pairs, discuss these questions.
1 Which aspects of your daily life are most stressful?
2 What good ways have you found to reduce stress?
3 What are the best 'third places' where you live?
4 Would you like to buy the MyThirdPlace app? Why/Why not?

Personal Best Describe the ideal third place for you.

3 LANGUAGE — phrasal verbs

3C To go, or not to go

1 Discuss the questions in pairs.
1 Do you prefer to go to popular tourist destinations or to places where tourists don't usually go? Why?
2 What are the most and least touristy places you've ever visited? What were they like?
3 What do you understand by the expression "mass tourism"?

2 Read the preview of a radio show about mass tourism. Is the situation similar or different in cities in your country? How?

Tourism heaven, tourism hell?

Barcelona, Venice, Prague, Dubrovnik – four of the most beautiful cities in Europe, and very popular tourist destinations. The cities are eager to attract visitors, who bring cities to life and greatly benefit local economies. But recently, in cities all over Europe, more and more residents have begun to voice their concerns about the impact of mass tourism. They're worried about issues such as the environmental impact of tourism and the increase in the cost of living for local people.
Barbara Vitez, a tour guide from Dubrovnik, in the south of Croatia, gives her views on tourism in her city.

3 A ▶ 3.11 Listen to the interview with Barbara. Which points below does she think are the benefits (B) and problems (P) of tourism in Dubrovnik?

1 the economic impact _____
2 the cultural life of the city _____
3 the number of tourists _____
4 the environmental impact _____
5 the cost of a place to live _____
6 the tourists in general _____

B Discuss the questions in pairs.
1 Why do you think each point in exercise 3A is a benefit or a problem?
2 What two things could local authorities do to reduce the negative impact of mass tourism?
3 Would you like to visit Dubrovnik?

4 ▶ 3.12 Complete the phrasal verbs in **bold** with the words in the box. Listen and check.

> come look grew throw

1 I _____ **up** in Dubrovnik.
2 The mayor of Dubrovnik has _____ **up with** a good idea.
3 We really need to _____ **after** our city.
4 They _____ their garbage **out** in the cans in the old town.

5 Look at the sentences in exercise 4 again and answer the questions below. Then read the Grammar box. Which sentences contain a phrasal verb with:

a an object after the phrasal verb? _____
b an object between the two parts of the phrasal verb? _____
c no object? _____
d three parts? _____

phrasal verbs **LANGUAGE 3C**

Grammar: phrasal verbs

Without an object:
We're going to **come back** very early tomorrow morning.
The plane **took off** twenty minutes late.

With an object (separable):
You can **try** the dress **on**.
The music's loud. **Turn** it **down**.

With an object (non-separable):
I'm **looking for** my phone. NOT ~~looking my phone for~~
I can't **do without** coffee. NOT ~~do coffee without~~

With three words (non-separable):
We've **run out of** sugar. NOT ~~run sugar out of~~
I **look forward to** Fridays. NOT ~~look forward Fridays to~~

Go to Grammar practice: phrasal verbs, page 117

6 A ▶ 3.14 **Pronunciation:** linking in phrasal verbs Listen to the sentences. Notice how the words in the phrasal verbs link together.
1 Ben and Julia have broken‿up.
2 We've run‿out‿of juice.
3 Adam's taken‿up yoga!
4 He grew‿up in the United States.
5 Did you hear about the game? They called‿it‿off.
6 There's no more shampoo. Sue used‿it‿up.

B ▶ 3.14 Listen again and repeat.

7 A Choose the correct option to complete the sentences. In two of the sentences, both options are correct.
1 I *take after my father / take my father after*. We're both cheerful.
2 Please *turn the lights off / turn off the lights* when you leave.
3 We have to *get off the bus / get the bus off* at the next stop.
4 Those jeans are great. Do you want to *try them on / try on them*?
5 Are you *looking forward the party to / looking forward to the party*?
6 I'm going to *throw out my old coat / throw my old coat out*.
7 I won't *put up your behavior with / put up with your behavior* any longer!
8 You've dropped some trash. *Pick it up / Pick up it*!

B ▶ 3.15 Listen and repeat the sentences in exercise 7A. Pay attention to how the words in the phrasal verbs link together.

Go to Communication practice: Student A page 159, Student B page 165

8 A Complete the questionnaire with the best answers for you.

When you go on vacation, do you usually …

1 a ☐ look forward to going away?
   b ☐ look forward to getting back?
2 a ☐ look up information before you go?
   b ☐ figure it out when you get there?
3 a ☐ come up with a plan for each day?
   b ☐ figure it out when you're there?
4 a ☐ go back to work the day after you get home?
   b ☐ show up at work after a few days' rest?
5 a ☐ get up early every day?
   b ☐ wake up late and relax?
6 a ☐ eat out once or twice?
   b ☐ go back to the same restaurant every day?
7 a ☐ get around by car?
   b ☐ do without a car and use public transportation?
8 a ☐ talk your friends into doing what you want to do?
   b ☐ put up with doing things you don't want to do?

B In pairs, discuss and explain your answers.

Personal Best Write a paragraph about a friend. Use five phrasal verbs.

3 SKILLS WRITING — writing a persuasive article ■ contrasting expectations with reality

3D A fantastic place to live

1. Look at the pictures below. What do you know about the city of Reykjavik, in Iceland?

2. Read the article. In your opinion, does the author make Reykjavik sound like a good place to live?

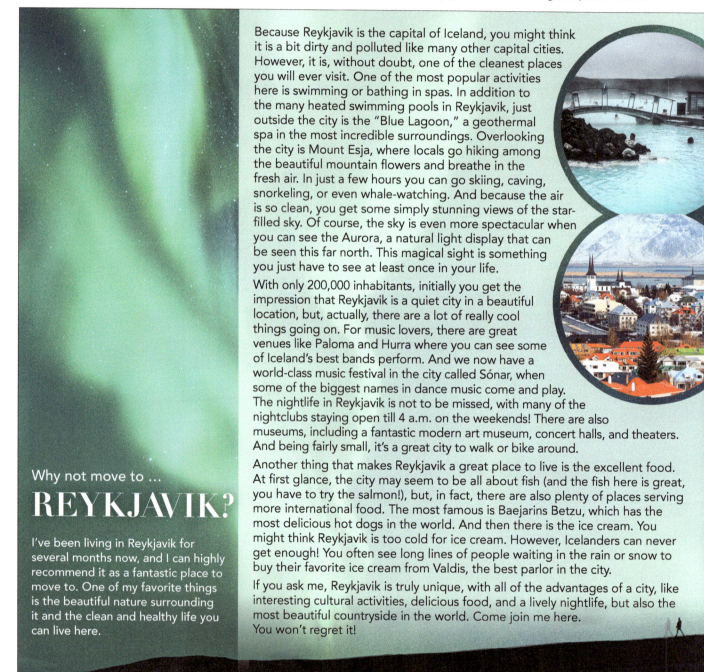

Why not move to …
REYKJAVIK?

I've been living in Reykjavik for several months now, and I can highly recommend it as a fantastic place to move to. One of my favorite things is the beautiful nature surrounding it and the clean and healthy life you can live here.

Because Reykjavik is the capital of Iceland, you might think it is a bit dirty and polluted like many other capital cities. However, it is, without doubt, one of the cleanest places you will ever visit. One of the most popular activities here is swimming or bathing in spas. In addition to the many heated swimming pools in Reykjavik, just outside the city is the "Blue Lagoon," a geothermal spa in the most incredible surroundings. Overlooking the city is Mount Esja, where locals go hiking among the beautiful mountain flowers and breathe in the fresh air. In just a few hours you can go skiing, caving, snorkeling, or even whale-watching. And because the air is so clean, you get some simply stunning views of the star-filled sky. Of course, the sky is even more spectacular when you can see the Aurora, a natural light display that can be seen this far north. This magical sight is something you just have to see at least once in your life.

With only 200,000 inhabitants, initially you get the impression that Reykjavik is a quiet city in a beautiful location, but, actually, there are a lot of really cool things going on. For music lovers, there are great venues like Paloma and Hurra where you can see some of Iceland's best bands perform. And we now have a world-class music festival in the city called Sónar, when some of the biggest names in dance music come and play. The nightlife in Reykjavik is not to be missed, with many of the nightclubs staying open till 4 a.m. on the weekends! There are also museums, including a fantastic modern art museum, concert halls, and theaters. And being fairly small, it's a great city to walk or bike around.

Another thing that makes Reykjavik a great place to live is the excellent food. At first glance, the city may seem to be all about fish (and the fish here is great, you have to try the salmon!), but, in fact, there are also plenty of places serving more international food. The most famous is Baejarins Betzu, which has the most delicious hot dogs in the world. And then there is the ice cream. You might think Reykjavik is too cold for ice cream. However, Icelanders can never get enough! You often see long lines of people waiting in the rain or snow to buy their favorite ice cream from Valdis, the best parlor in the city.

If you ask me, Reykjavik is truly unique, with all of the advantages of a city, like interesting cultural activities, delicious food, and a lively nightlife, but also the most beautiful countryside in the world. Come join me here. You won't regret it!

3. Read the article again and complete the notes in the chart about reasons for moving to Reykjavik.

Reason	Facts and examples
Healthy living	*Clean air, hiking, bathing in spas…*

writing a persuasive article ■ contrasting expectations with reality **WRITING** **SKILLS** **3D**

4 Look at this sentence from the article. Why do you think the writer uses exaggerated language like this?

This magical sight is something you just have to see at least once in your life.

> **🔧 Skill** **writing a persuasive article**
>
> **When you write a persuasive article, state your opinion about a subject and try to convince the reader to agree with you.**
> - Clearly state your point of view on the topic.
> - Give reasons for your opinion, and support them with facts and examples.
> - Use persuasive language to convince your reader, e.g., *fascinating*, *without a doubt*, etc.

5 Read the Skill box. Choose the correct option to complete the sentences below. Check your answers in the article.

1 I can highly recommend it as *an interesting / a fantastic* place to move to.
2 It is *without doubt / definitely* one of the cleanest places you will ever visit.
3 You get some *simply stunning / pretty* views of the star-filled sky.
4 And we now have a *very good / world-class* music festival in the city, called Sónar …
5 The nightlife in Reykjavik is *not to be missed / a lot of fun*.
6 The most famous is Baejarins Betzu which has *tasty / the most delicious* hot dogs in the world.

6 Complete the sentences with the words in the box. Then check your answers in the article.

> initially   first glance   might think   but, in fact   however   actually

1 Because Reykjavik is the capital of Iceland, you _____ it is a bit dirty and polluted like many other capital cities. _____ , it is, without doubt, one of the cleanest places you will ever visit.
2 With only 200,000 inhabitants, _____ you get the impression that Reykjavik is a quiet city in a beautiful location, but, _____ , there are a lot of really cool things going on.
3 At _____ , the city may seem to be all about fish … _____ , there are also plenty of places serving more international food.

> **🧩 Text builder** **contrasting expectations with reality**
>
> **We use the following expressions to contrast expectations and first impressions with the reality of a situation:**
> *… **initially you get the impression that** Reykjavik is a quiet city in a beautiful location, **but, actually,** there are a lot of really cool things going on.*
>
> ***At first glance,** the city may seem to be all about fish, **but, in fact,** there are also plenty of places serving more international food.*
>
> ***You might think** Reykjavik is too cold for ice cream. **However,** Icelanders can never get enough!*

7 Read the Text builder. Match the two parts to make complete sentences.

1 Initially you get the impression it's a busy place,
2 You might think it's too cold for a vacation destination.
3 At first glance, it seems a bit expensive,

a However, you can enjoy the various spas and hot springs most times of the year.
b but, actually, there are many budget hotels available.
c but, in fact, there are some lovely quiet back streets.

8 A **PREPARE** Think about a city you know well. Make a list of reasons why you think people should move there and make notes with examples and facts to support the reasons.

B **PRACTICE** Using your notes, write an article encouraging someone to move to the city. Use persuasive language and include some expressions for contrasting expectations with reality.

C **PERSONAL BEST** Exchange your article with a partner. Is the article persuasive? Why/Why not?

Personal Best Write a paragraph explaining why you would/wouldn't want to live in Reykjavik. 29

UNIT 4 Mind and behavior

LANGUAGE subject-verb agreement ■ personality and behavior

4A It really annoys me …

1 A What do the words in **bold** mean in the questions below? Discuss them in pairs.

1 When you're out on the street, what kind of behavior really **gets on your nerves**?
2 What kind of behavior do you think is **unreasonable** from neighbors?
3 Do you assume that strangers are kind, or that they are **mean** and will **take advantage of** you?

B In pairs, answer the questions in exercise 1A and compare your opinions.

Go to Vocabulary practice: personality and behavior, page 141

2 Read the blog post and answer the questions.

1 What three things does Jana get annoyed by in New York?
2 Is she still annoyed by these things in Tokyo? Why/Why not?
3 Do these three things annoy you? Why/Why not?

Home | Blog | Comment

JANA IN JAPAN

Pet peeves

Most of you reading this blog know that I moved from New York to Tokyo a few months ago. I usually post (or boast) about learning Japanese and discovering Japanese food, but today I want to tell you about something I never expected would happen: all my usual pet peeves have disappeared!

So, for instance, "subway behavior" drives me absolutely crazy at home in New York, but do you know what happens here in Tokyo? Everyone waits patiently as the train arrives and then moves to the center of the car. Even when the train is very crowded, no one blocks the door. People are so thoughtful.

Another pet peeve I no longer have is bad-tempered salespeople. In pretty much every store I've been to here, the staff has always been polite and charming. Plus, anything you buy as a gift is beautifully wrapped: all the salespeople must have taken courses in gift-wrapping and are so enthusiastic about it.

Pet peeve number three is noise. At home, people are so noisy, but many of the neighborhoods in Tokyo are surprisingly quiet. That's because commercial activity is concentrated near the train station, and because people really value peace and quiet.

Of course, no place is perfect, and eventually I'll probably develop some new pet peeves. But if you hate noise and rude behavior, my advice to you is … come join me in Tokyo!

3 Does a singular or plural verb form follow these words? Read the text again and check.

1 most of you _____
2 everyone _____
3 people _____
4 staff _____
5 anything _____
6 advice _____

30

subject-verb agreement ■ personality and behavior | LANGUAGE | **4A**

4 ▶ 4.3 Listen to two friends from New York talking about Jana's blog post. What two pet peeves do they have?

5 ▶ 4.4 Complete the sentences. Listen and check your answers. Then read the Grammar box.

In New York …
1 even the hairdresser is someone who _____ a tip for the holidays.
2 everyone in my building _____ to tip the postal worker.
3 more and more people _____ taxi apps these days.
4 have you ever been about to get into a taxi when a group of people _____ in front of you?
5 I can't believe anyone _____ that's OK!

Grammar: subject-verb agreement

Countable and uncountable nouns:
A lot of **news articles are** depressing.
Some of my friends' **advice isn't** very helpful.

Indefinite pronouns:
One of them **is** a doctor.
Everyone needs help from other people.

Collective nouns:
That new import-export **company is** hiring workers.

Asides:
Many **people**, including myself, **don't save** enough money.

Go to Grammar practice: subject-verb agreement, page 118

6 A ▶ 4.6 **Pronunciation:** *of* Listen to the conversations. When is *of* pronounced /əv/? When is it pronounced /ə/?

1 A Some **of** the trains here are incredibly crowded.
  B Yes, a lot **of** them are so bad I sometimes have to let two or three go by!
2 A Most **of** us have many pet peeves, don't you think?
  B Yes, I think so. Maybe one person out **of** a thousand people isn't annoyed by anything!

B ▶ 4.6 Listen again and repeat. Practice the conversations in pairs.

7 A Read the newspaper story about a pet peeve. Choose the correct answers.

Problem solved

In a small town in the UK, some families ¹*has / have* found a unique solution to their pet peeve. Everyone in the town ²*agree / agrees* that the speed of vehicles in residential areas ³*are / is* a danger, and what has made people so angry is that few drivers ⁴*pay / pays* any attention to the speed limit. Now, even children as young as ten ⁵*have / has* joined a unique speeding awareness campaign. People ⁶*have / has* been dressing in fluorescent jackets, and each of them ⁷*point / points* a hairdryer at the cars as they go by. This is a deterrent to drivers as the hairdryers look like police radar guns. The police ⁸*like / likes* the idea, but their advice to families ⁹*are / is* to be careful when standing by the side of the road. However, the local community still ¹⁰*feel / feels* that the solution to the problem is to install more speed cameras in built-up areas.

B ▶ 4.7 Listen and check. Then, in pairs, discuss possible solutions to one of your pet peeves.

Go to Communication practice: Student A page 159, Student B page 165

8 Complete the sentences. Then discuss your ideas in pairs. Does your partner feel the same way?
1 It drives me crazy when people …
2 What makes me really annoyed is when someone …
3 I can't believe anyone thinks it's OK when …
4 In my family, my …, as well as my …, are always …
5 It used to get on my nerves when everyone at school …
6 I don't think it's OK that the government …

Personal Best Write a paragraph about one of your ideas in exercise 8.

4 SKILLS | **READING** identifying attitude ■ conditionals for advice and suggestions

4B How to get along

1 Look at the title of the text on page 33. In pairs, make some suggestions for having good relationships with other people.

2 Read the text and choose the correct answer from a–d.

All of the writers ...
a tell their own story about friendship.
b make suggestions for readers.
c advise readers to listen and offer help.
d say how difficult it is to get along with people.

> **Skill** | **identifying attitude**
>
> **When reading a text, try to figure out the writer's attitude towards the topic. Attitude is not always explicitly stated, so try to understand the details of the text first, and then consider how the writer feels about the topic in general.**
> - Look for language that expresses opinions and feelings, which is often more explicitly stated than attitude.
> - If there are questions with the text, look for key words in the questions and find synonyms for these in the text. Then read that part of the text in detail.

3 A Read the Skill box. Then match questions a–f below with paragraphs 1–5. There is one question that you don't need.

Which person:
a believes in seeing things from other people's perspectives? _____
b feels we need to avoid offending people? _____
c feels people don't take friendship seriously enough? _____
d thinks everyone appreciates a little assistance from time to time? _____
e recommends paying close attention to what people are saying? _____
f likes finding things in common with others? _____

B <u>Underline</u> the parts of each paragraph that helped you choose your answers in exercise 3A.

4 Complete the sentences with the correct form of the verbs in parentheses. Scan the text and check.

1 If you really listen, you _____ (find) it makes a big difference.
2 If you _____ (want) to get along with people, remember that ...
3 If I were you, I _____ (offer) help whenever I can.
4 If you both like similar music, _____ (share) playlists.
5 If people _____ (want) to hear a good joke, they'd go to a comedy club.

> **Text builder** | **conditionals for advice and suggestions**
>
> **Zero conditional:**
> *If you're both sports fans, this is a great way to connect.*
>
> **First conditional:**
> *People will recall a conversation as being more interesting if you ask questions.*
>
> **Second conditional:**
> *If you wanted to ruin a friendship, an ill-advised comment would be the perfect way to go about it.*

5 Read the Text builder. Which types of conditional are the sentences in exercise 4?

6 Discuss the questions in pairs.

1 Which writers in the text do you have a similar attitude to?
2 In your opinion, which writer makes the most important point?
3 Do you disagree with anything that the writers say? Why?

32

identifying attitude ■ conditionals for advice and suggestions   READING   SKILLS   4B

Friends and colleagues:
essential tips for getting along

1 Martin

Sometimes we come up against problems that we can't work out on our own. Well, "A problem shared is a problem halved," as some of my British friends like to say. So whether I'm with a new acquaintance or an old friend, I always take the opportunity to give the person a hand if I can. The best kind of help is a favor you do for someone with no expectation of a favor in return. Doing people favors not only gives you a warm feeling inside, but it also sends the message that you can be trusted because you have that person's welfare in mind. If I were you, I'd offer help whenever I can because, as we say, "One good turn deserves another." You never know, your generosity may be repaid one day when you most need help from someone else. After all, "No man is an island."

The other day, I was in a face-to-face meeting with a colleague, and she'd sent three texts before I could even finish what I was saying. It drives me crazy when people don't listen, especially when they don't even look you in the eye. I was brought up to listen to people in order to understand them, not just in order to reply to them. If you really listen, you'll find it makes a big difference in understanding what motivates them, what worries them, and what they're enthusiastic about. You just have to ignore everyone around you, ignore your phone, and ignore that voice in your head that's thinking about how to respond. In no time, you'll find yourself connecting with people significantly better than before.

2 Magda

3 Nandeep

Are you familiar with the expression "six degrees of separation"? It's the theory that every person on the planet is connected to everyone else by a chain of no more than five personal connections. I'm not sure it's completely true, but there's definitely an element of truth in it. So when you meet someone new, find out about the person: ask where he/she is from, where he/she went to school, and where he/she works. You may well find that you have a mutual friend. Try comparing interests, too – if you're both sports fans, this is a great way to connect. I'm into bike riding, and I often connect with others using a cycling app called Strava. Similarly, if you both like similar music, share playlists via Spotify. For business contacts, why not send a message or share an article on LinkedIn? We live in a connected world, and you just have to find the connections.

Do you ever find yourself having a conversation, hearing someone say something pretty shocking, and wondering why on earth the person just said that? I do, and when it happens, I try to keep in mind where he or she is coming from. I'll ask myself something like, "Why does the person feel that way? Why is he or she saying that?" Obviously, you're allowed your own opinion, and you're not obliged to agree with everything someone says, but don't argue for the sake of it – that just causes friction. Try not to criticize or prove the other person wrong. Everyone is different, and if you want to get along with people, remember that someone else's experience isn't necessarily the same as yours. Try putting yourself in the other person's shoes.

4 Pascale

5 Kazuo

Having a laugh is essential, and I find humor is a great way to break the ice, ease tension, and get along with people. You can't force humor, though – in other words, you can't just switch on your funny side. Otherwise it might come out as awkward, and you could risk upsetting people, which you have to be very careful about. Humor is best when it comes from a laid-back and spontaneous place. I'd also be careful about what or who you make fun of because so much humor is based on being unkind to others. If you wanted to ruin a friendship, an ill-considered comment (humorous or not!) would be the perfect way to go about it. The safest way to enjoy humor is to make fun of yourself. And I don't recommend telling jokes: jokes are not the same as a sense of humor, and it's very hard to tell them well. If people wanted to hear a good joke, they'd go to a comedy club.

Personal Best Write another piece of advice about how you can connect better with friends and colleagues.

33

4 LANGUAGE perfect and past forms ■ word families

4C I see you've been busy!

1 In pairs, choose the correct option to complete the sentences. Then discuss the questions.
1. Do you consider yourself a *create / creative / creativity* person?
2. Describe three jobs that require a lot of *create / creative / creativity*. Would you like to do any of these jobs?
3. What would you prefer to *create / creative / creativity*: a painting or a hit song? Why?

Go to Vocabulary practice: word families, page 142

2 A Read the text. What is *procrastination*, and why can it sometimes be a good thing?

Procrastination and Creativity – the new link

Friends who know me well can always tell when I'm working to a deadline on an article or essay. Is it because I don't answer my phone, or because they never see me out and about? No. It's because my house is always impeccably neat, my nails beautifully painted, and my desk perfectly organized. "I see you've been doing the housework. When's the article due?" they say, or, "Wow, you've put all your books in alphabetical order. When do you have to hand the essay in?"

Yes, I'm a procrastinator, and I'm not alone. Many of us feel extremely guilty for putting off important tasks, but recent research has shown that procrastination is, in fact, fantastic for creativity.

Psychologist Adam Grant became interested in this area a few years ago when he found out that one of his most creative students, Jihae Shin, was a chronic procrastinator. Grant and Shin have been studying the link between procrastination and creativity ever since, and they've conducted a great deal of research. In one study, they asked a group of people to submit new business ideas. The people who played games like Minesweeper or Solitaire for five minutes before thinking about the task had the most creative ideas.

Professor Grant explains that procrastination lets the mind wander, and the ideas we have after procrastinating are more creative and innovative than the more conventional ideas we have when we start a task right away. He also claims that some of the greatest achievements of human history are examples of procrastination. For example, it took Leonardo Da Vinci 16 years to complete the Mona Lisa because he kept getting distracted by other things.

So, the next time you have an essay due or a deadline at work, spend five minutes doing something completely unrelated. The creative ideas you have afterwards may change the world!

B Read the text again. Answer the questions in pairs.
1. Which important tasks does the writer always leave to the last minute?
2. What activities does she do to put off completing these tasks?
3. How do the researchers explain the link between procrastination and creativity?
4. How long does the writer suggest we procrastinate for?

3 A Look at the pictures and sentences a and b below. Then answer the questions.

a I see you**'ve been doing** the housework.

b I see you**'ve done** the housework. It's so neat!

1. Which sentence emphasizes the result of a completed action?
2. Which sentence emphasizes the action (which may or may not be completed)?

B Read the text again and find four more present perfect or present perfect continuous sentences. What does each sentence emphasize, the action or the result? Then read the Grammar box.

perfect and past forms ■ word families **LANGUAGE** **4C**

Grammar: perfect and past forms

Present perfect:
I**'ve finished** my homework. Let's have dinner.
She**'s** always **been** extremely creative.

Present perfect vs. simple past:
I**'ve bought** a new laptop.
I **bought** a new laptop yesterday.

Present perfect continuous:
I**'ve been studying** all morning.
How long **have** you **been waiting**?

Present perfect vs. present perfect continuous:
He**'s** already **cleaned** the house, and it looks great!
He**'s been cleaning** the house, so he's tired now.

Go to Grammar practice: perfect and past forms, page 119

4 A ▶ 4.10 **Pronunciation:** sentence stress in perfect forms Listen to sentences 1–4.
Which of the words in the underlined phrases are stressed?

1 They have been doing an important research project.
2 Has he finished his psychology essay yet?
3 How long have you been working at the university?
4 The doctor has gone to the hospital. He's had an emergency.

B ▶ 4.10 Listen again and repeat.

5 ▶ 4.11 Choose the correct options to complete the texts. Listen and check.

SALLY

To be honest, I've always ¹*preferred / been preferring* to complete tasks as soon as I'm given them. I've never ²*liked / been liking* to wait until the last minute to do important things, especially at work. This morning, I've already ³*had / been having* a meeting with my boss, and he has ⁴*asked / been asking* me to prepare a sales presentation for next Monday. I've ⁵*prepared / been preparing* the presentation non-stop since the meeting. I would hate to wait until Sunday evening to start working on it. That would completely ruin my weekend!

RYAN

Personally, I've always ⁶*put off / been putting off* writing my college essays until just before the deadline. ⁷*I've done / I did* the same thing when I was in high school, and I still ⁸*managed / have managed* to get good grades every time. I think I'm one of those people who are most creative when they're under pressure. My final term paper's due next Wednesday, but I still haven't ⁹*been writing / written* anything. ¹⁰*I'm planning / I've been planning* it for the last two months, and I'm going to spend the next five days writing it, probably 24/7!

Go to Communication practice: Student A page 159, Student B page 165

6 Discuss the questions in pairs.

1 Which important tasks have you had to do this month? Have you finished them?
2 Which life changes have you been considering recently? Have you made a decision about them? Or have you put them off?
3 What's the most creative thing you've done in the last year? Does procrastination make you more creative?
4 What have you been worrying about recently? Have you found ways to deal with stressful situations?

Personal Best Write a paragraph about an experience when you procrastinated. Did it end well?

35

4 SKILLS SPEAKING responding to arguments ■ describing memorable experiences

4D Road rage

1 Look at the pictures. Discuss the questions in pairs.

1 What do you think the expression "road rage" means?
2 Is this a problem where you live?

2 A Look at the sentences below from the video. Predict what you think will happen.

1 I was waiting at a traffic light. … I didn't move immediately when the light turned green.
2 But then the woman behind me gets out of the car and …

B ▶ 4.12 Watch or listen to the first part of *Talking Zone*. How did Abigail react to the woman's behavior?

a She got out of her car and started yelling.
b She didn't get out of her car and kept driving.

3 ▶ 4.12 Watch or listen again. Fill in the blanks. Do Ben and Abigail seem to agree with each other?

Abigail When you're [1]_____, you're constantly under pressure.
Ben It's true. I think there's [2]_____ to it than [3]_____, though. … If you think of your car as an [4]_____ of your personality, you're more likely to lose your [5]_____ on the road.
Abigail I'm not sure I [6]_____ .
Ben If you see your car as part of [7]_____, anything that puts your car at [8]_____ is like a [9]_____ to you, personally.
Abigail That may be [10]_____ to a certain extent, but a lot of people … can lose [11]_____ of their [12]_____ when they get behind the [13]_____ .
Ben Yeah but why?
Abigail Perhaps it's because they try so hard to [14]_____ their [15]_____ in their day-to-day [16]_____ .
Ben No, sorry, I don't get that.

responding to arguments ■ describing memorable experiences   **SPEAKING**   SKILLS **4D**

Conversation builder — responding to arguments

Agreeing:
That makes a lot of sense.
I hadn't thought of that.

Disagreeing politely:
I think there's more to it than that, though.
That may be true to a certain extent, but …

Asking for clarification:
Sorry, I don't get that.
I'm not sure I follow.

4 Read the Conversation builder. In pairs, look at exercise 3 again. What language do Ben and Abigail use to agree or disagree politely? Look at the Conversation builder.

5 A Make notes to explain road rage, using arguments from exercise 3 or your own. Then, in pairs, practice a similar conversation to Abigail and Ben's. Start like this:

  A *Can you believe how many angry drivers there are?*
  B *Maybe it's because …*

B How many expressions from the Conversation builder did you use? Did you reach an agreement?

6 ▶ 4.13 Watch or listen to the second part of the show and answer the questions.

1 Where did Abigail meet the angry driver from Part 1 again?
2 How did Abigail feel when she met her?

Skill — describing memorable experiences

When we describe a memorable experience, we use various strategies to maintain the listener's interest:
• creating suspense: *You're not going to believe* / *You'll never guess what happened today!*
• describing your reaction: *I couldn't believe my eyes!*

When we respond, we can show interest by:
• guessing how the story will continue: *Let me guess – …?*
• showing surprise: *No way!*
• showing empathy: *That must have been so awkward.* / *I bet it was really uncomfortable.*

7 A Read the Skill box. What information (a–g) is prompted by the comments or questions in 1–7?

1 You're not going to believe what happened today. _d_
2 You'll never guess who was there! ___
3 No way! Did she recognize you? ___
4 That must have been so awkward. ___
5 Let me guess – road rage? ___
6 I bet it was really uncomfortable. ___
7 Are you serious? Was she angry? ___

a Tell me about it! And what was the first topic of the lesson?
b No, she apologized.
c Exactly. He showed us a video …
d You know I started that short course on safe driving this morning?
e As soon as she saw me. I couldn't believe my eyes!
f Our "friend" – you know, the angry driver!
g It was. And she came up to me at the end of the lesson.

B ▶ 4.13 Watch or listen again and check. Then in pairs, answer the questions.
1 Who says each sentence (1–7) in exercise 7A, Abigail or Ben?
2 Did you feel more sympathetic towards the driver in the end?

8 Practice Abigail and Ben's conversation from memory, using the sentences in exercise 7A to help you.

Go to Communication practice: Student A page 160, Student B page 166

9 A **PREPARE** Make notes about a real or imagined road-rage incident. Create suspense and describe your emotions. Prepare to tell your partner about it.

B **PRACTICE** Take turns practicing your conversations. Be sure to make your experience sound memorable.

C **PERSONAL BEST** Practice your conversation again. Did you change any details or use any new expressions?

Personal Best — Describe another memorable experience as if you were telling it to someone.

37

3 and 4 REVIEW and PRACTICE

Grammar

1 Choose the correct options to complete the sentences.

1 _____ leave now if you want to catch the bus.
 a You're supposed to
 b You're allowed to
 c You'd better

2 Be quiet! You _____ to talk in the library.
 a aren't allowed to
 b don't have to
 c are supposed to

3 Marta takes _____ her mother – they both have blue eyes.
 a up
 b after
 c on

4 I'm not going to put _____ his behavior any longer.
 a on with
 b up with
 c down with

5 One of my sisters _____ tennis really well.
 a play
 b are playing
 c plays

6 A lot of my friends, including Alberto, _____ for work at the moment.
 a is looking
 b are looking
 c look

7 I _____ in this house for 12 years.
 a have been living
 b live
 c am living

8 Sarah _____ her exams yet – she still has two left.
 a has finished
 b hasn't been finishing
 c hasn't finished

2 Choose the correct options to complete the sentences.

1 People that work *are allowed / have to* pay tax. If not, they *have to / they'd better* pay a fine.

2 All the classrooms, apart from this one, *is / are* already taken this afternoon.

3 Why didn't you answer your phone earlier? *I'm trying / I've been trying* to contact you all morning!

4 There are two groups of 12 students in my class. My group *want / wants* to watch the video now.

5 I think these shoes will look good on you. Why don't you try *them on / on them*?

6 You *should / have to* go to bed early tonight so you're ready for the exam tomorrow. That's my advice.

7 Oh no! I think we're going to *run out / run out of* gas!

8 I *have been looking / looked* for a job since I graduated.

3 Choose the correct options to complete the text.

I've ¹*done / been doing* a lot of traveling in my life and I've ²*learned / been learning* you ³*have to / are supposed to* be careful not to do the wrong thing when you're in a foreign country. My biggest mistake happened when I was teaching English in South Korea and I wrote some of the students' names in red ink. The whole class ⁴*was / were* very shocked because ⁵*you don't have to / you're not supposed to* do that. Years later, I spent a few months in a small village in the Philippines. I was surprised to discover that all the children in the village, including my daughter, ⁶*was / were* expected to bow to older people when they saw them. The funniest mistake I've ⁷*made / been making* in my life is to finish all the food on my plate at dinner parties, thinking I was being polite. For years, I couldn't ⁸*figure out / figure it out* why the host always gave me more food but not other people. Apparently, in many countries you ⁹*can't / shouldn't* finish everything on your plate because it means you're still hungry! But it's impossible to know all these cultural differences if nobody tells you. My advice is that you ¹⁰*ought / ought to* ask a local friend if there are any rules or customs you need to know about.

Vocabulary

1 Circle the word or expression that is different. Explain why.

1 harbor   traffic congestion   taxi stand   city hall
2 mean   stubborn   charming   unreasonable
3 persuasion   reliability   achievement   critical
4 business district   high-rise building   city hall   courthouse
5 creative   persuade   reliable   risky
6 drive someone crazy   get on someone's nerves   praise someone   upset someone

REVIEW and PRACTICE | **3** and **4**

2 Match the words in the box with definitions 1–10.

> poverty pretend persuasive achievement
> vandalism claim sensitive sensible
> considerate stubborn

1 having good judgment _____
2 a result gained by effort _____
3 the state of being very poor _____
4 say that something is true _____
5 not being prepared to change your mind _____
6 easily upset by things _____
7 causing damage to something on purpose _____
8 act as if something is true when it isn't _____
9 careful not to harm others _____
10 able to make other people do what you want _____

3 Choose the correct options to complete the sentences.

1 I couldn't go to the party, but I really didn't *mind / matter*. I was tired anyway.
2 The main problem in my town is *overcrowding / smog*. There just aren't enough houses!
3 Did you break that glass? You're so *silly / clumsy*!
4 We work as a team, but he always takes *credit for / advantage of* the final piece of work.
5 I know she gets on your nerves, but you have to take into *consideration / considerate* that she's had a really difficult year.
6 It isn't *sure / safe* to ride a motorbike without a helmet.
7 Remember you shouldn't drive too fast in *a residential / an industrial* area because there are often children around.
8 If you want to *success / succeed*, you need to start working harder.

4 Complete the text with the words in the box.

> bad-tempered nerves drive stand realize
> silly matter argue annoyed thoughtful

It's taken me a long time to ¹_____ it, but my best friend is my younger brother! When we were younger I couldn't ²_____ spending time with him. I would get so ³_____ because he was always doing stupid things and getting on my ⁴_____ . I suppose I was a pretty ⁵_____ child. We still ⁶_____ , but it doesn't ⁷_____ so much these days. Yes, he can be ⁸_____ , like when he dances around the kitchen, but he is also very ⁹_____ . He bought me flowers yesterday because I was upset about my job. So that's why, even though we ¹⁰_____ each other crazy sometimes, my brother is my best friend. Just don't tell him!

Personal Best

Lesson 3A
Give two rules and two pieces of advice for a new student in your class.

Lesson 4A
Write three sentences that begin with a countable noun, an uncountable noun, and a collective noun.

Lesson 3A
Write about four personal obligations you have for the next month.

Lesson 4A
Describe one person you like and one person you don't like.

Lesson 3A
Describe the three biggest problems that affect a city you know well.

Lesson 4B
Make three suggestions to someone new to your town using zero, first and second conditionals.

Lesson 3B
Name three pairs of words that are easily confused and explain their different meanings.

Lesson 4C
Describe one thing you have done this year and one thing you have been doing recently.

Lesson 3C
Write four things about what you usually do on vacation using phrasal verbs.

Lesson 4C
Name three adjectives from Lesson 4C and then name their verbs and nouns.

Lesson 3D
Describe a time when something was different to what you expected.

Lesson 4D
Write two sentences that create suspense about a memorable event.

39

UNIT 5 Our planet

LANGUAGE *so* and *such*; *so much/many, so little/few* ■ the environment

5A Going green

1 What can you do to help the environment? Make sentences using the prompts below.

drink cans   plastic bags   energy-efficient light bulbs   computers   eco-products

1 Turn off …   2 Stop using …   3 Switch to …   4 Recycle …   5 Use more …

2 Read Ida's first blog post. What is the *No Impact Experiment*? Would you like to try it?

Eco watch   Home | News | Forum | Contact us

Site of the month: noimpactproject.org
Climate change is real, and we must act now. This is why the No Impact Experiment is such a great initiative. Basically, it is a one-month "carbon detox" that will help you become more environmentally friendly and live a greener life. You can make simple changes like switching to energy-efficient light bulbs or turning off your faucet when you brush your teeth. I'm actually going to give the experiment a try. Stay tuned for my next post. [posted by Ida]

Go to Vocabulary practice: the environment, page 142

3 Read Ida's second blog post. How far is she into her *No Impact Experiment*?

a She's just started it.   b She's halfway through it.   c She's completed it.

As promised, this is a summary of my experience so far:

❶ I haven't switched to solar energy (not yet, anyway), but I've replaced all my light bulbs. I've heard that LED bulbs, for example, can reduce energy consumption by up to 90% and last around 100,000 hours, so you end up saving a lot of money in the long run. ¹_____

❷ I've stopped using plastic bags, which I'd actually thought about doing even before the experiment. They litter our cities, pollute our waterways, and kill wildlife. Sea turtles have been confusing jellyfish with plastic bags and choking as a result. ²_____ There's only one problem: I keep forgetting to take my reusable bag to the supermarket!

❸ I've been walking to work these past two weeks. I know I'm saving money on gas and burning fewer fossil fuels, but, honestly, I hate leaving my car at home. Before, it only took me ten minutes to get to work, but now it takes me an hour. ³_____

So far the *No Impact Experiment* has been harder than I thought, but I'm looking forward to the next two weeks. Maybe a greener lifestyle takes a little getting used to!

4 Fill in blanks 1–3 in the text in exercise 3 with a–e below. There are two extra sentences.

a It feels like such a waste of time!
b These are such important decisions.
c I just wish they weren't so expensive – and so bright!
d It's a shame there's so little time left.
e There have been so many shocking deaths you'll never use one again!

5 Read sentences a–e in exercise 4 again. Complete the rules with *so* or *such*. Then read the Grammar box.

1 Use _____ before nouns or adjectives followed by nouns.
2 Use _____ before adjectives.
3 Use _____ before quantifiers: *little, much, few,* and *many*.

so and *such*; *so much/many, so little/few* ■ the environment | **LANGUAGE** | **5A**

 **Grammar** *so* and *such*; *so much/many, so little/few*

So is followed by an adjective, *so many/few* by countable nouns, and *so much/little* by uncountable nouns:
Living green was **so** easy!
So many resources are being wasted, and there are **so few** people to help.
There's **so much** work to do and **so little** time.
Such a/an is followed by singular countable nouns, and *such* by plural countable nouns and uncountable nouns:
My diet was **such a** challenge.
I found **such** useful ideas online.
This is **such** important information!
So and *such* are often used in sentences that express cause and effect:
He made **so many** changes to his lifestyle **(that)** people couldn't recognize him.

Go to Grammar practice: *so* and *such*; *so much/many, so little/few*, page 120

6 A ▶5.4 **Pronunciation:** sentence stress with *so* and *such* Listen to the comments on the *No Impact Experiment*. Circle the stressed word in each underlined phrase.

1 This is such a great idea.
2 This is such a waste of time.
3 There's still so much to be done.
4 It's a such a shame that so few people take this seriously.

B ▶5.4 Listen and repeat. Then, in pairs, choose a sentence each and mention an environmental issue it applies to.

7 A Read the text and choose the correct options.

| Home | Articles | Blog | Log in |

What I learned from a 30-day social media "detox"
By John Seymour

Social media has been a massive part of my life for ¹*so / such* long that I can't remember when I became ²*so / such* a heavy user. Last month, though, I decided it was time to simplify my life, so I implemented a month-long detox, which was good for me and for the planet as well, since I used less electricity. Looking back, it was ³*such / such a* valuable experience. Now I realize that I was spending ⁴*so much / so many* time on social media that I no longer knew what real life was. Here are other insights I've had. …

B Read the rest of John's experience. Put *so* or *such* in the correct places and join the sentences together.

1 Social media was a big part of my life. I didn't know what to do with my time.
Social media was such a big part of my life (that) I didn't know what to do with my time.
2 I had very few "offline" hobbies. I had to learn how to have fun again.
3 I have many online connections. I don't know who they all are any longer.
4 I spent many hours online. My electricity bill was huge.
5 I spent a long time online. I stopped working out.
6 Doing a 30-day detox was good advice. I think I might extend it to 60 days.

Go to Communication practice: Both students, page 171

8 In pairs, predict how your life would change if you took part in the *No Impact Experiment*. Use *so* and *such*.

If I started biking everywhere, …
If I stopped using my washing machine, …
If I turned off my air conditioning/central heating, …
If I grew my own food, …
If I carried my own cup wherever I went, …
If I stopped using household cleaning products, …

If I started biking everywhere, I'd be in such great shape!

Imagine you did the *No Impact Experiment*. Write a paragraph about your experience.

41

5 SKILLS LISTENING identifying cause and effect ■ linking consonants and vowels ■ moods

5B Weather effects

1 A In pairs, imagine you've experienced one of these extreme weather events. Describe what it was like.

1 *The snow was so high we couldn't open our door!*

B Complete the sentences with the adjectives in the box. There is one extra. Can you think of other words to describe how you might feel?

desperate   exhausting   miserable   pessimistic

1 We've never had this much snow before! I'm feeling pretty _____ , stuck at home all day.

2 Third flood this year. I'm getting more and more _____ about climate change.

3 I heard on the news there's a fire coming our way. My family and I are _____ to escape.

Go to Vocabulary practice: moods, page 143

Skill identifying cause and effect

When listening, we often need to understand **why something happened** (the cause) and **what happened as a result** (the effect). Pay careful attention to:
- visual information that can help you understand what the speakers are saying.
- pronouns, so you don't get lost trying to understand what the speakers are referring to: *... it snowed the entire time.* **This** (the fact that it snowed) *resulted in our flights being canceled.*
- verbs that describe a result: *Weather always **impacts** mood.*

2 ▶ 5.7 Read the Skill box. Then watch or listen to the first part of *Talking Zone*. Number the effects of extreme weather in the order Joel mentions them.

a ☐ People sometimes help one another when a disaster happens.
b ☐ Extreme weather can put people under a lot of stress.
c ☐ The population, as a whole, is feeling more concerned about climate change.

identifying cause and effect ■ linking consonants and vowels ■ moods **LISTENING** SKILLS **5B**

3 **A** ▶ 5.7 Watch or listen again. Fill in the blanks with the words the speakers use to describe cause and effect.

1 As <u>these</u> stories become increasingly common, <u>it</u> _____ all of us.
2 Extreme weather can be so devastating that <u>it</u> can _____ every aspect of our lives. <u>This</u> has huge _____ for our emotional well-being.
3 Severe weather events can be very traumatic. <u>They</u> can _____ to feelings of stress and anxiety.
4 In 2012, Hurricane Sandy _____ New York to shut down. <u>It</u> was so severe in some areas that people's homes were badly damaged.

B What do the <u>underlined</u> pronouns in sentences 1–4 refer to?

4 Think about an extreme weather event. Discuss the questions in pairs.

1 Have you ever experienced extreme weather?
2 What caused it?
3 What happened as a result?
4 What can we do to prevent these events?

5 ▶ 5.8 Watch or listen to the second part of the show. Are the sentences true (T) or false (F)?

1 In the U.S., some people avoid leaving the house during the winter months. _____
2 S.A.D. affects more people in winter. _____
3 Joel says people should get as much sunlight as possible. _____
4 Tasha agrees with Joel that people in warm climates are more optimistic. _____
5 Joel doesn't see a connection between weather and mental health. _____

6 In pairs, discuss whether you think the weather can influence the character of the people that live in a particular country or city.

+|+ **Listening builder** **linking consonants and vowels**

When a word ends in a consonant sound and the next word begins with a vowel sound, we often move the consonant sound to the beginning of the next word. It can be easier to understand the two words if you think of them as a single word.

In part one, we looked at how global warming is changing our moods.
Weather affects our mood every single day.

7 **A** ▶ 5.9 Read the Listening builder. In pairs, guess the missing words in these sentences from the video. Listen and check.

1 My mood completely _____ the weather – just ask my friends! I get very grumpy _____ 's cold.
2 Study after study shows that people who _____ warm climates tend to be more motivated and optimistic, _____ turn makes them more _____ life.
3 So many scientific studies show that light _____ brain. There must be some _____ !
4 Movement _____ happy and energetic, and the _____ makes us grumpy and lethargic.

B ▶ 5.9 Mark the consonant-vowel links in the words you wrote in exercise 7A. Listen again and check. Then practice saying the sentences.

8 In pairs, discuss the best kind of weather for these activities.

play your favorite sport | visit your favorite vacation spot | do the housework

have a Netflix binge | go for a walk | do your homework

Personal Best Describe an experience where the weather has affected your mood. 43

5 LANGUAGE future predictions ■ adjective prefixes

5C In the year 2100 …

1 A Read the headlines below. Complete the words in **bold** with one of the prefixes in the box.

dis- in- mis- un-

1 COOLER SUMMERS ARE _____**LEADING** – CLIMATE CHANGE IS STILL A THREAT, SAYS EXPERT

2 New study finds that most global climate change policies are _____**effective**

3 Scientists warn there may be _____**expected** effects of climate change in future

4 NEW REPORT ACCUSES ENERGY INDUSTRY OF BEING _____**HONEST** ABOUT ITS ROLE IN CLIMATE CHANGE

B In pairs, discuss which headline worries you the most and explain why.

Go to Vocabulary practice: adjective prefixes, page 143

2 A Read the text. Which of the headlines in exercise 1A is the correct one?

Unless you've been avoiding the news for the past twenty years, you probably know that climate change is upon us and is going to continue to cause droughts and floods. And you know that glaciers are melting, sea levels are rising, and storms are definitely going to get more severe. But, get ready. There are other surprises coming our way by the year 2100.

More lightning

Worse allergies

Faster-growing trees

Some scientists predict that by 2100 lightning strikes will have increased by as much as 50%, which is bad news for areas where wildfires are a threat. And it won't be much fun if you're a frequent flyer: flights are likely to be bumpier, too, with an increase in turbulence. This is because if it's warmer, the atmosphere has more water vapor. And this vapor makes lightning and turbulence more likely.

When temperatures are high, plants release more pollen. This means that the amount of pollen will continue to increase as the Earth warms. In fact, according to a recent study, pollen levels might more than double by 2040, so if you're allergic, you'll be experiencing even more severe symptoms. And if you don't normally have pollen allergies, you may develop them.

You may not be aware of this, but over the past five decades, trees in Europe have been growing faster – by up to 70%, in some cases. A number of researchers believe that higher levels of carbon dioxide and nitrogen in the atmosphere are to blame, so we'll probably be seeing trees that are even taller in the coming decades. Having said that, taller trees absorb more carbon dioxide, which might help slow down climate change.

B Which of the three predictions brings good news, too?

3 A ▶ 5.11 Listen to two friends who have read the text. Why is the woman worried?

B ▶ 5.11 Match the two parts to make complete sentences. Then listen again and check.

1 Thanks to climate change, people
2 This rise in temperature
3 At the present rate, by 2050 the world
4 We can't be really sure. I mean, we
5 But I bet your favorite candy bar

a is going to make it too hot and dry for cocoa trees.
b will definitely be more expensive than it is today.
c will be eating less chocolate in the future.
d will have run out of all its chocolate.
e might still have chocolate.

future predictions ■ adjective prefixes   LANGUAGE **5C**

4 A Look at the sentences in exercise 3B again. Which sentences show …
  a predictions based on evidence? _____ _____
  b a personal opinion (low certainty)? _____
  c a personal opinion (high certainty)? _____
  d a future action in progress? _____
  e a completed future action? _____

B Find more examples of future forms in the text in exercise 2A. Then read the Grammar box.

| Grammar | future predictions |

Future with *will*, *going to*, *may*, and *might*:
I think the planet **will** probably **be** very hot in 50 years.
We **won't be** better at preventing climate change unless we act now.
I'm positive we**'re going to be** in big trouble!
Things definitely **won't get** better. In fact, they **may**/**might** even **get** worse.

Future perfect:
By the end of the century, we **will have used up** all our resources.
Won't we have developed new ways to save energy by 2100?

Future continuous:
We**'ll be living** in a very hot climate.
We **won't be enjoying** life very much.

Look! We can use *going to* when we're more certain of our predictions:
  I'm positive climate change **is going to be** worse in 50 years. (= very certain)
  I think climate change **will be** worse in 50 years. (= not as certain)

Go to Grammar practice: future predictions, page 121

5 A ▶ 5.13 **Pronunciation:** *will have* Listen to the predictions. Is the vowel /ə/ or /æ/ in *have*? Which sound don't you hear at all?

By 2030 …
1 climate change will have gotten out of control.
2 robots will have learned how to manipulate us.
3 we will have made contact with aliens.
4 sales of electric vehicles won't have increased.

B ▶ 5.13 Listen again and repeat each sentence. Do you agree with each prediction?

6 A Read Bill Gates's predictions for the future and choose the most logical option for each one.
  1 By 2030, two billion people who don't have a bank account today *won't be making / will be making* payments with their phones.
  2 Millions of people have already lost their jobs to robots, and I'm absolutely convinced that more jobs *might be / are going to be* lost to automation.
  3 In 2016, the world saw just 37 new cases of polio. Today, there are so few cases worldwide that by 2019, the disease *will have disappeared / will be disappearing* forever.

B Look again at the predictions in exercise 6A. How likely is each one? Discuss in groups.

Go to Communication practice: Both students, page 172

7 A Write questions based on the prompts. Use the future perfect or future continuous.

Do you embrace or **resist change?**

A year from today will you …
1 live / same / house?
2 still / study or work / same place?
3 change / hairstyle?
4 switch / phone brands?
5 hang out / same people?
6 listen / same kind of music?
7 change / your diet?
8 take up / new hobby?

B Interview two classmates and use future forms in your responses.
  A *So, a year from today, will you be living in the same house?*
  B *No, I don't think so. My neighborhood is getting too noisy, so maybe I'll start looking at other places.*

Personal Best Write six predictions for your town/city.

45

5 SKILLS WRITING writing an opinion essay ■ formal linkers

5D Let me persuade you …

1 Look at the advertisements. Which one do you like best? Why? Which one is more effective?

2 In pairs, think of two reasons why climate change campaigns are not very effective. Then read the essay. Were your ideas mentioned?

Are **global-warming** campaigns effective?

Gloria López

From 2015 to 2018, there were many climate change campaigns worldwide, and most people accept that global warming is real. However, they often don't change their behavior because they feel that experts may be exaggerating the problem and that rising temperatures are not an immediate threat. In general, environmental campaigns are not as effective as they could be, and we need to understand why.

One reason is the use of campaigns that use fear to motivate a person to change his or her behavior. For example, an environmental group might use images of environmental disasters so that people respond positively and take action. **Nevertheless**, they rarely do take action, since fear is an unpleasant emotion, and, **consequently**, people tend to ignore the things that make them afraid.

Similarly, the kinds of changes that people are asked to make are often too difficult. It is fairly easy, for instance, to recycle, take shorter showers, or use energy-efficient lightbulbs **as opposed to** more conventional ones. However, it is hard to give up meat, buy expensive organic food, or, in some cases, even leave your car at home. In other words, some changes are fairly easy, whereas others often require a lot of effort. The question is, how many people are willing to make these changes?

In sum, people do not respond well to fear or unrealistic demands. For an environmental campaign to be successful, it should encourage people to think about the issue of climate change in a positive and realistic way. In the words of author Ron Kaufman: "Convince people and you win their minds. Inspire people and you win their hearts." We need to do both.

3 A Is the answer to the question in the title *yes* or *no*?

  B Read the essay again. Does it give reasons:
  a for and against the main argument?
  b for the main argument, but not against?

writing an opinion essay ■ formal linkers **WRITING** **SKILLS** **5D**

🔧 Skill writing an opinion essay

One way to write an opinion essay is <u>only</u> to give reasons that <u>support</u> the main argument.
- In paragraph 1, write a thesis statement (a sentence that states the main point of your essay). A good thesis statement isn't too broad and clearly states the writer's position.
- In paragraphs 2 and 3, give arguments that support your thesis statement. Use examples, facts, figures, etc.
- Start each paragraph with a clear topic sentence (a sentence that introduces the main point of the paragraph).
- Summarize the key points in the concluding paragraph. Don't add any new arguments.

4 Read the Skill box. Then read Gloria's essay again and <u>underline</u>:

1 the thesis statement (paragraph 1).
2 the topic sentences (paragraphs 2 and 3).
3 an argument to support the thesis statement.
4 the summary sentence in the concluding paragraph.

5 **A** Choose the best thesis statement for each essay question.

1 Should pop artists take environmental issues more seriously?
   a Environmental issues are very important, and we should all take care of the environment.
   b Influential pop artists should use their fame to encourage people to protect the planet.
2 Is a college degree really necessary?
   a If Steve Jobs, one of the most influential people in history, did not graduate from college, it could be argued that a college education is not essential.
   b In my country, more and more people are dropping out of college because of the high tuition fees.
3 Do violent video games cause behavior problems?
   a I have loved video games ever since I can remember.
   b Violent games can have a negative impact on children.

B In pairs, how would you answer each question? Think of two arguments to support your opinion.

🧩 Text builder formal linkers

Two similar arguments: *Climate change can be difficult for some people to understand.* ***Similarly****, a lot of people feel confused when scientists disagree with each other.*

A comparison: *People should be encouraged to buy electric cars,* ***as opposed to*** *gas or diesel ones.*

A result: *Fear about the future of the planet is a negative emotion.* ***Consequently****, we tend to reject it.*

A contrast: *People should respond positively to climate change campaigns.* ***Nevertheless****, they rarely do.*

A conclusion: ***In sum****, people do not usually respond well to environmental campaigns.*

6 **A** Read the Text builder. Find the **bold** formal linkers in the essay in exercise 2.

B Complete the sentences below with the linkers in **bold** from the Text builder.

1 Many families are less well off these days. _____ , a lot of students are dropping out of college because they cannot afford the tuition fees.
2 Many people say that children are not easily influenced by violent video games. _____ , a lot of research suggests that this is not true.
3 Some pop stars have millions of followers on social media. _____ , millions of people watch their favorite stars on TV.
4 To be successful, you need to be smart, creative, and have good interpersonal skills. _____ , these three critical traits are necessary for success.
5 Video games should encourage creativity and cooperation, _____ violence.

7 **A** **PREPARE** Choose an essay question from exercise 5A. Write a thesis statement and make notes of the supporting arguments.

B **PRACTICE** Use the Skill box to help you write your essay. Use topic sentences at the start of each paragraph and connect your ideas using formal linkers.

C **PERSONAL BEST** Exchange essays with a partner. Choose the best argument(s) supporting the thesis statement, and think of one additional one.

Personal Best Think about the essay question, "Are advertising campaigns successful?". Write two different thesis statements.

47

UNIT 6 Habits and change

LANGUAGE the habitual past ■ expressions with *time*

6A My best decade

1 In pairs, ask and answer questions about your interests when you were younger. Use the ideas in the box.

> Music   Food   TV shows   Clothes   Gadgets

2 A Read the text about people's past habits. Which of the interests in exercise 1 are mentioned?

A sign of the times

We all look back fondly on what was in fashion when we were younger. You know that old song you still sing along to in the car **from time to time** when no one is looking? Or that comfortable pair of sweatpants you're ashamed to admit you still love to wear? Looking back on previous decades, what do we think of them now? Mary, Bob, and Raul share their memories from three very different decades.

2000s: *Glee*

For some time in my teens, I watched it in bed till late at night. My mom was always coming into my room, though, so I would quickly change channels and pretend I was watching National Geographic. As the "intellectual" in the family, I had a reputation to maintain, and *Glee*, with all its strange dance moves and questionable song choices, was a no-no. It still influences so many of the "teen shows" we watch today.
(Mary, Chicago)

1990s: Cooking shows

In the 1990s, I couldn't afford to eat out very often, so I had to learn how to cook. Cooking shows were big then, so when I was making dinner, I used to pretend I was hosting my own show! I often invited a friend to "co-host" and we would use a camcorder to video our "cooking show." It's only **a matter of time** before one of those videos appears on YouTube. *(Bob, Boston)*

1980s: Abba

My dad used to be a huge Abba fan at one time, so I grew up listening to their songs, and eventually got hooked, too. My friends were always teasing me, of course, but I bet some of them secretly sang along to *Dancing Queen* in the shower! I still have a Spotify playlist with all their hits, which I'd memorized **at the time.**
(Raul, São Paulo)

B Look at the expressions with *time* in **bold** in the text. Match 1–4 with meanings a–d.

1 from time to time   _____   a then
2 for some time   _____   b sometimes
3 (only) a matter of time (before) _____   c for a period of time
4 at the time   _____   d certain that something will happen

Go to Vocabulary practice: expressions with *time*, page 144

3 A Complete the sentences about the text in exercise 2. Use past forms and include adverbs if necessary.

1 Mary _____ *Glee* in bed till late at night.
2 She _____ channels when her mom entered her room.
3 Bob _____ he was the host of a cooking show.
4 Raul's dad _____ a huge Abba fan.
5 Raul's friends _____ him.

B Look at the sentences in exercise 3A and complete the rules below. Then read the Grammar box.

1 *Used to / Would* is used to talk about past states.
2 The simple past *can / can't* be used to talk about past habits.
3 The past continuous with *always* is used to talk about *annoying / positive* past habits.

48

the habitual past ■ expressions with *time*   **LANGUAGE   6A**

 Grammar   the habitual past

used to and *would*:
I **used to play** video games all the time. I **would spend** hours in front of the computer.
Did you **use to be** a good student? I **didn't use to like** studying at all.

Simple past:
I **didn't play** any sports when I was younger. I **hated** sports.

Past continuous with *always*:
My little sister **was always interrupting** us. And she **was always making** noise, too.

would vs. *had*:
I**'d** (I **would**) **eat** chocolate every day.
That Thursday, I**'d** (I **had**) **eaten** a whole bar by the time my mother came home.

Look!   You cannot use *would* to talk about past states:
When I was younger, I **was**/**used to be** a huge fan of horror movies. NOT ~~I would be~~

Go to Grammar practice: the habitual past, page 122

4 A ▶ 6.3   **Pronunciation:** *use* and *used* Listen to the conversation. Notice how *use* and *used* are pronounced.

A Can I **use** your phone? My battery is dead, and I need to call my sister in Spain.
B Yeah, sure. But didn't you **use** to Skype her? That way you can **use** the camera, too.
A Well, I **used** to have a Skype account, but I haven't **used** it in years, and I've forgotten my password!
B Here, **use** my phone, instead.

B ▶ 6.3   Listen again and repeat. Practice the conversation in pairs.

5   Read the opinion poll. Decide if <u>one</u> or <u>both</u> options are possible.

What was the worst decade for music? Click on a decade and tell us why.

2010s 6 votes   Vote
"The early 2000s ¹*were / would be* amazing, but I can't stand the stuff they're playing on the radio these days. In the 2000s, I ²*was always spending / used to spend* hours listening to the radio, and at least 7 out of 10 songs were good. But now …" (Linda, San Francisco)

2000s 10 votes   Vote
"I was a teenager in the 2000s, and I remember how I ³*was always complaining / would complain* about bands like Coldplay and Keane. At least the 2000s gave us Lady Gaga, who ⁴*had / used to have* her first hit in 2009." (Juan, Mexico)

1990s 15 votes   Vote
"I grew up in the 1990s, and I ⁵*liked / used to like* rock and heavy metal. But my parents ⁶*used to listen / would listen* to people like Celine Dion and Mariah Carey – every single day. What a nightmare the 1990s were for me!" (Cynthia, New York)

Go to Communication practice: Student A page 160, Student B page 166

6   In pairs, ask each other at least three questions. Use the simple past, *used to*, *would*, and the past continuous with *always* in your answers.

| Do you think the | 1980s
1990s
2000s | were good for | music?
movies?
TV?
video games?
soccer?
fashion? |

I think the 1980s were terrible for fashion. People used to wear some really weird clothes!

Write a paragraph about when you were a child. Use a variety of past forms.

6 SKILLS

READING understanding non-literal meaning ■ contradicting

6B Healthy living: myths and facts

1 What is your healthiest eating habit? Do you have any bad eating habits? Discuss in pairs.

2 Look at the four myth headings about food in the text on page 51. Why do you think these may be myths?

3 Read the text and look carefully at "the facts" for each myth. Choose the correct summary of each fact.

Myth 1   **a**   Not all types of fiber are equally beneficial.
           b   Certain types of fiber are dangerous.
Myth 2   **a**   Organic food is safer to eat, but not necessarily more nutritious.
           b   Organic food isn't necessarily more nutritious or safer to eat.
Myth 3   **a**   What you eat is more important than when you eat.
           b   Eating at night can actually help you lose weight.
Myth 4   **a**   Water is not your only source of hydration.
           b   Drinking too much water can be dangerous.

🔧 Skill   understanding non-literal meaning

Writers use words with abstract, non-literal meanings to give the text more impact. When you are reading, pay attention to:

- **exaggeration:** *My doctor gave me a **never-ending** list of foods to avoid.* (= huge)
- **comparisons:** *I lost weight and now this dress looks **like a balloon**.* (= round)
- **personification:** *Four food myths that just won't **die**.* (= cease to exist)
- **idioms:** *I hate dieting, but you know what they say, **no pain, no gain**.* (= no hard work, no success)

---

4 **A** Read the Skill box. Look at this sentence from the introduction. What kind of non-literal language is used?

We are faced with a flood of information.

B Look at the underlined phrases 1–8 in the text. What kind of non-literal language in the Skill box is used in each one?

5 **A** In Myth 1, find the question "Does this mean you can stop eating broccoli … ?". Read the next sentence. What expression tells you the answer is "no"?

◆⊪ Text builder   contradicting

We use the expressions in bold to contradict something that was said.

*Does this mean you can stop eating broccoli like a health freak? **On the contrary**, most experts are skeptical.*
*If you buy organic food because it's "free from pesticides," keep in mind that **the opposite is true**.*
***The truth of the matter** is that it's the extra calories that lead to weight gain.*
***Contrary to popular belief**, you don't need to drink eight glasses of water a day.*

B Read the Text builder and find the expressions in **bold** in the text. Complete sentences 1–4 with two words.

1 Contrary to _____ , not everybody needs eight hours of sleep every night.
2 Some people say you should work out every day, but _____ is true. It's better to work out every other day so your body can recover.
3 We don't only use 10% of our brain. On _____ , we use most of it most of the time.
4 Spending too much time in the cold air doesn't make you sick. The _____ the matter is that you're more likely to get sick indoors, where germs are easily passed around.

6 Discuss the questions in pairs.

1 Were you aware of the myths in exercise 5B? Which one surprised you the most?
2 Do you know any other popular health myths? Why do people continue to believe in them?

50

understanding non-literal meaning ■ contradicting   READING   SKILLS   6B

Four food myths *that just won't die*

Whether at the grocery store, at a restaurant, or in our own kitchens, we are faced with a flood of information about what we should eat. Social media makes it easier than ever to spread myths and half-truths, so how much do we *really* know about the choices we are making when we eat? Our specialists have their say.

Myth 1: The more fiber you eat, the better.

The facts: Your grandparents probably used to tell you about the importance of fiber, but they had no idea just how popular "fiber-rich" foods would become. These days, it seems that food manufacturers are adding specific types of fiber to just about everything – from cereal bars to yogurt and even water! So does this mean you can stop eating broccoli [1]like a health freak? **On the contrary,** most experts are skeptical that processed fiber offers the same benefits as whole grains, fruits, and vegetables, which contain natural fiber. So when it comes to fiber, it's quality not quantity that matters.

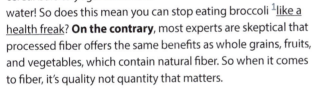

Myth 2: Organic food is better for you.

The facts: [2]Organic foods have shot up in popularity over the last decade. It seems that wherever you shop, every other food item you see also comes in an organic, health-conscious version. So, is it worth spending your hard-earned cash on the apples with the "organic" sticker on them? Recent research suggests the answer is no, since there is no significant nutritional difference between organic and conventional foods. And if you buy organic foods because they're "free from pesticides," keep in mind that **the opposite is true** – organic farms do use pesticides. And while organic foods may taste a little better, the only difference is that it's produced using natural, rather than synthetic, pesticides.

Myth 3: Eating at night makes you gain weight.

The facts: My mother was always telling me not to eat anything after 10 p.m. because evening meals would "make me fat." In certain countries, some people take this idea so seriously that they think twice before eating late in the evening [3]even if they're starving. It may be easy to believe our bodies have an internal clock set to store anything we eat at night as fat, but it's not as simple as that. **The truth of the matter** is that it's the extra calories – not when we consume them – that lead to weight gain. So if you tend to eat late in the evening, you don't have to [4]eat like a horse – just be selective. Stick with vegetables, lean proteins, and complex carbohydrates if you can.

Myth 4: You should drink eight glasses of water a day.

The facts: [5]This is another stubborn myth that has been around for decades, and [6]it just won't go away. Every summer we are flooded with media reports warning us about the dangers of dehydration and urging us to drink lots of water, even if we're not thirsty. But these fears are exaggerated. **Contrary to popular belief**, you don't need to drink eight glasses of water a day, since water is also present in tea, coffee, ice cream, and fruits and vegetables – you name it. In other words, while it's very important to drink water when the weather is hot, we may be less likely to dehydrate than pseudo-science would have us believe.

On a subject where a lot of people [7]talk as if they were experts, there is no shortage of bad health advice out there, so please remember, whatever you read, [8]to take it with a grain of salt.

Personal Best Write a paragraph about some food myths that you believe. Use linkers for contradicting.

6 LANGUAGE
be used to and *get used to* ■ expressions with prepositions

6C My generation and me

1 Think about your own family, and then discuss the questions below in pairs.
1. How many generations are there in your family? Do you all share the same values?
2. Who do you talk to and what about? Are there any subjects you avoid?
3. Complete the sentences:
   a. Unlike my parents, I (don't) care about …
   b. Unlike my parents, I (don't) approve of …
   c. Unlike my parents, I'm (not) fed up with …
   d. Unlike my parents, I (don't) feel I am entitled to …
   e. Unlike my parents, I'm (not) comfortable with …
   f. Unlike my parents, I'm (not) anxious about …

Go to Vocabulary practice: expressions with prepositions, page 145

2 Read the text about "Generation Y." How does the writer answer questions 1–3: *yes* or *no*?

MILLENNIALS: more to them than meets the eye?

When older people think of millennials, also known as "Generation Y," a few images often come to mind: lazy, living in their parents' basement, and addicted to social media. It's easy to get things wrong about those born from 1980 to 1995. Here are three common stereotypes.

1 Is it true that they need constant encouragement?
Research shows most millennials feel they are entitled to regular, immediate feedback from their managers, as opposed to formal reviews. This comes as no surprise. As they were growing up, millennials were constantly evaluated in school and taught how to improve their skills – perhaps more than their parents ever were. So, if millennials are constantly seeking regular feedback, _____ .

2 Do they care about owning a home?
Some of my friends in their 20s say, "_____ and all the work that comes with it. I'd rather spend my time – and money – doing something I actually enjoy." Fair enough. I'm not sure that's representative of most millennials, though. According to a recent survey, nearly 70% of those aged 18–34 want to own a home and still haven't bought one simply because they can't afford it.

3 Have they given up on marriage?
It seems that in some countries, at least, people are waiting longer to get married. At one time, young people in the U.S., for example, used to get married in their early 20s. Last year, the average age was 28. But just because millennials are putting off getting married doesn't mean they have no interest in marriage. Some are waiting to marry until they're more financially secure. Or maybe _____ of being married. That can take a while!

3 A Fill in the blanks in the text with a–d below. There is one extra item.
a. I'd never <u>get used to</u> a big house
b. they're still <u>getting used to</u> the idea
c. they <u>were not used to</u> long-term relationships
d. that's because <u>they're used to</u> it

B Which <u>underlined</u> expressions in exercise 3A mean:
1. be accustomed to?
2. become accustomed to?

4 A ▶ 6.6 Listen to two friends discussing the text. Do the man and the woman feel the same way about marriage?

B ▶ 6.6 Listen again and complete the sentences. What verb form follows *be used to* and *get used to*? Then read the Grammar box.
1. I'm used to _____ time alone and to _____ my own decisions.
2. I guess I'm used to _____ .
3. He'd never get used to _____ his life with another person.
4. Presumably, some people feel they can get used to _____ !

be used to and get used to ■ expressions with prepositions

LANGUAGE 6C

Grammar be used to and get used to

be used to:
Many young people **are used to** living alone.
My first year in Canada was tough because I **wasn't used to** long winters.

get used to:
I **haven't gotten used to** living with a roommate.
I don't think I**'ll** ever **get used to** college, no matter how hard I try.

Look! be/get used to are followed by the -ing form or a noun.

Go to Grammar practice: be used to and get used to, page 123

5 ▶ 6.8 **Pronunciation:** sentence stress with be used to and get used to Listen and repeat. Notice the /ə/ sound in to.

1 My cousin got used to living in a big city.
2 We're used to short summers now.
3 I'm not used to dealing with badly behaved children!
4 My parents are getting used to retired life.

6 A Choose the correct options to complete the text.

GENERATION Z, the term often used to describe those born after 1995, is essentially a global, social, visual, and technological generation. Here are some common stereotypes often associated with today's teens and young adults.

1 Generation Z was born into a world filled with technology, so they *used / are used* to the technology that millennials had to learn how to use.
2 Generation Z processes information faster than other generations because they are used to *communicate / communicating* with apps like Snapchat.
3 Multitasking is not a problem. They *used to do / are used to doing* it with great skill.
4 The downside is that they can be easily distracted because, over the years, they *get / have gotten* used to *focus / focusing* on too many things at the same time.

B In pairs, discuss which ideas from exercise 6A you think are true for people of your age.

7 A Complete the sentences with the correct form of be and get. There may be more than one answer.

1 The best age to learn how to drive is in your early 20s. In your late teens, your reflexes are still developing, so *you probably* _____ *used to fast responses in traffic*.
2 The best age to find a roommate is from your mid- to late 20s. It's not always easy to share your space with someone else, especially if *you* _____ *used to your independence*.
3 The best age to become a manager is in your mid-30s. I got promoted at 24, and it was a disaster, partly because *I* _____ *used to so much pressure*.
4 The best age to live abroad is in your late teens. *Young people tend to* _____ *used to new experiences more easily*.
5 When you're older, *it's harder to* _____ *used to another country*.

B Rewrite the words in *italics* in exercise 7A with *used to* and verbs 1–5.

1 make   2 have   3 work under   4 have   5 live

1 You're not used to/You haven't gotten used to making fast responses in traffic.

Go to **Communication practice:** Student A page 160, Student B page 166

8 In pairs, answer the questions.

1 Do you agree with the suggested ages in exercise 7A? Why/Why not?
2 What is the best age to do the things below?

[leave home] [have your first boyfriend/girlfriend] [have children]

[get your first job] [get married] [retire]

The best age to leave home is 18. We should get used to living alone as soon as possible!

Personal Best Describe something you never thought you'd get used to, but are used to now.

53

6 SKILLS SPEAKING challenging assumptions ■ solving problems

6D A suitable roommate

1 In pairs, choose the three most important characteristics of a roommate. Use the ideas in the box.

fun   honest   organized   quiet   responsible   the same age   the same values

2 ▶ 6.9 Watch or listen to the first part of *Talking Zone*. Write *Ben* or *Abigail*.

1 _____ suggests finding a roommate.
2 _____ thinks the age gap might be a problem.
3 _____ begins to change his/her mind a little towards the end.

3 A Match the two parts to make complete sentences from Ben and Abigail's conversation.

1 Just because he's older doesn't mean
2 But hanging out is one thing, sharing an apartment
3 True, but it might be nice
4 Responsibility has nothing
5 But what if he doesn't
6 People can get along no matter
7 But how do you know he won't mind

a to do with age!
b we can't get along.
c watch the same TV shows we do?
d to have someone older and more responsible around.
e sharing an apartment with people half his age?
f quite another.
g how different their tastes are.

B ▶ 6.9 Watch or listen again and check. What does Ben say to change Abigail's mind?

Conversation builder — challenging assumptions

Just because you like her doesn't mean you should be roommates.
Being friends is one thing, living together (quite) another.
True, but it's still important to get along.
Honesty has nothing to do with age.
But what if we have different tastes?
People can get along no matter/regardless of how different their tastes are.
But how do you know he won't mind helping with the chores?

4 Read the Conversation builder. Imagine you and your partner are looking for a roommate. Take turns challenging the assumptions below.

1 "She's only 20. She's probably too immature."
2 "He has two cats. We've never had a pet around here."
3 "She's a vegetarian. Planning our meals will be a nightmare."
4 "He works from home. He'll never leave the house."
5 "He's into classical music. He'll listen to Mozart all day long."

54

challenging assumptions ■ solving problems **SPEAKING**   SKILLS **6D**

5 ▶ 6.10 Watch or listen to the second part of the show. What do Ben and Abigail agree on?

1 The potential roommate who came to their apartment will probably say "No."
2 Spending less on the Internet will help solve their financial problems.
3 Spending less on electricity is a solution, too.
4 Since the rent is going up, they'll probably need a third roommate.

Skill | **solving problems**

When you try to solve a problem, you can use some of the following conversation strategies:
- Make a point: *If you ask me, we should hire a nanny.*
- Suggest alternatives: *We could either sell the car or move to a cheaper place./We could always sell the car./Why not see if we can sell the car?/We could sell the car instead of moving.*
- Ask for or offer clarification: *Like what? You mean sell the car? The point I'm making is …*
- Challenge someone to keep thinking: *Is it worth it, though? But is it really a good idea? What difference would it make?*

6 ▶ 6.10 Read the Skill box. Guess the missing words in Ben and Abigail's sentences below. Then watch or listen again and check.

1 We'll _____ have to look for another roommate _____ find a way to save some money.
2 _____ ? We're pretty economical when it comes to food and stuff.
3 _____ switch to a cheaper Internet provider.
4 But even if we save 10 or 20 dollars, _____ would it _____ ?
5 Like, _____ use LED lights _____ normal bulbs?
6 _____ the ones that are cool to touch?
7 Is it _____ ? They're so expensive to buy.
8 _____ is that if we're serious about saving money, every little bit counts.

7 Which problem-solving strategy does each sentence in exercise 6 use?

1 *suggest alternatives*
2 _____
3 _____
4 _____
5 _____
6 _____
7 _____
8 _____

Go to Communication practice: Student A page 161, Student B page 167

8 A PREPARE In pairs, imagine you belong to the same family. You need to solve a problem together. Prepare a conversation, using one of the ideas below.

(an overdue bill) (noisy neighbors) (sharing the family car)

(apartment cleaning schedule) (walking the dog) (doing the weekly food shopping)

B PRACTICE Practice the conversation. Make sure you make suggestions and offer/ask for clarification. Were you able to solve your problem?

C PERSONAL BEST Choose a new problem and practice the conversation again. Did you suggest practical solutions? What improvements can you make?

Personal Best | Write a paragraph describing a problem you or someone you know has had, including how it was solved. | 55

5 and 6 REVIEW and PRACTICE

Grammar

1 Cross (**X**) the sentence that is NOT correct.

1 a I ate so much food I'm not hungry.
 b I ate such a big lunch I'm not hungry.
 c I ate so big lunch I'm not hungry.

2 a I lived in Norway when I was a child, but I never got used to the cold weather.
 b I lived in Norway when I was a child, but I couldn't be used to the cold weather.
 c I lived in Norway when I was a child, but I didn't use to like the cold weather.

3 a There are so much different phones on sale.
 b There are so many different phones on sale.
 c There are such a lot of different phones on sale.

4 a There will be so few guests at the wedding.
 b There will be so little guests at the wedding.
 c There won't be many guests at the wedding.

5 a By the time I'm 30, I will have saved enough money to buy a car.
 b By the time I'm 30, I'm going to be saved enough money to buy a car.
 c By the time I'm 30, I might have saved enough money to buy a car.

6 a Our teacher had yelled at us all the time.
 b Our teacher would yell at us all the time.
 c Our teacher used to yell at us all the time.

7 a I may never get used to waking up at such an early time.
 b I may never get used to waking up so early.
 c I may never get used to wake up so early.

8 a My children never slept on vacation.
 b My children wouldn't sleep on vacation.
 c My children didn't used to sleep on vacation.

2 Use the words in parentheses to complete the sentences so they mean the same as the first sentence.

1 The kitchen was a complete mess, so I ordered a pizza, instead.
 The kitchen _____ a pizza instead. (such)

2 My mother would make us sweet tea when we were sick.
 _____ sweet tea when we were sick. (used)

3 She doesn't think she's going to be able to go to work tomorrow.
 _____ able to go to work tomorrow. (might)

4 I never became accustomed to working during the night.
 I never _____ during the night. (used)

5 Will robots be doing all of our jobs by 2050?
 _____ doing all of our jobs by 2050? (going)

6 There were hardly any cars on the road because of the snow.
 _____ because of the snow. (so)

7 My brother and his friends used to wear the same clothes every day.
 My brother _____ the same clothes every day. (would)

8 We will have four meetings between now and next Friday.
 _____ by next Friday. (had)

3 Choose the correct options to complete the text.

▶ INTERVIEW   Thursday, January 4

My name is Marie and I'm 75 years old. I ¹*used to live / have lived* my whole life in the outskirts of Lyon in the south of France. I have ²*so many / so much* wonderful childhood memories. My friends and I ³*used to / were used to* walk to and from school every day, and when it was warm, we ⁴*were playing / would play* outside all evening. In the summer, we ⁵*used to / got used to* swim in the lake near my house. The water was ⁶*so / such* a cold at first, but you ⁷*got used / are used* to it after a few minutes. I had ⁸*so / such* a happy childhood, but I'm rather worried about children today. They seem to spend ⁹*much / so much* time in front of their computers and so ¹⁰*few / little* children today walk to school these days. And there are so many problems in the world! I ¹¹*wouldn't / won't* be here in 50 years, but my grandchildren ¹²*will have been / will be*. But with all this climate change, what ¹³*will be / is going to* happen to the environment? And employment will be very different, too. In 50 years, a lot of people ¹⁴*are going to / may have* lost their jobs because robots ¹⁵*will be / may* doing all the work!

Vocabulary

1 Circle the word or expression that is different. Explain why.

1 inaccurate irregular improbable impatient
2 waste time in time for on time for some time
3 passionate lethargic motivated eager
4 grumpy energetic positive enthusiastic
5 wildfires drought heatwave wildlife
6 impolite illegal immature irregular
7 motivated down miserable pessimistic
8 climate change solar energy endangered species toxic waste

REVIEW and PRACTICE 5 and 6

2 Match the words and expressions in the box with definitions 1–10.

> fed up with illogical dynamic misleading
> obsessed with entitled to insist on sth
> distressing accuse sb of sth informal

1 say that somebody did something wrong _____
2 full of energy and new ideas _____
3 unhappy or annoyed about a situation that has been happening for a long time _____
4 thinking about something, all the time _____
5 have the right to do or have something _____
6 causing anxiety or sadness _____
7 not making sense _____
8 having a relaxed nature or style _____
9 giving the wrong idea _____
10 demand something and not accept refusal _____

3 Choose the correct words from the box to complete the sentences.

> improbable advised eager energy consumption
> optimistic grumpy suspicious irrelevant

1 When my father is hungry, he gets really _____ and starts yelling at everybody.
2 My friend Elena is a very _____ student, and she always asks questions in lectures.
3 I'd love to get the job, but I'm not _____ because the interview went very badly.
4 My teacher said my essay contained a lot of _____ information that wasn't connected to the title.
5 Karina tells some great stories, but I find a lot of them pretty _____ . I think she exaggerates.
6 My roommates and I are trying to reduce our _____ , so we always turn off the lights when we leave a room.
7 I wanted to apply for the manager's position, but my friends _____ me against it.
8 I'm always _____ of news stories because I think journalists often invent things.

4 Choose the correct options to complete the text.

> Many people are rightly [1]*distressing / concerned* about [2]*climate change / solar power* as it is only a [3]*matter / waste* of time until it becomes the most important issue on the planet. In fact, it is [4]*irrelevant / irresponsible* not to discuss the issue. However, while it is encouraging to hear politicians being sympathetic [5]*of / to* the environmental cause, we should all be suspicious [6]*of / with* government policies which seem too perfect. Although some of these ideas can be beneficial, most of them are [7]*immature / ineffective*. Instead of [8]*wasting / taking* time on short-term solutions, governments need to look at the bigger picture.

Personal Best

Lesson 5A
Write four sentences about your life using *so / such, so much / so many* and *so little / so few*.

Lesson 6A
Describe four habits or routines from your childhood using *would* and *used to*.

Lesson 5A
Name four environmental issues that affect our planet.

Lesson 6A
Write four sentences about yourself and people you know using different expressions with *time*.

Lesson 5B
Name four "mood" adjectives and for each one, say when you last felt this way.

Lesson 6B
Describe an experience using exaggeration, comparison, and an idiom.

Lesson 5C
Make four predictions using *will, going to, may/might*, the future perfect, or the future continuous.

Lesson 6C
Describe two things you are used to and two things you can't get used to.

Lesson 5C
Write four sentences using words with these prefixes: *dis-, ir-, im-, mis-*.

Lesson 6C
Use four different adjectives followed by prepositions to describe your generation.

Lesson 5D
Write three pairs of sentences. Begin the second one with *similarly, consequently*, and *nevertheless*.

Lesson 6D
Write four sentences in which you challenge assumptions about an important topic.

UNIT 7 Lifelong learning

LANGUAGE   relative clauses ■ collocations with *attend*, *get*, *make*, and *submit*

7A Unique college programs

1 In pairs, discuss the statements below about college programs. Do you agree?
1. You won't get ahead in life if you don't go to college.
2. It makes a big difference exactly which college you go to.
3. At college, it's better to study online than to attend classes.
4. No one should need to submit a college application. The transition from high school should be automatic.

Go to Vocabulary practice: collocations with *attend*, *get*, *make*, and *submit*, page 145

2 A Read the text. In pairs, say which program you like the best and explain why.

B Do the underlined sentences in the text mean the same as sentences 1–4 below?
1. In Surf Science and Technology, students only learn how to make a surfboard.
2. Comic Art appeals to a specific group of potential students.
3. Comic Art only teaches students how to express themselves artistically.
4. Ethical Hacking students will learn how hackers gain access to information illegally.

Undergraduate programs you didn't know existed!

Struggling to choose a career? Not interested in traditional options like engineering, education, or business administration? I have good news! If you have a passion or a hobby, there's a chance you can get a degree in that subject, which means you can make the most of your hobby or interest, doing something you love! Here's a list of our favorite unusual-but-cool programs.

Surf Science and Technology:
Cornwall College, UK

If you're into surfing, this two-year program is just what you need. It covers the history of surfing, explores the psychology of being a successful surfer, and investigates people's attitudes to fitness. [1]There are both lectures and practical modules focusing on surfboard building, so, yes, you'll need to attend the classes. This program won't teach you how to surf, though!

Comic Art:
Minneapolis College of Art and Design, U.S.

[2]Anyone interested in comics should take a closer look at this innovative program. Graduates may even find the job of their dreams in the comic industry or on TV. [3]The program includes courses focusing on both the history of comic art and artistic expression. As you learn about storytelling techniques, you'll also learn how to use colors and lines to get people's attention – and keep them interested.

Ethical Hacking:
University of Abertay Dundee, UK

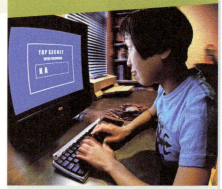

This four-year program teaches you everything about computer hacking! [4]Students enrolling in the program will study the techniques hackers use to obtain illegal information. The course covers areas such as breaking into web servers, stealing information, and remotely controlling someone's computer. The aim is to show students how illegal computer attacks are carried out, and how to prevent them.

relative clauses ■ collocations with *attend*, *get*, *make*, and *submit*   **LANGUAGE** **7A**

3 Read the text again and complete the tasks below. Then read the Grammar box.
1 Rephrase the underlined sentences using *that* or *who*.
2 Underline the *which* clause in the text. Does it refer only to the word immediately before *which* or to a complete idea?

 Grammar relative clauses: reduced and comment clauses

Defining relative clauses – reduced clauses:
Students (who are) living at home sometimes have a long commute to school.
I got an e-mail containing further information about the program.
Anyone (who is) caught cheating will be suspended immediately.

Non-defining relative clauses – comment clauses:
The test was easy, which explains why so many students passed.
The program was too hard, which is why I quit.

Look! *Students attending* (= Students who attend) *classes should arrive on time!*

Go to Grammar practice: relative clauses; reduced and comment clauses, page 124

4 A ▶7.3 **Pronunciation:** comment clauses Listen to the conversations. Insert a comma when you hear a pause in B's responses. After *which*, does the intonation go up or down?

1 A So you're getting a degree in surfing?
 B I am! And it's a serious program which most people don't really expect.
2 A How's college?
 B Great! I love creating comics. And I'm good at it which shows I picked the right program.
3 A I can't believe I'm graduating next month!
 B And you've gotten lots of job offers which means the market needs "ethical hackers."

B ▶7.3 Listen again and repeat. Then practice the conversations in pairs. Replace the underlined words with your own ideas.

5 A Find the relative clauses in sentences 1–6 below. Then rephrase them using reduced clauses.

SCHOOL RULES from around the world

1 At one school in the U.S., students who skip classes aren't punished.
2 A Canadian school banned hard balls because of a parent who was hit by a ball.
3 Many students who attend high school in Japan have to wear uniforms.
4 In Sweden, students who are aged 10–15 can't use their phones in class.
5 A school in the UK has created a policy that bans students from having best friends.
6 There's a rule in some schools in Australia and the UK that states that students' papers should be graded using green ink.

B In pairs, give your own opinion of each rule, using comment clauses.

… which is a good/terrible idea because …   … which means that …   … which makes a lot of/no sense because …

… which explains why …   … which makes me wonder if …

At one school in the U.S., students skipping classes aren't punished, which is a terrible idea because …

Go to Communication practice: Student A page 161, Student B page 167

6 Think of two high school/college/workplace rules that you don't agree with. Discuss your ideas in groups.

Students attending …   Employees arriving …   Anyone caught …   People absent from …

Personal Best Write five rules for a school or work poster.

7 SKILLS LISTENING identifying sequence ■ reduced forms ■ ability

7B Successful learning

1 A Read the comments. In pairs, decide if any of these sentences are true for you.

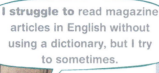

> **I struggle to** read magazine articles in English without using a dictionary, but I try to sometimes.

> **I keep looking up** the difference between *will* and *going to*, but **I can't quite manage to** understand it!

> **I'm pretty good at** listening. I watch movies in English, and I understand a lot of what is said.

B In pairs, summarize your top three tips for learning English.

Go to Vocabulary practice: ability, page 146

2 A ▶ 7.5 Watch or listen to the first part of *Talking Zone*. What is a Polyglot edutainer? How does Cameron reach his students?

B Check (✓) the language learning tips that are mentioned.

a Listen to songs so you can learn new words. ☐
b Watch TV programs like soap operas to help you learn. ☐
c Don't worry about making errors when you speak. ☐
d Follow the news and watch movies with subtitles.
e Find a pen pal you can write to every week.
f Keep practicing!
g Be sure to study grammar also.

Skill   identifying sequence

When someone gives you tips or advice, they often follow a sequence, and are in the form of commands. These are some ways to identify the steps you should follow.

- When two activities are mentioned together, think about which one logically comes first: *Once you've saved some money, you can buy a new car.* (First you save some money, then you buy a car.)
- Listen for expressions that tell you what to do first: *Don't wait until level 5 before you try to understand movies.* (You can try to understand movies before level 5.)
- Remember previous advice and pay attention to intonation: *Finally, don't give up!*

3 ▶ 7.5 Read the Skill box. Then watch or listen again and complete the sentences with *before* or *after*.

1 Cameron thinks you should make friends in your new language _____ you become fluent.
2 He says you should correct your mistakes _____ you try to speak the language.
3 Cameron studied foreign languages _____ he turned twenty, but was more successful _____ that age

identifying sequence ■ reduced forms ■ ability **LISTENING** SKILLS **7B**

4 In pairs, think of three excuses people sometimes use for not learning a language.

5 ▶7.6 Watch or listen to the second part of the show. Are any of your ideas from exercise 4 mentioned?

6 ▶7.6 Watch or listen again. Complete the notes with one or two words in each blank.

As a kid: short attention span – Cameron couldn't ¹_____ .
Babies: ²_____ languages easily, but adults can learn, too!
Adults: very good at learning ³_____ .
Difficulty: could be easy or difficult – depends on your ⁴_____ language.
Important: adults can learn if they're ⁵_____ .
Common excuse from ⁶_____ : "I don't have that kind of brain!"
Important slogan: Make it ⁷_____ !

Listening builder | reduced forms

In natural spoken English, words like *to*, *for*, *as*, *do/does*, *was/were* and *can* may be hard to understand because they are usually pronounced as a "schwa" /ə/.

I had **to** /tə/ change my mindset.
It's too late **for** /fər/ me!
We do that **as** /əz/ adults, too.

Does /dəz/ he speak another language?
It **was** /wəz/ totally addictive.
You **can** /kən/ correct your mistakes later.

7 A ▶7.7 Read the Listening builder. Then listen and complete each sentence from the show with two words. Which words that you filled in have reduced forms?

1 People come up with a lot of reasons not _____ a language.
2 If a baby _____ it, why can't I?
3 There are languages that are trickier to learn _____ .
4 As _____ we're motivated, we do that as adults, too.
5 Thank you, Cameron, and thank you _____ .

B Practice saying each sentence.

8 In pairs, rank skills a–d from 1 (easy to learn) to 4 (hard to learn). Explain the reasons for your ranking with real examples.

a swimming

b speaking in public

c drawing or painting

d dancing

Personal Best Describe something you found difficult to learn. Include some tips.

7 LANGUAGE present and future real conditions ■ mind and memory

7C If I remember correctly …

1 A Look at the pictures for 10 seconds. Close your book and make a list of everything you remember. In pairs, compare your lists.

B In pairs, discuss the questions. Which of you has the best memory?
1. How many pictures were you able to recall? What do you think made them memorable?
2. How did you try to remember the pictures?
3. In general, do you find it easy to learn things by heart?

Go to Vocabulary practice: mind and memory, page 146

2 Read the text. Which suggestions do you follow? Did any of the information surprise you? Discuss in pairs.

3 simple ways to improve your memory

Your brain is constantly changing. Every day it can grow new cells, form new connections, and help you remember things more easily – provided you give it a little help. Here are three examples of daily habits that can boost your memory.

1. Students occasionally stay awake before a big test, but it's better to get a good night's sleep. Your brain receives lots of information when you're awake, and it uses the time you're asleep to process this information. Unless you get enough sleep, your mind might go blank the next day.

2. Listening to music before you start studying is a good way to help you recall new facts – as long as the music is relaxing and provided it's not too loud! But once you start work, turn the music off. Research has shown that any kind of background noise can be distracting.

3. "Nuts are good for your memory! Avoid sweets!" Does this sound familiar? As it turns out, it's not only what you eat that affects your memory – it's also what you drink! Our brains are over 70% water, so keep in mind that dehydration can interfere with both attention and memory. Drink lots of water throughout the day, even if you're not particularly thirsty.

3 A Statements 1–4 below are all false. In pairs, underline the evidence in the text.
1. A lack of sleep won't interfere with your memory.
2. Any kind of music can help you remember information.
3. Music can boost your memory, and volume isn't important.
4. You should only drink water when you feel like it.

B Look at the sentences you underlined. Which words below can replace *as long as*? Then read the Grammar box.

a provided   b unless   c even if

present and future real conditions ■ mind and memory   **LANGUAGE** **7C**

Grammar: present and future real conditions

Zero and first conditionals:
If/When I **study** every day, I **do** better on tests.
If you **want** to pass this exam, you**'ll need** to study hard.

Future time clauses:
I**'ll finish** my paper as soon as I **get** home.
I **tend** to forget new words until I **see** them again.

Alternatives to *if*:
As long as you **review** your notes, you**'ll remember** what you've learned.
Provided (that) you **study**, I**'m** sure you'll pass.
Unless you **practice** every day, you **won't learn** to play an instrument.
Even if your memory **is** good, you still **need** to take notes.

Go to Grammar practice: present and future real conditions, page 125

4 A ▶ 7.11   **Pronunciation:** sentence stress in conditional sentences Listen to the sentences. Which are the two stressed words in each underlined phrase?

1 Oh, all right, you can borrow it, as long as <u>you promise to be careful</u>!
2 I'll be there at about 10, provided <u>the bus is on time</u>.
3 Unless <u>you tell her a story</u>, she won't go to sleep.
4 You should exercise every day, even if <u>it's only for ten minutes</u>.

B ▶ 7.11   Listen again and repeat. Then, in pairs, think of a question that would produce each sentence as a response.

5 A Read the text and choose the correct options.

... Five tips to help you remember new vocabulary
Which ones would work best for you?

1 Before you can use a new word confidently, you need to see it again and again. *Unless / As long as* you have a really good memory, constant review is essential.

2 Repeating words out loud is a simple but powerful way to help you remember vocabulary – *even if / provided that* you know what the words mean, of course!

3 Try to "play" with the new vocabulary. For example, to learn the expression "keep an open mind," imagine your brain and an open window, *even if / as long as* it feels a bit strange!

4 When you learn a new word or expression, close your eyes and try to visualize it, *even if / as long as* it's an abstract concept such as "love" or "peace."

5 You can remember new words more easily *unless / as long as* you learn them with words they go with. For example, instead of simply learning "boost," try to memorize "boost your memory."

B ▶ 7.12   Listen to a teacher and student discussing the tips in exercise 5A and check your answers. In pairs, say which tip you like the best.

Go to Communication practice: Both students, page 172

6 In groups, share your suggestions for getting ready for exams. Use the ideas below to help you, and use present real conditions in your suggestions.

The day before the exam	The day of the exam	During the actual exam
How many hours of review? Breaks? Alone? Background music? Bedtime?	Last-minute review? What kind of food? Any physical exercise? Tea or coffee?	Relaxation techniques? Easy questions first? Memory problems? Timing?

On the day before the exam, I spend as much time studying as I can, even if I have to go to bed at 2:00 a.m.!

Using alternatives to *if*, complete this sentence in four different ways: *I will become fluent in English ...*

7 SKILLS WRITING writing a set of guidelines ■ linkers to add ideas

7D It's never too late to learn!

1 A Look at the categories below. What would you like to learn in the next two years? Add two ideas to each category.

Sport
"I'd like to become a better tennis player."

Music
"I've always wanted to play the guitar."

Art
"I'd love to draw better than a five-year-old."

Technology
"I want to design phone apps and sell them."

B In pairs, compare your answers. Which goals sound the easiest? Which sound the most difficult?

2 A Read Ann's blog post, ignoring the blanks. Then match headings a–d below with tips 1–4 in the text.

a Work hard
b Choose something you care about
c Establish concrete goals
d Get a good teacher

B Which tip seems most useful?

Learning a new skill

BLOG   ABOUT   PROFILE

There are a lot of reasons why you might want to learn a new skill. Maybe you're trying to get a promotion. Perhaps you want to keep your mind active. Or you might just be looking for a new challenge. No matter what you want to learn and why, these four tips will help you.

1 _____

Even if you want to learn three sports, pick one you're truly passionate about. If you choose a sport you're not really interested in, the chances are you won't be very good at it! (a) _____ , you'll find it hard to keep yourself motivated. Trust me – I've quit soccer practice three times!

2 _____

It's easier to accomplish goals that are realistic. When I learned Portuguese, instead of saying, "I want to learn Portuguese," I told myself, "I want to be able to communicate in everyday situations when I go to Brazil."
(b) _____ , I gave myself a deadline ("in six months"), which helped.

3 _____

You can learn a new skill on your own, but it's easier when you have someone guide you. For example, you can create a professional-looking website by watching online tutorials, but a teacher helped me speed up the process.
(c) _____ , he or she will give you feedback, which is a good thing.

4 _____

Research shows that talent has less to do with your genes and more with your attitude. For example, I'm taking art lessons, and I'm not naturally good at drawing or painting. (d) _____ , I'm making good progress, and people seem to like my work. My secret? Two hours of practice every day.

Lastly, here's my most important piece of advice for you: keep in mind that making mistakes is a normal part of the learning process. As an adult, you're good at lots of different things, and it's difficult to be a beginner again. (e) _____ , we all need to learn to start over and get things wrong before we get them right. Good luck!

Posted by Ann   Share   Like   Comment

writing a set of guidelines ■ linkers to add ideas **WRITING** **SKILLS** **7D**

3 Think of something you've learned to do well. Make a list of three strategies that helped you. Then discuss them in pairs. Were any of your ideas mentioned in the blog post?

Skill **writing a set of guidelines**

Guidelines or tips that give advice on how to do something should be easy to follow, friendly, and interesting.
- Organize your tips into short paragraphs.
- Give each tip a title summarizing the advice.
- Make sure each tip includes the reason why it's important.
- Include examples or personal experiences to help you make your point.
- "Speak" to the reader directly, using "you" and "your."

4 Read the Skill box. Then read tips 1–4 in Ann's blog post again and <u>underline</u> …
1 the reason behind each of Ann's four tips.
2 Ann's personal experience.

5 Choose the correct option for three additional points for the Skill box. Check your answers in Ann's blog post to help you.

- Write a [1]*short / detailed* introduction explaining the purpose of your post.
- Write [2]*one / two* tip(s) per paragraph. You [3]*can / shouldn't* number the paragraphs.
- Decide where to put the most important tip. You [4]*can / can't* include it in the conclusion.

Text builder **linkers to add ideas**

We use the linkers *besides*, *in addition*, and *moreover* to connect similar ideas:
*Practice helps you play better. **Besides**, it can boost your confidence.*
*I'm fluent in Spanish. **In addition**, I speak very good German.*
*It's a good idea to watch YouTube tutorials. **Moreover**, reading on the subject is useful, too.*

Look! When the words in **bold** in the sentences above connect two independent clauses, always start a new sentence:

*I'm a skilled drummer. **In addition**, I can play the guitar quite well.*
NOT *I'm a skilled drummer, in addition, I can play the guitar quite well.*

6 Read the Text builder. Choose the correct linkers for blanks a–e in the blog post.
a *Besides / Although*
b *Moreover / Though*
c *In addition / Despite*
d *Besides / However*
e *In addition / However*

7 Write two sentences for each item 1–4 below. Connect them using a linker in the Text builder.
1 Health: yoga / good / health – can boost / memory
Yoga is good for your health. Besides, it can boost your memory.
2 Hobbies: good idea / watch YouTube videos – try / follow experts / social media
3 Singing: important / warm up / voice when you sing – don't forget / drink / plenty / water
4 Language learning: no "right" age / learn / foreign language – no "right" method

8 A **PREPARE** Choose something you've learned or would like to learn to do well. Decide on three important tips.

B **PRACTICE** Use the Skill box to help you write a blog post. Add ideas using linkers.

C **PERSONAL BEST** Exchange posts with a partner. Rank the tips in order of importance. Would you change the order of any of them?

Personal Best Can you learn a new skill completely on your own? Write a paragraph answering this question.

65

UNIT 8 The changing media

LANGUAGE using linkers (2) ■ the media

8A TV in the 21st Century

1 Read the responses from a survey. In pairs, say which ones are true for you.
  a "I prefer to get my news from independent sources, which I think are less biased."
  b "There are so many good shows on TV that I don't know which ones to follow!"
  c "I love to watch the evening news, especially when there's breaking news."
  d "I rarely watch regular TV. I prefer to stream shows and watch them when I feel like it."

Go to Vocabulary practice: the media, page 147

2 Read the text and fill in the blank in the first line with "In some ways" or "No, not at all."

Is this the end of TV as we know it?

"_____," says media expert Jane Midler, who has just released the results of a survey she conducted recently.

The role of television in our lives has changed a lot. Viewing habits in the U.S. are very different from ten years ago, and we can expect even more changes in the near future.

1 Fewer shows in the future

¹In 2010, media companies produced about 200 original TV shows, whereas seven years later this number had more than doubled. ²While variety is a good idea, most of the people I have interviewed about this trend say there is now too much to choose from, and this creates a problem for TV networks. ³Since there are too many shows for too few viewers, audiences tend to be small, which means fewer ads and less money. As a result, the number of shows will probably drop in the near future.

2 More subscription services

I have interviewed nearly 100 people between the ages of 16–22, and most of them have grown up watching less TV than their parents. So, ⁴unlike older adults, it seems that teens and young adults are abandoning television. When they want to watch a show, they simply go online and watch it on their phone or computer – anywhere, any time. ⁵Due to this desire for flexibility, services like Netflix will undoubtedly remain popular for many years to come.

3 The death of the evening news as we know it

My survey has also revealed that fewer people seem to trust the evening news. Words like "fair," "objective," and "accurate" rarely came up in their opinions, and it is not hard to understand why. ⁶Viewers have access to hundreds of sites and online channels where they can compare different perspectives and form their own opinions. Therefore, they have become more critical. Unless the evening news reinvents itself, networks will continue to lose viewers.

3 Match sentences a–d in exercise 1 with sections 1–3 of the text. There is one extra sentence.

4 Look at the underlined sentences 1–6 in the text. What kind of idea does each one express: contrast/comparison or reason? Then read the Grammar box.

66

using linkers (2) ■ the media | LANGUAGE | 8A

 Grammar using linkers (2)

Expressing a contrast or comparison:
Only 50% of teens say they watch TV, **whereas/while** the rest use streaming services.
While/Whereas every home had a TV in the 90s, today some homes don't have one.
Unlike the younger generation, some adults still prefer to read print newspapers.

Expressing a reason:
Since/As technology has changed so quickly, the press has had to adapt.
Due to/Because of/As a result of advances in technology, e-books are easier to read than before.
I rarely watch the news. **Therefore/As a result**, I don't know what's going on in the world.

Go to Grammar practice: using linkers (2), page 126

5 A ▶8.3 **Pronunciation:** emphatic stress Listen to the sentences. Notice how the underlined words are stressed to emphasize a contrast or a reason.

1 I watch *The Simpsons* regularly, <u>unlike</u> most of my friends.
2 I can stream my favorite films. <u>As a result</u>, I've been going to the movies less often.
3 I like to watch subtitled movies, <u>whereas</u> my brother prefers the dubbed versions.
4 Reading is a unique experience, and, <u>therefore</u>, movies based on books are never very good.

B ▶8.3 Listen again and repeat. Then choose a statement that is true for you and discuss it in pairs.

6 ▶8.4 Choose the correct options to complete the text. Listen and check.

How **virtual reality** might change the movie industry

¹*Because of / As* rising costs and recent improvements in home entertainment technology, movie attendance has declined over the past few years. However, the movie industry has been quick to respond, and now audiences can enjoy advanced 3D projections, complete with surround sound.
But ²*since / whereas* movie tickets are still expensive, studios are now trying to change people's experiences of going to the movies. And this is where 360-degree virtual reality comes in. Soon moviegoers will be wearing special glasses that, ³*whereas / unlike* 3D glasses, will make them feel as if they are "surrounded" by the movie. ⁴*Due to / Therefore*, audiences will feel closer to the action and more connected with the characters. ⁵*As / While* none of this is guaranteed to bring viewers back, it seems like a step in the right direction.

7 Rewrite each person's reason for not going to the movies anymore in two different ways. Use the words in parentheses.

1 "Movie theaters are too expensive, and this is why I prefer to watch movies at home." (since / as a result)
2 "Movies from the 1990s were great. Today's movies are silly." (unlike / whereas)
3 "I don't go to movie theaters anymore because people always talk during the movie." (as a result / since)

Go to Communication practice: Student A page 161, Student B page 167

8 Choose a picture and think about the questions below. Then, in pairs, answer the questions using linkers to express contrast/comparison or give reasons.

a   b   c   d

1 How often do you/your friends/your family use this piece of technology?
2 In general, is it more/less popular than it used to be? Why?
3 What do you think will happen in the next ten years or so? Why?

Most of my friends still have laptops. They're still very popular since they've become much lighter and easier to carry. I don't think many people will have them in 10 years as tablets have become more popular, too.

Personal Best Choose a different piece of technology and answer the questions in exercise 8.

8 SKILLS

READING inferring meaning using related words ■ generalizing

8B Digital media for you

1 Look at the pictures on page 69 showing people using various kinds of social media. Which opinion best represents you? Why?

2 Look at the title. What is the purpose of the text? Choose from a–c. Read the introduction and check.

   a to describe the results of a survey   **c** to report a news event that has happened
   b to help readers deal with a problem

3 Check (✔) the sentence (1 or 2) that best summarizes each person's main point. Then match it with his/her advice a or b.

Larry

  1 ☐ Social media platforms don't give us the opportunity to see things in different ways.
  2 ☐ We allow social media to spy on us.

  a We should be willing to consider ideas we may disagree with.
  b We should spend less time on social media.

Sue

  1 ☐ Serious news sources are disappearing.
  2 ☐ Today, it's hard to distinguish real news from fake news.

  a We should read or watch the news critically.
  b We should never depend on online sources.

🔧 Skill   inferring meaning using related words

When you are trying to infer the meaning of unknown vocabulary, look for related words. These are often:
- in the same sentence as the unknown vocabulary item.
- synonyms or near-synonyms to the vocabulary item.
- the same part of speech as the vocabulary item (e.g.,both are adjectives).

4 **A** Read the Skill box and the example below. Then <u>underline</u> a synonym (or a word with a similar meaning) for each word in **bold** in the text.

*Digital news platforms make it easier than ever to find information about <u>almost</u> any topic on **virtually** any device.*

B Complete the sentence below with the correct option.

Related words, such as synonyms or the same part of speech, can be found *before / after / either before or after* the word they refer to.

🧩 Text builder   generalizing

We can use the expressions in bold below to make generalizations:
***Generally speaking**, news sources in my country are trustworthy.*
***On the whole**, I consider myself tolerant of other people's opinions.*
***As a rule**, I don't read or watch the news in English.*
***For the most part**, I get my news from Facebook and Twitter.*

5 Read the Text builder. Complete each sentence from the text with the appropriate expression.

  1 Are we getting a balanced perspective? Apparently, _____ , no.
  2 _____ , people prefer to watch or read things they agree with.
  3 _____ , though, it's easy to be deceived by misleading, one-sided, or fake stories.
  4 _____ , unknown sites may not be trustworthy.

6 **1** Which sentences in exercise 5 do you agree with? Has the text made you change any of your opinions?

  2 In pairs, modify the sentences in the Text builder so they are true for you.

inferring meaning using related words ■ generalizing   READING   SKILLS   8B

FACTS or "FACTS"?

Digital news platforms make it easier than ever to find information about almost any topic on **virtually** any device. But are we getting a balanced perspective? Apparently, for the most part, no. Social media experts Larry Jones and Sue Herrera explain why this is so and what we can do about it.

Unbelievable! I've got to share this.

That's it! I'm not following this site anymore.

I just love my Facebook friends!

LARRY JONES

Research has shown that, generally speaking, people prefer to watch or read things they agree with. As a result, algorithms – the secret codes that power social media platforms – tend to show us what *they* think we want to read or watch, based on who we interact with, what we've read in the past, and the sites we visit. This means that the version of the world we find every day in our own personal newsfeed has been pre-selected to confirm our opinions and **reinforce** our beliefs. In a sense, it's as if we're all **trapped** inside social media's walls, stuck in our own bubbles. So it's no surprise that we're sometimes tempted to block people whose tastes and opinions are different from ours. However, we actually should do the exact opposite: actively follow people who don't necessarily share our point of view, and try to see things from *their* **perspective**. Not only is this a good exercise in empathy, it will also get algorithms "confused" and stop media platforms from flooding our newsfeed with ideas and opinions that are identical to ours.

SUE HERRERA

In the newsfeed on your phone, most stories look believable – whether or not they come from a "serious" source. True, some fake news sites are so bad they're easy to spot: missing references, no authors' names, spelling and grammar mistakes. As a rule, though, it's easy to be deceived by misleading, one-sided, or fake stories, which are sometimes read and watched even more widely than real stories. So here's what you should do so you don't get **fooled**.

First, if you're reading or watching the news on an unknown site, check out other articles and videos the site has posted. On the whole, unknown sites may not be **trustworthy**, and you may need to look for a more reliable source so you can compare different news outlets that report the same piece of news. Second, when you're reading an article, be sure to read past the headline and also go **beyond** the opening paragraph, which are usually designed to sound convincing and may mislead you. Last but not least, please remember: If a news story sounds **phony**, don't share it because sharing fake news generally makes it go higher up in search-result pages. This, ironically, will make even more people read or watch it!

Personal Best — Write a paragraph about your general views on digital news platforms.

8 LANGUAGE   -ing forms and infinitives ■ expressions with *at*, *for*, *in*, and *on*

8C Binge-watching

1 Think about how we use technology or the media today. Complete the sentence in three different ways.
I don't think it's healthy to …
I don't think it's healthy to play video games for more than two hours.

2 A Look at the picture and read the entry from an online encyclopedia, ignoring the blanks. How often do you binge-watch?

Binge-watching

In 2013, Netflix did something no other media company had done before: instead of showing only one episode of a series each week, they released the complete season – all ¹_____ ! This allowed viewers to be ²_____ of what, when, and how much TV they wanted to watch, which meant they could sit through a whole season of their favorite show for hours and hours. Interestingly, according to a recent survey, though, it seems that typical "viewing marathons" consist, ³_____ , of four episodes. Still, that can be defined as binge-watching, ⁴_____ .

B Complete the text in exercise 2A with the expressions in the box.

> for sure   at once   in control   on average

Go to Vocabulary practice: expressions with *at*, *for*, *in*, and *on*, page 148

3 A ▶ 8.7   Listen to Anna and Fred talking about binge-watching. Who likes/dislikes it? Who changes his/her mind in the end?

B ▶ 8.7   Listen again and complete each sentence with one or two words.
1 I'm going to stay home _____ some rest if it's OK.
2 When I finish an episode, I can't help _____ the next one.
3 _____ for a new episode is fun, too. It makes me look forward to it even more.
4 I'm sick and tired of _____ spoilers.

4 Look at exercise 3B again. Match sentences 1–4 with rules a–d. Then read the Grammar box.
Use the:
a *-ing* form if a verb is the subject of a sentence.   _____
b *-ing* form after an expression with a negative meaning.   _____
c infinitive to give a reason.   _____
d *-ing* form after a preposition.   _____

-ing forms and infinitives ■ expressions with *at*, *for*, *in*, and *on* **LANGUAGE** **8C**

📖 Grammar — *-ing* forms and infinitives

-ing forms

1 after prepositions and certain verbs:
   I'm not **into playing** computer games, but
   I **enjoy streaming** movies.

2 as the subject of a sentence:
   Watching horror movies is fun.

3 in expressions with a negative meaning:
   There's no point/It's no use trying to stop.
   I **have trouble staying** away from social media.

Infinitives

1 after certain verbs:
   I **decided to go** to the movies.

2 after adjectives:
   It's **impossible** not **to cry** during this movie.

3 to give a reason:
   I went home early **to catch** my favorite show.

Infinitive vs. base form:
   I **encouraged** her **to take** a look at the news.
   I **made** him **put** the phone down.

Look! *Stop* has a different meaning when it is followed by an infinitive rather than by an *-ing* form:
   I **stopped** for a second **to check** my messages. (I stopped what I was doing to check them.)
   I **stopped watching** TV, and now I'm a lot happier. (I don't watch TV anymore.)

Personal Best

Go to Grammar practice: *-ing* forms and infinitives, page 127

5 A ▶ 8.9 **Pronunciation:** *to* Listen to the sentences. Notice the unstressed pronunciation of *to*.

1 No, it's no use trying to convince her.

2 Well, I can't help feeling that you're lying to me.

3 Yes, I'd love to spend a week there.

4 Well, I only stopped by to say "hi."

B ▶ 8.9 Listen again and repeat.

6 A Complete the sentences in *italics* with the correct form of the verbs in the box. Add *not* if necessary.

answer   eat (x2)   pick up   save   spend   try

● ● ●

My three favorite **obsessions**

by Jake Sullivan

» **Binge-texting:** On average, I send and receive about 100 text messages per day. No matter where I am, if I get a new message, *I can't help* ¹_____ *the phone so I can read it.* When I'm with friends and family, *I try my best* ²_____ *text messages, though.*

» **Binge-eating:** ³_____ *a slice of cake every once in a while is normal,* I know, but I eat at least three slices of banana cake every day. *My mother tries to encourage me* ⁴_____ *healthier food,* but *it's no use* ⁵_____ *to convince me* to cut down on sugar. Life's too short!

» **Binge-shopping:** *I've always found it hard* ⁶_____ *money,* but it feels as if I might be getting worse! *I can't stop* ⁷_____ *money on things I don't need,* especially new pens. Yes, pens of all kinds! Thank goodness I've never ended up in debt.

B Rephrase the sentences in *italics* from exercise 6A with the words below. In pairs, say which of Jake's habits are true for you.

1 It's hard not

2 I avoid

3 It's normal

4 My mother tries to make

5 There's no point

6 I have trouble

7 I keep

Go to Communication practice: Student A page 161, Student B page 167

7 What are *your* three favorite addictive habits? Share your ideas with your partner.

> I try my best not to … , but I can't help …

> I find it hard not to …

> I've always had trouble …

> I know it's no use trying to …

> I should definitely stop …

Personal Best Write four sentences saying what your parents encouraged you to do/made you do as a child.

71

8 SKILLS | SPEAKING expressing annoyance and indifference ■ clarifying and reacting

8D Ads to drive you crazy

1 Discuss the questions in pairs.

 a
 b
 c
 d
 e
 f
 g
 h

1 What ads do you like/hate on TV or online?
2 What are "infomercials"? Do you ever buy anything after watching them?

2 ▶ 8.10 Watch or listen to the first part of *Talking Zone*. Ben and Abigail are talking about an exercise machine Ben saw on an infomercial. Check (✓) the arguments that they make.

Infomercials ...

1 make products sound affordable. ☐
2 use psychology to convince us. ☐
3 work better with younger audiences. ☐
4 have good arguments. ☐
5 can be funny. ☐

3 ▶ 8.10 Complete sentences 1–4 with the expressions in the box. Watch or listen again and check.

however hard I try   whatever it takes   whatever way you look at it   whenever I watch

1 "Call now, and we'll double the offer!" They'll do _____ to convince you!
2 They're manipulating you. _____ , that's what it's all about.
3 It's just that _____ an infomercial, something strange happens.
4 It's almost as if I've been hypnotized. _____ , I can't help it.

Conversation builder | expressing annoyance and indifference

Expressing annoyance:
I end up buying **whatever** (product) they advertise.
However effective these ads may be, they're sometimes dishonest.
These ads follow me **wherever** I go.
Whenever an infomercial comes on, I mute the TV.

Expressing indifference (or dismissing what someone says):
People say I should spend my money more wisely. Well, **whatever**.

Words with *-ever* include *whatever* (= any thing), *however* (= any way), *wherever* (= any place) and *whenever* (= any time).

expressing annoyance and indifference ■ clarifying and reacting **SPEAKING**   **SKILLS** 📷 **8D**

4 A Read the Conversation builder. Rank a–d from 1 (least annoying) to 4 (most annoying).

a an <u>infomercial</u> about the latest cleaning product ☐

b a musical <u>jingle</u> for a TV advert ☐

c a <u>pop-up</u> ad from your favorite shoe company ☐

d a <u>trailer</u> at the beginning of a film ☐

B Share your opinions with your partner.

I can't stand jingles. However hard I try to forget them, they keep playing in my head!

5 ▶ 8.11 Watch or listen to the second part of the show. Choose the main point.

a Regular TV is becoming less and less popular.

b Ads may work even if you're not paying attention.

c Repetitive ads are annoying.

6 ▶ 8.11 Watch or listen again and number sentences a–f in the order you hear them.

a ☐ So, what's the point of running a TV ad if most viewers might not even notice it?

b ☐ I see what you mean, in theory, but I'm not sure that happens.

c ☐ You see, here's what I don't get. How do they ever sell any products?

d ☐ I think it's all about creating familiarity. It's kind of subliminal.

e ☐ It's hard to tell, but I think ads might work even if you don't remember seeing them.

f ☐ Yeah, that makes sense. It's the same principle as a song that keeps replaying in your head.

🔧 **Skill** **clarifying and reacting**

When you discuss something concrete, you may need to clarify what you say and react to what others say.

• You can express doubt about something: *What's the point of answering? Jamie never listens. Here's what I don't get...*

• You can offer an explanation, even if you're not sure: *It's hard to tell why Bill hasn't called, but maybe it's because he's been sick.*

• You can acknowledge a point/what someone has said: *Yeah, that makes sense. Let's invite a few more people over. I see what you mean in theory, but...*

7 Read the Skill box. Look at the sentences in exercise 6 again. In pairs, decide which expressions Ben and Abigail use to clarify and react. <u>Underline</u> them and identify the function of each one.

8 ▶ 8.12 In pairs, order sentences a–f to make a conversation. Listen and check.

a ☐ Good question. I think it's all about making your product known, no matter how.

b ☐ Neither do I. Here's what I don't get. What's the point of trying to get people to buy something by annoying them?

c ☐ 1 I often find flyers on my windshield or in my mailbox. It really gets on my nerves.

d ☐ Flyers? They drive me crazy, too. And I never want or need whatever they're advertising.

e ☐ I think most people do. But flyers are cheap, if two or three customers call, maybe that's better than nothing.

f ☐ Yeah, that makes sense, but don't people throw those flyers away as soon as they see them? I know I do.

Go to Communication practice: Student A page 162, Student B page 168

9 A PREPARE Think of three really annoying things you see on TV (an ad, a show, the news, etc.) Choose one and prepare a conversation about it.

B PRACTICE In pairs, practice the conversation. Take turns clarifying how you feel and reacting to your partner's comments.

C PERSONAL BEST Choose another idea and practice a similar conversation. Can you improve the way you clarify and react?

Personal Best   Write a paragraph about an annoying problem in your neighborhood.   73

7 and 8 REVIEW and PRACTICE

Grammar

1 Choose the correct options to complete the sentences.

1 The most famous broadcaster in the UK is the BBC, _____ is funded by the public.
  a which
  b who
  c that

2 My sister likes going out _____ , I prefer staying in.
  a unlike
  b as
  c while

3 I spent a long time preparing for the interview _____ myself a good chance of getting the job.
  a by giving
  b to give
  c while giving

4 _____ the snow, most trains will be running late.
  a Because
  b Since
  c Due to

5 That man _____ the street was my first music teacher!
  a crossing
  b who crosses
  c crossed

6 I don't take my phone out in the evening because I'm afraid of _____ it.
  a lose
  b losing
  c to lose

7 I got the highest grades, _____ made me very proud.
  a as
  b which
  c that

8 We stopped _____ the car with gas because we had almost run out.
  a filling
  b by filling
  c to fill

2 Complete the sentences with the correct forms of the verbs in parentheses.

1 I'm very tired today, so I _____ (go) to bed as soon as I _____ (finish) my homework.
2 _____ (live) in Spain is more fun than _____ (live) in the UK.
3 As long as you _____ (not call) me after 9 p.m. tonight, I _____ (answer) the phone.
4 It's no use _____ (ask) me to change my mind because I've decided _____ (quit).
5 If there _____ (not be) any buses running tomorrow, I _____ (have to) walk to work.
6 We _____ (have) our classes outside every Friday unless it _____ (not be) warm enough.

3 Choose the correct options to complete the text.

Will we need teachers in the future?

Two experts give their predictions about the classrooms of the future.

Expert 1: [1]*Whereas / Since* many professions have been replaced by machines in recent years, teachers should generally feel safe [2]*therefore / due to* the nature of their work. [3]*Unlike / Whereas* factory workers or store cashiers, teachers require skills [4]*who / that* machines do not currently have. [5]*While / As* robots can perform many physical and logical tasks, they are not able to do things [6]*require / that require* emotional intelligence. [7]*Unless / If* a robot is invented that can do these things, teaching [8]*continues / will continue* to be done by humans. And [9]*even if / provided* a robot is invented with these qualities, people would rather be taught by a human than by a machine.

Expert 2: In just ten years, machines [10]*will be / are* a lot more intelligent than they are today, [11]*that / which* should really worry teachers. These new machines will listen to the voices of learners and read their faces. [12]*Therefore, / Since* they will be able to adapt their teaching methods to each individual student. [13]*As soon / As soon as* these machines [14]*are / will be* available in schools, teachers will simply become classroom assistants in charge of discipline and responsible for setting up equipment. [15]*Learning / To learn* will take place in an environment managed by robots.

Vocabulary

1 Circle the word or expression that is different. Explain why.

1 can't seem   fail   can't manage   succeed
2 host   tabloid   press   headlines
3 learn by heart   cross your mind   recall   remind
4 report   application   proposal   conference
5 viewer   tabloid   broadcast   television
6 every day   once in a while   at once   on a regular basis

74

REVIEW and PRACTICE — 7 and 8

2 Match the words and expressions in the box with definitions 1–8.

> keep an open mind   memorable   get ahead
> get hold of   keep something in mind
> make the most out of   can't quite manage
> change your mind

1 easy to remember _____
2 just unable _____
3 have a new, different opinion to before _____
4 become successful in life or in a career _____
5 wait before making a judgment _____
6 successfully contact _____
7 use to the greatest advantage _____
8 remember and think about something _____

3 Choose the correct options to complete the sentences.

1 That was awful! I had studied hard, but when the exam started, *I kept an open mind / my mind went blank.*
2 My friend knows a website where you can *stream / host* live soccer games for free!
3 It's funny that we've become such good friends because at *once / first,* we didn't get along.
4 I don't trust any news channels because they're all *biased / objective.*
5 Yesterday you said "Yes," but today you're saying "No." I wish you would *make up your / keep an open* mind!
6 I've come to pick up some medicine *for the sake of / on behalf of* my mother.
7 If you want to *make the most out of / get hold of* your time in college, you should live with other students.
8 Could you *recall / remind* me to call my brother today? It's his birthday.

4 Complete the text with the words in the box.

> struggling   matters   at   hard   across
> of   breaking news   in

One of the most significant recent trends in media has been the decrease in newspaper sales. Until quite recently, many newspapers were pretty successful [1]_____ getting their message [2]_____ to their readers, but today they are [3]_____ to survive. Several national newspapers are finding it [4]_____ to sell enough copies and are [5]_____ debt, while some have closed down completely. One of the reasons for this is the rise in the number of online news sites, which are capable [6]_____ delivering [7]_____ much more quickly. To make [8]_____ worse for the newspaper industry, people are less willing to pay for their news and are increasingly turning to free news sites online.

Personal Best

Lesson 7A
Describe four recent events. Use a relative clause to comment on each one.

Lesson 8A
Write four sentences about a well-known media organization in your country.

Lesson 7A
Name two things you can do with these verbs: *attend, make, get, submit.*

Lesson 8A
Write three sentences about current news stories using these linkers: *due to, whereas, unlike.*

Lesson 7B
Describe something you struggle to do, have a talent for, have succeeded at, and are very bad at.

Lesson 8B
Describe how you use the Internet, using four different generalizing expressions.

Lesson 7C
Name four possible future events or situations. Describe the consequences of each.

Lesson 8C
Name five expressions which use these prepositions: for, *on, at, in.*

Lesson 7C
Write two sentences containing the word *memory* and two containing the word *mind.*

Lesson 8C
Write four sentences about your classmates: two with *-ing* forms, and two with infinitives.

Lesson 7D
Write three pairs of sentences. Begin each second sentence with *besides, in addition,* and *moreover.*

Lesson 8D
Describe four situations in your life using these words: *whatever, whenever, however, wherever.*

75

UNIT 9 The power of design

LANGUAGE position of adverbs ■ collocations with *have* and *take*

9A Steps to a better life

1 Imagine a happy day in your life. Where are you? Who are you with? Why are you there? What are you doing? Now tell your partner.

2 Match quotes a–c with sentences 1–3. Which is your favorite quote?

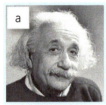

a "A table, a chair, a bowl of fruit, and a violin; what else does a man need to be happy?" (Albert Einstein)

b "If you don't like something, change it. If you can't change it, change your attitude." (Maya Angelou)

c "Be happy for no reason, just like a child." (Deepak Chopra)

1 To be happy, you should **have an open mind** and **take responsibility for** your life.

2 If you want to be happy, don't **take things too seriously**.

3 If you're **having trouble** being happy, **take pleasure in** the small things.

Go to Vocabulary practice: collocations with *have* and *take*, page 149

3 Read the text. Which sentence (1–3) from exercise 2 best summarizes it?

Happiness by design

How many times have you seen this meme on social media this past month? Probably more than once or twice, right? People <u>sometimes</u> dislike their colleges, their jobs, or their lifestyles, but feel that if they just live one day at a time, something will <u>magically</u> change. But you don't need to live on autopilot – you can live by design! The key is to establish clear goals and create a plan to achieve them. Here are three "musts" to take into account when setting goals.

I HATE MONDAYS

1 They must be <u>personally</u> important to you. You <u>probably</u> won't do everything necessary to achieve a goal unless it's something that you're <u>really</u> passionate about.
   WRONG: *Learning how to play the piano might be fun. I guess I could give it a try.*
   RIGHT: *I <u>truly</u> love the sound of the piano, and I'd really like to learn how to play it <u>well</u>.*

2 They must be something you can visualize. Otherwise, your brain will have trouble getting the message.
   WRONG: *I want to have my own business.*
   RIGHT: *I'd like to create a start-up and sell clothes online.*

3 They must be specific and measurable. <u>Ideally</u>, you should give yourself a deadline. If you don't, you won't feel your goal is urgent.
   WRONG: *I need to lose some weight.*
   RIGHT: *I want to lose seven pounds by April.*

One last important point: people <u>often</u> forget that goals must be realistic. You won't go from couch potato to marathon runner in a week. Or become fluent in a foreign language in six months, even if you live abroad. So you should take care not to set goals that you can't <u>realistically</u> achieve.

76

position of adverbs ■ collocations with *have* and *take* LANGUAGE 9A

4 Find the underlined adverbs in the text in exercise 3. Check (✓) the correct option(s) below. Then read the Grammar box.

Adverbs can go _____ of a sentence.
a at the beginning ☐   b in the middle ☐   c at the end ☐

Grammar position of adverbs

Beginning of a sentence:
Fortunately, I have a stress-free life. (comment)

Middle of a sentence:
He has an *extremely* positive outlook on life. (degree)
She *quickly* adopted a healthier lifestyle. (manner)
I've *often* thought about changing my diet. (frequency)

Look! We cannot place an adverb between the verb and its object:
She *quickly* adopted a healthier lifestyle. NOT ~~She adopted *quickly* a healthier lifestyle.~~

End of a sentence:
I'd like to learn to play the guitar *well*. (manner)

Go to Grammar practice: position of adverbs, page 128

5 A ▶ 9.4 **Pronunciation:** syllable stress with adverbs of degree Listen to the sentences. Mark the stressed syllable in the underlined words.
1 I thought Stephen King's novel *It* was surprisingly good.
2 My nephew's birthday party was terribly boring.
3 It's unusually cold for this time of year.
4 My grandfather is remarkably active for a 90-year-old man.
5 Kelly Clarkson is a truly talented artist. She sings amazingly well.

B ▶ 9.4 Listen, check, and repeat. Then, in pairs, choose two sentences and change the details to make the sentences true for you.

6 A Insert the adverbs in parentheses into the correct places in the sentences or phrases in *italics*.

Five simple steps to a **happier you**

❶ **Keep learning new things.** *Learning affects your well-being in lots of positive ways*. (not surprisingly) It exposes you to new ideas and encourages curiosity.

❷ **Stop saying, "I'll do it later – maybe next month."** *Procrastinating tends to have a negative impact on your well-being.* (extremely)

❸ **Do things for others.** *Helping other people makes us happier and healthier*. (usually) *It's not all about money.* (obviously) We can also offer others our time, ideas, and energy.

❹ **Take care of your body.** Your body and your mind are connected, so *being active is important*. (physically) *It can change your life*. (easily)

❺ **Be comfortable with who you are.** Nobody's perfect, but we forget that! (often) *If you accept yourself*, (truly) *you'll be a lot happier*. (probably)

B In pairs, discuss the tips above and decide which ones you like best.

Go to Communication practice: Student A page 162, Student B page 168

7 How can you plan for a happier life? Choose two of the ideas below and tell your partner how each one will make you happier. Use some of the adverbs in the box.

| fortunately   easily   extremely   obviously   personally   realistically   truly |

| spending quality time with your family | making a lot of money | learning when to say "no" | having a stress-free lifestyle |

Obviously, my job's very important to me, but I think I could spend more quality time with my family.

Personal Best Write a paragraph about your plan for a happier life in exercise 7.

77

9 SKILLS LISTENING understanding key points ■ silent *h* ■ colors

9B Good or bad design?

1 A Discuss the questions in pairs.

 a

 b

 c

1 Which chair looks the nicest?
2 Which one looks the most comfortable?
3 Which one would look better in a different color?
4 Which one would you never consider buying?

B Match descriptions 1–3 with pictures a–c.

1 a brownish-green 1950s style armchair
2 a dark green rocking chair with a wooden frame
3 a light green armless designer chair

Go to Vocabulary practice: colors, page 150

Skill   understanding key points

When listening, it's important to understand the speaker's key points and differentiate them from supporting details and examples. Speakers often:
- repeat a key point more than once, using different words.
- explain it using an example or comparison.
- stress certain key words for emphasis.

2 ▶9.6 Read the Skill box. Then watch or listen to the first part of *Talking Zone*. Check (✓) the key point Ava makes about good design.

a Use is more important than style. ☐
b Use is less important than style. ☐
c Use is as important as style. ☐

Ava

3 A ▶9.6 Ava repeats her key point several times during the program. Can you remember the missing words? Watch or listen again and check.

1 A lot of people still seem to think that _____ is always second to function.
2 Design and function are like a pair of _____ – you can't have one without the other!
3 The look and _____ of a product should work together.
4 Tupperware might not be _____ for the way it looks, but I think it's a fantastic example of good design.
5 And that's what good design is all about. Creating something that is both _____ and efficient.

B Look at the sentences in exercise 3A. Which sentences:
- offer a comparison ____
- provide an example ____
- make the same point with different words ____ ____

4 In pairs, look at exercise 2 again. Discuss which statement best matches your own opinion.

understanding key points ■ silent *h* ■ colors **LISTENING** **SKILLS** **9B**

5 ▶ 9.7 Watch or listen to the second part of the show. Check (✓) the picture that Ava describes as an example of bad design.

Modern London Underground map

Sydney Opera House

6 ▶ 9.7 Watch or listen again. Choose the correct options.
1 Early London underground maps were *more* / *less* accurate than today's maps.
2 Harry Beck made his version of the map more *detailed* / *practical*.
3 The Sydney Opera House has poor *acoustics* / *visibility* so it's hard to *hear* / *see* well.
4 The Guangzhou Opera House in China is a *good* / *bad* example of design and function working together.

Listening builder   silent *h*

When the letter *h* isn't pronounced, speech can be harder to understand. It is almost always silent in pronouns or auxiliaries after a consonant: ask *him*, tell *her*, must *have*. In fast speech, it is sometimes silent:
- in pronouns that start a sentence: *He didn't call.*
- when the main verb is *have*, even after a vowel: *She has a new car.*
- in content words, especially after consonants: *I was hungry.*

However, it is never silent when a word is emphasized: *I said I wanted hot coffee, not iced coffee.*
When in doubt, always pronounce the letter *h*, especially when speaking slowly.

7 A ▶ 9.8 Read the Listening builder. Then listen to the sentences from the video. Cross out the letter *h* when you don't hear it pronounced.
1 Today I'm with Ava Janssen to talk about **h**er brilliantly written book.
2 They were messy and much, much **h**arder to read.
3 **H**e straightened the lines and put the stations equal distances apart.
4 Most metro stations **h**ave symmetrical, color-coded maps.
5 It's the Sydney Opera **H**ouse.
6 I cannot recommend the book **h**ighly enough.

B In pairs, practice saying each sentence.

8 In pairs, discuss two objects or places that each match one of the categories below. Can you support your opinion with examples or analogies?
a It's both beautiful and practical.
b It's beautiful, but not practical.
c It's practical, but not beautiful.
d It's neither beautiful nor practical.

Personal Best Describe something in your home where function and design work well together.

9 LANGUAGE
passives and causative *have* ■ dimensions and weight

9C Extreme designs

1 A Look at the house in the picture. Do you think it's a piece of art or a real house? Read the text and check.

Unconventional design: this week's top picks

If you like unconventional architecture, you will love House NA, a 914-square-foot home made almost entirely of glass! That's 85 square meters.

Located in the Koenji neighborhood in Tokyo, this three-story house is unlike anything you've ever seen. Instead of walls or doors, there are large floor-to-ceiling windows, which means that just about everything can be seen from the outside!

House NA was designed as a modern version of an adult treehouse, where all the different "rooms" are connected to each other. I'd love to have a house like this designed specially for me and my family.

This house is so special it's been featured in dozens of specialized magazines since it was built in 2011. It's definitely worth checking out, though the owners probably won't let you in!

B How big is your home in square feet? Multiply the length by the width to find out. Describe it to your partner.

Go to Vocabulary practice: dimensions and weight, page 151

2 A ▶ 9.11 Listen to a couple talking about House NA. Who thinks it would make a good office?
the woman ☐   the man ☐   both ☐   neither ☐

B ▶ 9.11 Listen again and complete the sentences.
1 They _____ a famous Japanese architect _____ it.
2 It looks as if it _____ _____ simply as a concept. You know, like modern art.
3 This glass building really makes us think about how a house should _____ _____.
4 I'm guessing they probably _____ blinds _____ up or something.
5 Save money? You mean because the lights would _____ _____ _____ during the day?

3 Match sentences 1–5 from exercise 2B with patterns a–c. Are patterns a and b active or passive? Then read the Grammar box.

a *be* + past participle
b *have* + object + past participle
c *have* + object + base form

passives and causative *have* ■ dimensions and weight   LANGUAGE **9C**

 Grammar passives and causative *have*

Passives:
The building **was designed** by a very famous architect.
When we got to the airport, all the flights **had been canceled**.
The new expressway **will have been finished** by 2025.
More houses **should be built**.

Causative *have*:
They **had** me **write down** every word they said. (active)
We **had** our house **designed** by a well-known architect. (passive)
It's important to **have** your eyes **tested** from time to time. (passive)

Go to Grammar practice: passives and causative *have*, page 129

4 A ▶ 9.13 **Pronunciation:** stress in passive and causative *have* sentences Listen to the sentences. Which of the underlined words is stressed?
1 My phone <u>was stolen</u> last month.
2 I've <u>been interviewed</u> for lots of jobs this year.
3 My hair's too long. I should probably <u>have it cut</u>.
4 I think I should have <u>been given</u> a pay raise.

B ▶ 9.13 Listen again and repeat. Then, in pairs, tell your partner if any of the sentences are true for you.

5 Rewrite the <u>underlined</u> phrases using the passive or causative *have*.

What's the most practical innovation of the last 25 years?

1 I think people installing home surveillance cameras is really practical. I like to <u>protect my home</u> from burglars, 24/7.

2 I love postal tracking. I sent a package yesterday, and they let me know exactly what time <u>they had delivered it</u>. How great is that?

3 I love the fact that, before you choose a hotel, you can go online and find out whether <u>other guests have recommended it</u>.

4 Definitely bitcoin. I wonder, though, if by 2030, <u>people will replace it</u> with other payment methods.

5 Online shopping. I like <u>other people delivering stuff to my door</u>!

6 Here's something that <u>they should have invented</u> by now: a device that automatically throws balls for dogs to catch.

Go to Communication practice: Student A page 162, Student B page 168

6 In pairs, think of three more innovations and describe them, using passives or causative *have*. Say what makes them practical.

Personal Best Write sentences about things you're going to have done in the next month, e.g. *I'm going to have my hair cut.*

81

9 SKILLS WRITING writing a magazine article ■ articles: *a*, *an*, *the*, zero (–)

9D Accessible spaces

1 A Look at the three pairs of pictures below. Then, in pairs, identify two advantages of picture a over picture b.

1a
2a
3a
1b
2b
3b

B Read the article. Which of your ideas were mentioned?

Universal design

Our city is one of the state's most important tourist destinations, and it's easy to understand why: We have the best parks, museums, and restaurants in the region. The proposed shopping area next to (a) <u>Luna Park</u> will be open seven days (b) <u>a week</u> when it opens in 2022. But, unlike most of the tourist attractions we have now, it should be designed to be accessible.

1 _____ ?
(c) <u>The new streets and buildings</u> that are planned should meet the needs of all users, including people who may have a physical or learning disability. They should also be practical. Here are a few simple examples:
- Wheelchair-friendly entrances with no steps, which are also safer for (d) <u>the visually-impaired.</u>
- Larger restroom stalls, which provide easier access for wheelchairs.
- Clear signs that use well-known symbols to help people who can't read.

2 _____ ?
Firstly, making "universal" design decisions means fewer expensive changes in the future. Secondly, these decisions can benefit both people who are physically disabled and those who are not. For example, entrances that don't have steps and larger restroom stalls are more practical for those with suitcases or strollers. User-friendly signs can also be more easily understood by (e) <u>people</u> who don't understand English very well.

3 _____ ?
Our government has recently passed a law on universal access, and now we have a chance to test its success. Sign this online petition now to remind our leaders that all new buildings and streets must be accessible to everyone.
As a society, we have (f) <u>a moral obligation</u> to everyone who lives here. People need to be able to access and use public spaces and buildings safely and comfortably.

2 Match headings a–c with blanks 1–3 in the article in exercise 1B.

a What are the benefits?   b What can *you* do to help?   c What do we need to do?

writing a magazine article ■ articles: *a*, *an*, *the*, zero (–) **WRITING** | **SKILLS** | **9D**

🔧 Skill   writing a magazine article

To write an effective magazine or newspaper article, it is important to catch and hold the reader's attention.
- Give your article an interesting title.
- Avoid talking about yourself. You are writing for the general public.
- Introduce the topic in an opening paragraph that readers can relate to.
- Develop your ideas in two or three paragraphs. You can use headings to keep the reader interested.
- Summarize your ideas in the last paragraph. Don't add any new information.

3 Read the Skill box. What is the purpose of each paragraph in the article in exercise 1B?

4 In pairs, make a list of four ways to make your city or neighborhood more accessible to those with disabilities.

5 Look at the headings in the article again. In pairs, summarize the answer to each question.

🧩 Text builder   articles: *a*, *an*, *the*, zero (–)

- **Use the indefinite article (*a/an*):**
1 to talk about something/someone for the first time: *A new plan is needed.*
2 in expressions of frequency: *This entrance is used several times **a** day.*

- **Use the definite article (*the*):**
3 before a collective group: *He's collecting money for **the** homeless.*
4 when something has already been mentioned, or is specific: *I really like **the** car across the street.*

- **Don't use an article (–):**
5 before uncountable and plural nouns in general: (–) *Street signs should be easy to read.*
6 with most proper nouns and cities: (–) *Fifth Avenue is in* (–) *New York*.

6 Read the Text builder. Then match <u>underlined</u> examples a–f in the article with rules 1–6.

7 A Fill in the blanks in the text below with *a/an*, *the*, or zero (–).

Four ways to make your city a better place now

❶ Support culture. _____ great way to support your community is through _____ art because _____ artists and _____ writers can tell _____ story of a city better than anyone else.

❷ Bike to work. Commuting can be _____ frustrating experience. Taking _____ public transportation helps to reduce _____ traffic – and your carbon footprint!

❸ Volunteer. We know you're busy, but any time you can spare could make _____ huge difference to _____ city you live in.

❹ And last but not least, show _____ friendly face. You should treat _____ other people the way you would like to be treated.

B In pairs, rank the ideas in exercise 7A in order of importance for your city. Add two new suggestions.

8 A **PREPARE** Think of how you want to improve your city or neighborhood, e.g., a stronger community or a better environment and three ways to achieve it.

B **PRACTICE** Write your article, using the Skill box to help you develop your ideas. Pay attention to the use of definite and indefinite articles.

C **PERSONAL BEST** Exchange articles with a partner. How many similar ideas did you have?

Personal Best | How accessible is your house or apartment? Write a paragraph answering this question. | 83

UNIT 10 The business world

LANGUAGE quantifiers ■ trends and business

10A Careers on the rise

1 A Look at the pictures and read the information about U.S. job trends. Are the numbers increasing or falling?

a Health care professionals
2010: 14 million   2020: 18 million

b Mail carriers
2010: 315,000   2020: 280,000

c Elementary school teachers
2010: 1.5 million   2020: 1.7 million

B In pairs, discuss the information in exercise 1A. Can you think of a reason for each trend? Are the job trends the same in your country?

Go to Vocabulary practice: trends and business, page 152

2 Read the text. Which job would you most/least like to have?

Are these **professions** for you?

Jobs in some traditional professions are decreasing, while in new fields they're increasing! Whether you're launching your career for the first time or setting up a new business, here are a few options you might like to consider.

1 Video game developers
Have you ever considered a career in game development? If so, you'll probably have little trouble finding a well-paid job. Game designers are in high demand, and the reason is your phone. Mobile technology has created a need for new games, and experts expect to see a major increase in the gaming industry over the next decade.

2 User-experience designers
Would you like to study people's reactions when they use a new product or system, and find ways to improve it based on their feedback? There are few qualified professionals available, so demand is high and growing steadily. Average salaries have nearly doubled in the past decade. Expect quite a few exciting opportunities in the coming years.

3 Health and wellness educators
These days, most people work under a great deal of stress. As a result, an increasing number of companies are hiring health and wellness educators to look after their employees' physical and mental well-being. These specialists offer individual advice and guidance, which usually increases productivity for the company.

3 A Are the sentences true (T) or false (F)? Read the text again and underline the four sentences that contain the relevant information.

1 Game developers usually earn high salaries. _____
2 It's relatively easy to find good user-experience designers. _____
3 The job market for user-experience designers is likely to increase. _____
4 Most employees have stressful jobs. _____

B Find the expressions of quantity in the sentences you underlined. Which ones describe large quantities? Which ones describe small ones? Then read the Grammar box.

quantifiers ■ trends and business   **LANGUAGE 10A**

 Grammar quantifiers

Large quantities
1 countable:
   I sent my résumé to **quite a few** companies.
   A large number of professions are growing.
2 uncountable:
   A great deal of/A lot of time is needed to apply for jobs.
   He has **a fair amount of** experience in web design.

Small quantities
1 countable:
   I have **a few** business contacts in Japan.
   There are **few/not many** good candidates for this position.
2 uncountable:
   I can invest **a little** money in your company.
   There's **little/not much** information on the website.

Look! We use **both/neither** when referring to two people or things, and **all/none** for more than two people or things:
Both my parents work. **Neither** (of them) is very happy.
All my friends are unemployed. **None** (of them) have found work.

Go to Grammar practice: quantifiers, page 130

4 A ▶ 10.4 **Pronunciation:** *(a) few* and *(a) little* Listen to the conversations. Notice how *a few*, *few*, *a little*, and *little* are pronounced.

1 **Ann** So, how was your first day at work?
   Luke There were quite **a few** friendly faces, but I had very **little** time to socialize.
2 **Bob** So, how was your last day at work?
   Sue Very **few** people came to say good-bye, so I did **a little** work, instead.

B ▶ 10.4 Listen again and repeat.

5 Read the text and choose the correct options. Can you think of other jobs at risk?

Declining careers: Is your job at risk?   Search

Telemarketers: In the past ten years, job opportunities have fallen by more than 10%, and the reason is simple. [1]*Few / A few* people enjoy receiving sales calls, and as call-blocking technology has improved, [2]*a large number of / a fair amount of* companies are now looking for other ways to reach customers.

Bank tellers: [3]*Quite a few / A great deal of* tellers will lose their jobs in the next few years, and [4]*not much / not many* can be done about it. Improvements in mobile banking are to blame, as there's [5]*little / a little* that can't be done online.

Reporters: Newspapers have lost [6]*a large number of / a great deal of* money in recent years, and if this trend continues, reporters and other media professionals might lose their jobs. Social media sites, which have changed the way people get their news, are [7]*all / both* responsible for this.

6 A Rewrite sentences 1–6 below using the words in parentheses.
1 Lots of small stores have gone out of business in my neighborhood. (quite)
2 I had a lot of information about the job market when I finished college. (fair)
3 I don't know many people who raise money for charity. (few)
4 Both my parents are working under a lot of stress right now. (deal)
5 I didn't have much experience when I got my first job. (little)
6 Last year, all my job interviews were unsuccessful. (none)

B Choose two of the sentences and make them true for you, using quantifiers from the Grammar box.

Go to Communication practice: Student A page 162, Student B page 168

7 Look at the trends below. Have the activities increased, decreased, or remained stable?

| dropping out of college | emigrating | using Facebook | watching sports on broadcast TV |

I think quite a few people have dropped out of college in recent years. This is probably because …

Personal Best Write a paragraph describing one of the trends in exercise 7.   85

10 **SKILLS** **READING** understanding text development ■ complex negative sentences

10B Starting your own business

1 If you wanted to start your own business, which of these ideas would you consider? Give reasons.

an interior design company · a café or tea shop · selling used books

a computer repair shop · a health and fitness center · a marketing business

2 What are the advantages and disadvantages of starting your own business when you're young? In pairs, add an idea to each column below.

Advantages	Disadvantages
(+) You have fewer responsibilities.	(−) You have less time to study.
(+) You can make your parents proud.	(−) It can be hard to raise money.
(+) _____	(−) _____

3 **A** Read the text, ignoring the blanks. Complete the title with *best* or *worst*.

B In pairs, discuss the text. Which ideas from exercise 2 are mentioned? Which would be true for you?

🔧 Skill — understanding text development

In a text, sentences are often related to each other. When you recognize the connections, you can understand the text better.

• related words: *Feeling under **pressure**? Here are three strategies to help you deal with job-related **stress**.*
• reference words: *I have two college **degrees**. Neither of **them** has helped me get a job.*
• time and contrast words: ***At first**, I hated my job. **However**, I **soon** got used to it.*

4 Read the Skill box. Fill in blanks 1−5 in the text with a−e below, paying attention to the words in **bold**.

a I **eventually** leased a new car, bought a house, and got my hours down to 50 or 60 hours a week.
b I'm sure that my parents would have **lent** me the $13,000 I needed to start my little shop, but I was committed to doing it myself.
c **In spite of** these **advancements**, the core risks and worries for young entrepreneurs have not changed.
d If I were to risk **it all** now, I'd have a lot to lose.
e **While** I suffered from **both**, I overcame them with blood, sweat, and tears – and time.

✦ Text builder — complex negative sentences

Negative sentences are easier to understand if you try to rephrase them:
*He had **no one** to trust **but** his parents.* = He **only** trusted his parents.
*He was **never unsure** of what to do.* = He was **always sure** of what to do.
*His **lack of** money was a problem.* = He **didn't have** any money, and that was a problem.
*Worrying **does little to** solve problems.* = Worrying **doesn't really** solve problems.

5 Read the Text builder. What do the underlined sentences (a−c) in the text mean?

6 Discuss the questions in pairs.

1 When you choose a career, how important is it to do what you really love? Why?
2 Can you imagine making a decision like the author's? Why/Why not?

86

understanding text development ■ complex negative sentences   READING   SKILLS   10B

Why starting a business at 19 was one of the _____ decisions I ever made

Special to The Globe and Mail Published Tuesday, Sep. 17, 2013   CHRIS GRIFFITHS

I started my first business when I was 19 years old, and that was long before youth entrepreneurship was celebrated the way it is now. I had a retail showroom and a service shop, employees, inventory, bank debt and all the joys and stresses that came with them.

I remember getting a fair bit of attention for starting a business at that age, but it didn't seem like a big deal to me. To me it made perfect sense; after all, I was single, had no dependents and was still living at home. My future seemed like a blank page that allowed me to write my own story.

Being young wasn't helpful when it came to raising capital, I can assure you. (a) Having nothing but a high school education and a well-written business plan did little to calm the nerves of my family's bank.

1_____ Although I was very nervous about getting into debt, a wise man reminded me that $13,000 is a small car payment for most people, and for that amount of risk, you get to try and make a dream come true that could impact the rest of your life.

He was right. The thought of not doing it, and spending the rest of my life wondering "What if?" was riskier than borrowing the money. I sold my rusty Ford and rented a small spot in the center of town. I was officially in business.

Taking the city bus to your own business and scheduling appointments around when you can borrow your parents' car wasn't the glorious start to entrepreneurship I had imagined, but it was a start. In my first year of business, I regularly booked 95-hour work weeks, seldom went out with friends and paid myself only $781 for the entire first year.

Every dollar went back into the business as I needed a strong foundation to build upon. Over time, things started to improve. 2_____ Getting to this point took years, and to be honest, I don't know how I would have done it if it weren't for the advantages of my youth.

You see, I started with the burden of the two most common reasons for business failure: lack of experience and lack of capital. 3_____

I was able to risk all that I had because I didn't have anything. That gets tougher to do later in life. Now I have a marriage, a mortgage and three kids. 4_____ I also don't have the ability to work 95 hours a week or accept $781 as an annual salary. Starting a business later in life requires better planning and more support systems. Sure it's possible, but I definitely benefited from the flexibility that came with starting a business in my youth.

The great thing about starting a small business in my 20s was that I was able to make mistakes on a small scale and learn from them. The more experience I gained, the more the business grew. (b) I was using my youth to my advantage and never really saw it as a disadvantage.

Today I see a lot more support systems for young entrepreneurs and I am pleased to see it become a hot topic and a celebrated achievement. 5_____ (c) They worry about their own lack of experience and lack of ability to raise capital. They worry about taking on such responsibility and risk at a young age.

My advice is always the same: imagine yourself not pursuing your passion; decades from now, will you be looking back on today's opportunity and wondering "What if?"

Chris Griffiths is the Toronto-based director of *fine tune consulting*, a boutique management consulting practice. Over the past 20 years, he has started or acquired and exited seven businesses.

Personal Best   Write a paragraph about someone you know who took a risk.   87

10 LANGUAGE — comparison ■ word pairs

10C Job interview tips

1 Read the text. Complete blanks 1–4 with a–d below. In pairs, discuss why you shouldn't say a–d in a job interview.

a "I hated my last company."
b "Well, it's on my résumé."
c "I'm really nervous."
d "Things are difficult right now."

Four things you should never say in a job interview

The big day has come. The company has looked through dozens – if not hundreds – of résumés, and one of its managers wants to meet you. So now it's your turn to make an impression! Here are four things you should never ever say!

1 _____ The person interviewing you is aware of that. But even if you're more anxious than you've ever been, please don't say it out loud **over and over**! Companies want to hire people who are confident and who can use self-control.

2 _____ No matter how bad a job was, criticizing a former employer in an interview is one of the worst mistakes you can make. Negativity should be avoided during job interviews, so focus on what you learned while working there.

3 _____ While it's true that the interviewer has this information, he or she needs to listen to you and see if you are as good as your résumé says. How good are your communication and social skills? Can you express yourself clearly? Do you make eye contact? Use the question you're asked as your chance to impress.

4 _____ **Sooner or later**, we all have to face life's **ups and downs**, and most interviewers would be sympathetic to someone who's having a family crisis. But even if you think you may need to take time off, now is not the time to give the impression that your personal life might affect your performance. So, remember: the less you talk about your personal issues, the better.

Do you have an interview coming up? <u>Click here</u> for more advice on how to get your dream job!

2 Match the **bold** expressions in the text above with their definitions 1–3.

1 at some future time _____
2 good and bad experiences _____
3 repeatedly _____

Go to **Vocabulary practice:** word pairs, page 153

3 A ▶ 10.7 Listen to two friends, Tony and Claire, discussing a job interview. Complete the sentences. Which mistake from the text in exercise 1 did Claire make?

1 For starters, the traffic was slightly _____ _____ usual, so I got there ten minutes late.
2 She was really friendly – by far _____ _____ person ever to interview me.
3 She asked me why I'd left my previous job, and I tried to be _____ _____ _____ possible.
4 But _____ _____ details I gave, _____ _____ she smiled.

B Look at sentences 1–4 in exercise 3A again. Choose the correct option to complete each sentence below.

1 The traffic was *a little* / *a lot* worse than usual.
2 *Some* / *None* of the other interviewers were this friendly.
3 I was *completely* / *mostly* honest.
4 The interview ended *better* / *worse* than it started.

comparison ■ word pairs **LANGUAGE 10C**

4 Find four sentences expressing comparison in the text in exercise 1. Which one is a superlative sentence? Then read the Grammar box.

Grammar | comparison

Comparatives:
The interview was **far easier than** I'd imagined.
It's important to listen **more carefully than** usual.

the ... the:
The less prepared you are, **the worse** you'll do.
The more questions she asked, **the more** nervous I became.

Superlatives:
That was by far **my worst** interview.
I was clearly **the least experienced** candidate.

as ... as:
The interview went **as well as** I'd expected.
The experience wasn't quite **as bad as** I'd thought it would be.

Look! After *one of* + a superlative, we use a plural noun:
He was **one of** the best **candidates** in the group. NOT ~~one of the best candidate~~

Go to Grammar practice: comparison, page 131

5 A ▶10.9 **Pronunciation:** sentence stress with *the ... the* comparisons Listen to the sentences. Which words are stressed in each one?
1 The more I study English, the more I like it!
2 The more chocolate I eat, the happier I get!
3 The less I exercise, the more tired I feel!

B ▶10.9 Listen again and repeat. Then, in pairs, change the sentences so they are true for you.

6 A Read the text. Complete the sentences with patterns from the Grammar box, using the correct forms of the prompts in parentheses.

New job? Here's your survival guide for the first few weeks.

- **Dress professionally.**
  Research shows that people make a judgment about you almost ¹_____ (soon / they / meet) you. So, to make a good first impression, ²_____ (few / things / important) than dressing professionally.

- **Learn people's names.**
  ³_____ (fast / you / learn / everyone's name / easy) it will be to get along with your coworkers. If you're bad with names, google some memory tricks you can use to help you.

- **Arrive early and leave late.**
  During the first few weeks, make sure you ⁴_____ (arrive / early / leave / late) than most of your coworkers.

- **Listen more than you talk.**
  This can be ⁵_____ (one / hard / skill) to learn, but if you talk too much, you may sound arrogant.

- **Avoid gossip.**
  There may be a lot of gossip at work, but try not to get involved. Repeating gossip is probably ⁶_____ (one / productive / way) to spend your time at work.

B In pairs, discuss the tips in exercise 6A. Which ones are also helpful for college?

Go to Communication practice: Both students, page 172

7 In pairs, think of two tips for each topic. Give reasons using comparisons.

Things you should never say or do:
- when talking to a police officer
- on a first date
- when meeting your in-laws for the first time

On a first date, you should never ...
The more you ... , the less you ...

Personal Best Write three sentences comparing yourself to a family member.

89

10 SKILLS SPEAKING discussing pros and cons ■ being supportive

10D Two job offers

1 A What's most important to you when choosing a job? Take the survey. Rank each factor from 1 (not important) to 5 (very important).

My dream job would have …

1	a boss I respect. ____	4	lots of room for growth. ____
2	coworkers I get along with. ____	5	above-average pay. ____
3	a low level of stress. ____	6	excellent benefits. ____

B In pairs, discuss your answers. How many were the same?

2 ▶ 10.10 Watch or listen to the first part of *Talking Zone*. Write S (Synergy) or FB (Future Bytes) for each sentence.

1 ____ was the second company to approach Ben.
2 ____ has a more relaxed working atmosphere.
3 ____ is closer to his home.
4 ____ pays less.
5 ____ offers room for growth.

3 A ▶ 10.10 Watch or listen again to Ben talking about the two companies. Write P (Pros) or C (Cons) next to each of the things he mentions.

Synergy
____ creativity   ____ hours
____ distance   ____ atmosphere

Future Bytes
____ distance   ____ benefits
____ pay   ____ atmosphere

B How did Ben discuss the two jobs? Complete sentences 1–5 with the words in the box.

Each one has its pros   I can't make up my mind whether   I'm torn between
I'm leaning towards   One of the drawbacks of

1 _____ to take it or not.
2 _____ the two jobs.
3 _____ and cons.
4 _____ working there … is that it's really far.
5 _____ Future Bytes.

🧩 Conversation builder   discussing pros and cons

We use a variety of phrases to weigh up and consider our options.
I'm torn between working at home and taking an office job.
Each option has its pros and cons.
I can't make up my mind whether to stay with John or break up.
One of the drawbacks of my current job is the pressure.
I'm leaning towards going away for the summer.

4 A Read the Conversation builder. In pairs, ask and answer questions 1–4, using the words in parentheses.

1 I hear you're buying a new car. Congratulations! Have you picked a model? (*I'm leaning … ,*)
2 I'm thinking of renting a house near you. What do you think? (*… pros and cons/One of the drawbacks …*)
3 Any plans for New Year's Eve? (*I can't make up …*)
4 So, have you chosen the baby's name? (*I'm torn …*)

B In pairs, discuss something you haven't made up your mind about yet.

90

discussing pros and cons ■ being supportive **SPEAKING**   **SKILLS** **10D**

5 ▶ 10.11 Watch or listen to the second part of the show. Why is Ben less enthusiastic about Future Bytes than he was after the first interview? Choose the correct answer.
  a He was misled in the first interview.
  b He didn't do well on the second interview.
  c He got a better offer from another company.

6 ▶ 10.11 Watch or listen again. Are the sentences true (T) or false (F)?
  1 If he does an MBA, Future Bytes will not pay the full tuition fee. ____
  2 Future Bytes has changed its mind about the salary. ____
  3 Ben hasn't given Synergy a final answer yet. ____
  4 Ben made a decision he regrets. ____

🔧 **Skill** being supportive

To be supportive when talking to someone who has a problem, you can:
• listen carefully, nod, and make eye contact.
• show sympathy: *I really sympathize.*
• show the positive side of the problem: *Look on the bright side. The pay is good.*
• make a suggestion: *You could always call them.*
• try to cheer the other person up: *Don't let it get you down.*

7 ▶ 10.12 Read the Skill box. Listen to conversations 1–3. Check (✓) the strategies used in each one.

Strategy	1	2	3
show sympathy	☐	☐	☐
show the positive side of a problem	☐	☐	☐
make a suggestion	☐	☐	☐
cheer the other person up	☐	☐	☐

Go to Communication practice: Student A page 163, Student B page 169

8 **A** PREPARE In pairs, imagine you're upset about something. Prepare a conversation, using one of the ideas below. Think about the pros and cons of the situation, as well as how you feel.

You stained your favorite shirt, and it's difficult to clean.

You can't get tickets for a concert you really wanted to go to.

You haven't heard from a friend for a long time.

You had an accident and damaged your bike.

B PRACTICE Practice the conversation. Take turns explaining why you're upset and being supportive.

C PERSONAL BEST Can you improve the way you show support to each other? Practice again with a new partner. Talk about a different idea.

Personal Best Choose a new situation from exercise 8 and write about the pros and cons of the situation.

9 and 10 REVIEW and PRACTICE

Grammar

1 Cross (**X**) the sentence that is NOT correct.

1 a Unfortunately, my mother slipped on the ice and fell.
  b My mother slipped unfortunately on the ice and fell.
  c My mother slipped on the ice and fell, unfortunately.

2 a Elena has two children, but neither of them go to the school across from their house.
  b Elena has two children, and all of them go to the school across from their house.
  c Elena has two children, and both of them go to the school across from their house.

3 a He has a good memory, extremely.
  b He has an extremely good memory.
  c His memory is extremely good.

4 a A fair amount of people I know work from home.
  b A fair number of people I know work from home.
  c Quite a few people I know work from home.

5 a My boss had me work until 8 p.m. yesterday!
  b I was worked by my boss until 8 p.m. yesterday!
  c I had to work until 8 p.m. yesterday!

6 a The more money you make, the more taxes you should pay.
  b If you earn a lot of money, you should pay a lot of taxes.
  c As much money you make, as much taxes you should pay.

7 a We had our plants watered while we were away.
  b A neighbor watered our plants while we were away.
  c Our plants had watered while we were away.

8 a Lima is by far the biggest city in Peru.
  b Lima is one of the biggest city in South America.
  c Lima is much bigger than all the other cities in Peru.

2 Use the words in parentheses to complete the sentences so they mean the same as the first sentence.

1 Our house is the same size as my cousin's house.
  Our house _____ my cousin's house. (big)

2 I realized a thief had stolen my bag.
  I realized _____ a thief. (stolen)

3 Schools spend a lot of money on books.
  Schools spend _____ on books. (deal)

4 If I go to bed late, I feel tired in the morning.
  The later _____ in the morning. (more)

5 Did you know that Alex has cut Yolanda's hair?
  Did you know that _____ Alex? (had)

6 She doesn't leave the house very often anymore.
  She _____ . (rarely)

3 Choose the correct options to complete the text.

To:
From:

This is a photo of the house we bought three years ago. As you can imagine, we ¹*immediately started / started immediately* making a lot of changes. Since we bought it, ²*we have / we've had* a ³*great deal / large number* of work done to the house. Before, there was very ⁴*few / little* light downstairs, but that problem ⁵*solved / was solved* by having one of the walls ⁶*took / taken* out. We also ⁷*added / had added* some new windows in the living room. Our friends thought we were really crazy when we bought it, but now ⁸*they say always / they always say* it's ⁹*a / the* most beautiful house they've ever been in! And, actually, my husband and I agree that the work was far ¹⁰*more / most* enjoyable than ¹¹*all / either* of us had expected. We didn't have as ¹²*many / much* arguments ¹³*than / as* we could have had! In my view, the more work you ¹⁴*have done / had done* on a house, the ¹⁵*most / more* pride you take in it.

Vocabulary

1 Circle the word or expression that is different. Explain why.

1 ruby   multi-colored   maroon   teal
2 ounce   gallon   pint   quart
3 mile   inch   foot   ton
4 light green   reddish   lavender   dark blue
5 lengthen   widen   deep   shorten
6 once or twice   side by side   ups and downs   sick and tired

92

REVIEW and PRACTICE — 9 and 10

2 Complete the text with the words in the box.

> seriously   account   peace
> over   cons   taking   clue   raise

A lot of my friends in college spend their weekends at the beach or having each other [1]_____ for lunch, whereas I volunteer at the local hospital with three other students. In addition to [2]_____ turns looking after patients, we help manage projects to [3]_____ money for the hospital. There are pros and [4]_____ to volunteering, but I take my role very [5]_____ . Working means I have a good understanding of real-life issues, while most of my friends don't have a [6]_____ about life outside college. I think my experience at the hospital will definitely be taken into [7]_____ by future employers when I start to apply for jobs after I graduate. But although I enjoy volunteering, I have to admit I enjoy the [8]_____ and quiet on my days off!

3 Choose the correct options to complete the sentences.

1   I wish our teacher would type his comments because I *have trouble reading / take care not to read* his handwriting.

2   Sara submits her essays late every week, but she always has *nothing to do with it / an excuse*.

3   He's not a very nice person. He takes *pleasure / pride* in other people's bad luck.

4   *Sooner or later / Now and then* I drive to work, but I usually take the bus.

5   Maria is normally home by 6 p.m., so I don't have *a clue / an open mind* why she isn't here yet.

6   At first I could hardly speak a word of English, but *by and large / little by little* I picked it up, and now I'm pretty fluent.

7   Did I tell you I'm *setting up a / going out of* business? If it's successful, I'll be rich!

8   They're planning on *lengthening / widening* the road here so there's more space for cars to pass.

4 Put the words in the box under the correct headings.

> teal   increase   fall   turquoise   ounce   foot
> drop   go up   violet   rise   ton   go down
> grow   decrease   inch   bronze

Positive trends	Colors
_____ _____	_____
_____ _____	_____

Length and weight	Negative trends
_____ _____	_____
_____ _____	_____

Personal Best

Lesson 9A
Write four sentences using adverbs of comment, degree, manner, and frequency.

Lesson 10A
Name two things you have in large quantities and two you have in small quantities.

Lesson 9A
Write five sentences about yourself or people you know using collocations with *have* and *take*.

Lesson 10A
Describe three current business or economic trends in your country.

Lesson 9B
Describe objects you own that are silver, multicolored, reddish, or light blue.

Lesson 10B
Write three complex negative sentences about yourself or people you know.

Lesson 9C
Name three things you have had done in the past year.

Lesson 10C
Describe four things that are very good, very bad, very strange, and very funny, using superlatives.

Lesson 9C
Describe the length and weight of four things you own.

Lesson 10C
Write four sentences using word pairs.

Lesson 9D
Write three sentences about your classroom using a definite article, an indefinite article, and a zero article.

Lesson 10D
Describe the good and the bad aspects of a situation you know about.

93

UNIT 11 Fact and fiction

LANGUAGE present and past modals of deduction ■ science

11A It can't have been real!

1 A Look at the headlines of three articles. Then match the words in **bold** with their definitions a–d.

1 Mind-reading experiment **carried out** on live TV!
2 New **data** to be **gathered** in horoscope study
3 Major **breakthrough** in UFO sightings

a development _____
b done _____
c collected _____
d factual information _____

B Which of the three articles would you like to read most? Do you believe in any of these things?

Go to Vocabulary practice: science, page 154

2 A Read the blog post. Which headline in exercise 1A does it refer to?

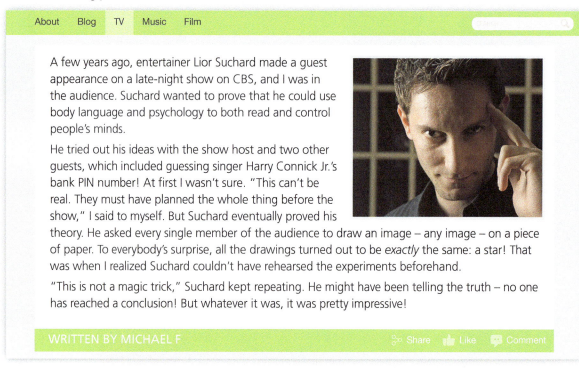

About Blog TV Music Film

A few years ago, entertainer Lior Suchard made a guest appearance on a late-night show on CBS, and I was in the audience. Suchard wanted to prove that he could use body language and psychology to both read and control people's minds.

He tried out his ideas with the show host and two other guests, which included guessing singer Harry Connick Jr.'s bank PIN number! At first I wasn't sure. "This can't be real. They must have planned the whole thing before the show," I said to myself. But Suchard eventually proved his theory. He asked every single member of the audience to draw an image – any image – on a piece of paper. To everybody's surprise, all the drawings turned out to be *exactly* the same: a star! That was when I realized Suchard couldn't have rehearsed the experiments beforehand.

"This is not a magic trick," Suchard kept repeating. He might have been telling the truth – no one has reached a conclusion! But whatever it was, it was pretty impressive!

WRITTEN BY MICHAEL F   Share   Like   Comment

B Choose the correct option to complete the sentence below.

By the end of the show, Michael *thinks he knows / has no idea* how Suchard did his trick.

3 A ▶ 11.4 Listen to a couple watching the show on TV. Who's more skeptical, Mitch or Jane? Do both people agree in the end?

B ▶ 11.4 Who said these sentences, Mitch (M) or Jane (J)? Listen again and check.

1 Oh, come on! <u>They must be pretending</u> they're surprised.
2 Of course not. <u>The man must have known the numbers</u> before the show.
3 <u>He might have known them</u>, but who knows? How can you be so sure?
4 Well, <u>you might be right</u> about ghosts, but "no UFOs"? Come on!
5 No way! <u>That couldn't have been a UFO</u>!

94

present and past modals of deduction ■ science   LANGUAGE   **11A**

4 A Match meanings a–c with the underlined phrases in sentences 1–5 in exercise 3B.
  a Definitely. I'm sure. _____
  b Definitely not. I don't think it's true. _____
  c Maybe, but I'm not sure. _____ _____

B Which underlined phrases are in the present? Which are in the past? Then read the Grammar box.

  Grammar   **present and past modals of deduction**

Something you think is/was true:
You **must be reading** my mind. That's exactly what I think.
What was that noise? You **must have heard** it.

Something you think is/was possibly true:
You **could be** right, I guess. I'll take your advice.
I think I **might have made** a mistake. Sorry!

Something you don't think is/was true:
Are you kidding? This story **can't be** real!
Bad weather? That **must not be** the reason.
It **couldn't have been** Joe you saw. He's on vacation.

5 Read the text in exercise 2A again and find more examples of modals of deduction.

Go to Grammar practice: present and past modals of deduction, page 132

6 A ▶ 11.6 **Pronunciation:** reduction of past modals Listen to the sentences. Notice how *have* is pronounced.
  1 You must **have** seen it – it was right there!
  2 She might **have** forgotten – who knows?
  3 It could **have** been Michael on the phone.
  4 She couldn't **have** left the office yet. It's only 4 p.m.

B ▶ 11.6 Listen again and repeat. In pairs, add a line before each sentence to create a conversation.

7 A Rewrite the two possible underlined responses to 1–5 using modals of deduction.
  1 "What's that bright light in the sky? It doesn't look like an airplane to me!"
    a "Relax! I'm sure it's an airplane."
    b "Weird, isn't it? Maybe it's a UFO or something."
  2 "I just read my horoscope. Tough week ahead!"
    a "You're definitely kidding, right? Who believes in that stuff?"
    b "You mean astrology.com? I'm sure they know what they're talking about."
  3 "I dreamed about my aunt last night, and she called me this morning!"
    a "I'm sure it was a coincidence."
    b "Wow! Maybe she read your mind."
  4 "Who do you think built the pyramids?"
    a "The Egyptians definitely built them. Who else?"
    b "It definitely wasn't anyone on this planet!"
  5 "Homeopathy cured my constant headaches, you know."
    a "Homeopathy? You're definitely not serious!"
    b "I used to suffer from insomnia, and maybe homeopathy cured me, too."

B In pairs, discuss the responses to 1–5 in exercise 7A. Which response, a or b, would you give?

Go to Communication practice: Student A page 163, Student B page 169

8 Look at the three pictures. Who are the people? Where are they? What might have happened in each picture? Use modals of deduction in your answers.

Personal Best Write some sentences explaining what you think happened during the TV show in exercise 2.

95

11 SKILLS LISTENING identifying conclusions ■ the "flap" in American English ■ opposite adjectives

11B Fake news

1 In pairs, complete the headlines so they are fake news (= news that isn't true). Use your imagination!

1. **Scientists create plant that ...**
2. **A new study reveals that people who ...**
3. **Facebook reveals plans to ...**
4. **The government has announced that ...**

2 Why is fake news such a big problem these days? In pairs, decide what you think the two most important reasons are.
1. Some journalists are **irresponsible** and don't check their facts.
2. Fake news isn't necessarily **illegal**.
3. **Controversial** news stories attract more clicks.
4. Fake news can sound **believable** sometimes.

Go to Vocabulary practice: opposite adjectives, page 155

3 ▶ 11.8 Watch or listen to the first part of *Talking Zone*. Which ideas from exercise 2 are mentioned? What is Alan's job?

Alan

Skill identifying conclusions

When you listen to informal conversations where lots of ideas are mentioned quickly, it can sometimes be hard to identify the conclusions. It is helpful to listen for:
- a logical order – for example, a problem is usually described before advice is given.
- expressions that show a key point is being repeated: *it's important to point out*, *you should always*, *whereas ... now ...* , etc.
- words related to the main theme: *fake news*, *propaganda*, *social media*, etc.
- expressions that imply a consequence: *If you don't do x, then y*; *always do x*, etc.

4 ▶ 11.8 Read the Skill box. Then watch or listen again. Number the conclusions below in the order you hear them.
a ☐ Fake news is not a recent phenomenon.
b ☐ It's getting harder and harder to know if a news story is true.
c ☐ You may need to do research in addition to reading the article.
d ☐ There are ways to find out if a news story is fake.
e ☐ Anyone can now create fake news easily.

5 Have you ever accidentally shared fake news stories on social media? How did it happen? Discuss with your partner.

identifying conclusions ■ the "flap" in American English ■ opposite adjectives LISTENING   SKILLS   11B

6 A ▶ 11.9 Watch or listen to the second part of the show. What story did Alan create?

B What happened to the story? Choose the correct answer.
a Everyone quickly realized that it wasn't true.
b It appeared on a TV news program.
c Alan sent it to various news organizations.

7 ▶ 11.9 Watch or listen again. Put the sentences in the correct order.
____ He created his website 'fakenewsspotter.com'.
____ He shared it with a fake social media account.
____ The story broke on 'real' TV news.
____ He created a fake picture and news story.
____ The story went viral very quickly.
____ Alan was surprised and tried to deny the story was real.

Listening builder   the "flap" in American English

In American English, when the sound /t/ follows a vowel and the next word begins with a vowel, the /t/ can sound like a very light *d* to listeners, or even an *r*. This also occurs when there is a /t/ in the middle of a word, e.g. *better*. This sound is called a "flap."

I wish I could help you, **but I** *can't.* [bəraɪ]
Grab a coat and **put it on**. [pʊrɪɑn]

8 A ▶ 11.10 Read the Listening builder. Then listen and (circle) the flap in the underlined part of each sentence from the video.
1 It's gotten <u>a lot of attention</u>!
2 <u>It was about a polar bear</u>, wasn't it?
3 And were you surprised <u>by the reaction at all</u>?
4 So, did you do anything <u>after you saw it on the news</u>?
5 It must have been frustrating <u>that it spread so fast</u>.

B In pairs, practice saying the sentences.

9 In pairs, create a fake news story using one of the photos below. Share your story with another pair. Whose is the funniest? Whose is the most believable?

a

b

c

Personal Best Describe a fake news story you've heard that many people believed.

97

11 LANGUAGE
reported speech patterns ■ sleep

11C The science of sleep

1 A Match the words in **bold** in the survey with pictures a–d.

Do you have a sleep problem?

Answer each question with a number from **3** (all the time) to **0** (never).

Do you ever:
1 **oversleep**? _____
2 **snore** so loudly it wakes people up? _____
3 wake up often in the middle of the night? _____
4 **doze off** at work/school? _____
5 wake up feeling tired and spend the whole day **yawning**? _____

If you scored more than 10 points, you might have a sleep problem!

B Take the survey in pairs. Who has more trouble sleeping: you or your partner?

Go to Vocabulary practice: sleep, page 156

2 Read the text. Check (✔) the correct answer. Short-sleeping is …
a probably genetic. ☐
b pretty common. ☐
c fully understood by science. ☐

SHORT-SLEEPING: Is it always a problem?

Jimena Sánchez, a 28-year-old teacher, has been living on about four hours of sleep every night for as long as she can remember. Early this year, her husband persuaded her to look for a sleep specialist, and the diagnosis took everyone by surprise.

Dr. John Scorsone, a researcher from the sleep-disorder clinic she attended, assured Jimena she didn't have a sleep problem. After a series of tests, Dr. Scorsone concluded that Jimena was a "short sleeper" – someone who only needs a few hours' sleep each night.

Jimena claims she fits that description: "I go to bed at midnight, wake up at around four, and I never feel tired," she says. Jimena's previous doctors had suggested sleeping pills, but she refused to take them: "I'm glad I said no. Now I know that I'm not sleep-deprived. I just don't need much sleep – that's all."

Dr. Scorsone based his diagnosis on a 2009 study at the University of Utah that discovered a rare gene in a mother and daughter who were able to function well on very little sleep. Since then, other studies have been carried out, but scientists are "only just beginning to understand this phenomenon," Dr. Scorsone claims.

It has been estimated that 1%–3% of the population consists of short-sleepers. For example, former UK Prime Minister Margaret Thatcher supposedly claimed she needed just four hours' sleep a night.

I asked Jimena if she felt short-sleeping was a problem: "No, not at all. It's so peaceful and quiet when I get up. I love it!"

3 A Complete the sentences with the verbs in the box. Then read the text and check.

assured   claimed   persuaded   refused

1 Jimena's husband _____ her to look for a sleep specialist.
2 Dr. John Scorsone _____ Jimena she didn't have a sleep problem.
3 Jimena's previous doctors had suggested sleeping pills, but she _____ to take them.
4 Margaret Thatcher supposedly _____ she needed just four hours' sleep a night.

reported speech patterns ■ sleep   LANGUAGE 11C

B Match a–d with sentences 1–4 in exercise 3A. Then read the Grammar box.

a verb + (*that*) + clause: *He said (that) he was bored.* ____
b verb + object + (*that*) + clause: *She told me (that) she hadn't been there before.* ____
c verb + infinitive: *My parents agreed to lend me some money.* ____
d verb + object + infinitive: *My doctor advised me to lose some weight.* ____

Grammar | reported speech patterns

Direct statements:
"You need more sleep." →
"OK, I'll pick up the kids." →

Reported statements:
He said (that) I **needed** more sleep.
She agreed (that) she**'d pick** up the kids./She agreed **to pick up** the kids.

Direct questions:
"Did you call Tim?" →

Reported questions:
She asked me if/whether I **had called** Tim.

Direct commands:
"Apologize to your boss." →

Reported commands:
She urged me **to apologize** to my boss.

Go to **Grammar practice:** reported speech patterns, page 133

4 A ▶ 11.14 **Pronunciation:** /t/ and /d/ Listen to the sentences. When are /t/ and /d/ fully pronounced in the underlined phrases?

1 He <u>told me</u> he was selling his car, but I <u>told him</u> I wasn't interested.
2 She <u>urged me</u> to see a doctor, and I <u>promised I</u> would.
3 I <u>asked a</u> simple question, but his explanation <u>confused me</u> even more.
4 My brother <u>asked me</u> to help him, but I <u>said I</u> was busy.

B ▶ 11.14 Listen again and repeat. In pairs, choose two sentences from exercise 4A and create short conversations that include them.

5 ▶ 11.15 Read the conversation and report what Ann and Roy said, using the verbs in parentheses. Listen and check.

Ann You look tired. ¹(tell)
Roy I've been sleep-deprived for weeks. ²(explain)
Ann Oh, is something wrong? ³(ask)
Roy It's just work-related stress. ⁴(assure)
Ann I've been under a lot of stress, too. ⁵(mention)
      My boss is a very difficult person. ⁶(say)
Roy Really?
Ann Yes, and I have a secret. ⁷(confess)
Roy What?
Ann I won't tell you. ⁸(refuse)
Roy Why not?
Ann You'll laugh at me! ⁹(think)
Roy I won't laugh! ¹⁰(promise)
Ann I listen to Solfeggio frequencies on YouTube. ¹¹(admit)
      You should definitely give them a try. ¹²(encourage)

1 *Ann told Roy he looked tired.*

Go to **Communication practice:** Both students, page 173

6 A What strategies have you used to achieve the following?

  [quit an unhealthy habit]   [stick to an exercise program]

  [deal with a difficult person]   [get over stress at school or work]

B Report some of the things your partner told you to the rest of the class.

Gloria told me she was trying to eat less sugar. She explained that …

Personal Best Write four things people have told you today using reported speech.

11 SKILLS | WRITING writing a personal recommendation ■ order of adjectives

11D I first met Julia …

1 A When was the last time you recommended the following?

(a restaurant) (a person) (a book)

(a movie) (a music track) (a tourist site)

B Discuss with your partner and give details.

2 Read the personal recommendation below. What does the writer feel is important in a roommate?

To: Sue Parker

Subject: Julia Bannon

Dear Sue,

1 Julia Bannon has asked me to recommend her as a roommate, and it is with pleasure that I do so. I first met Julia five years ago when I was her geology professor. Last summer, Julia returned to our town for a summer job and lived with me and my family.

2 When she stayed with us, Julia was a cooperative, considerate roommate. She always kept her room neat and clean, helped with the housework, and sometimes even cooked delicious Italian meals for us. Also, Julia is one of the most thoughtful people I have ever met. She was always willing to help, even when we made last-minute requests. Once, my husband and I had to go on an emergency trip, and Julia offered to babysit for us even though she had made other plans.

3 Julia is an easygoing young woman with a great sense of humor. At the same time, she is extremely responsible and hardworking. As a geology major, Julia worked on a number of challenging environmental projects in my classes, and I was impressed by how carefully she gathered and analyzed data before reaching a conclusion. In her personal life, she also avoids reaching quick conclusions and tries to find something in common with everyone she meets. She tries her best to understand people, and, as a result, she has many friends.

4 My experience with Julia Bannon was entirely positive, and I would not hesitate to recommend her as a roommate. Please feel free to contact me at 205-555-3246 with any questions.

Sincerely,

Gloria Winfrey

3 Answer the questions below.

1 How does Gloria know Julia?
2 Does Gloria know Sue, do you think?
3 Is the recommendation written in a formal or informal style?

writing a personal recommendation ■ order of adjectives **WRITING** **SKILLS** **11D**

🔧 Skill writing a personal recommendation

To write an effective personal recommendation, it's important to:
- explain how you know the person: *I first met Julia five years ago.*
- share details about someone's relevant personal qualities: *She was one of the most thoughtful people I have ever met.*
- give specific examples of those qualities: *She offered to babysit for us even though she had made other plans.*
- offer to provide more information: *Please feel free to contact me.*

4 A Read the Skill box. In which paragraph (or paragraphs) does Gloria:

1 say how Sue can get in touch with her? _____
2 say what kind of person Julia is? _____
3 explain how she knows Julia? _____
4 give specific examples of Julia's behavior? _____

B Find at least two examples of points 2 and 4 above in the recommendation in exercise 2.

⇆ Text builder order of adjectives

When we use more than one adjective before a noun, adjectives of opinion come before adjectives of fact:
*Julia is an **easygoing young** woman.*
*She cooked **delicious Italian** meals for us.*
*Julia worked on a number of **challenging environmental** projects.*

Look! Always use a comma between two adjectives of the same kind, e.g., two adjectives of opinion:
*Julia was a **cooperative, considerate** roommate.*

5 A Read the Text builder. Then read the extracts from some personal recommendations below. Correct the mistakes in the underlined phrases.

1 Mike's a <u>hardworking reliable member</u> of our team, who is famous for his <u>French classic dishes</u>.
2 Christina is a <u>young bright woman</u> who provided excellent customer service when she worked for us.
3 Kevin is a <u>polite friendly person</u>. He has loved animals since he was a young boy, and dreams of becoming a vet.
4 I met Giselle in high school, and we have developed a <u>close meaningful friendship</u>. She has always been great with children, and I can't think of a better person for the job.
5 As <u>an undergraduate motivated student</u>, Pablo wrote dozens of <u>literary interesting essays</u>, and he has achieved a very high level of English.

B Use the adjectives in exercise 5A to talk about people you know.

6 A Match the people in sentences 1–5 of exercise 5A with positions a–e below.

a sales representative _____
b chef in a restaurant _____
c English teacher _____
d dog walker _____
e babysitter _____

B Now match these adjectives with the positions. There is more than one answer.

> caring creative responsible gentle energetic
> outgoing amusing lively supportive trustworthy

7 A **PREPARE** Choose one of the positions in exercise 6A and think of someone you would like to recommend.

B **PRACTICE** Write your recommendation, using the Skill box to help you develop your ideas. Include some examples of adjectives of opinion and fact.

C **PERSONAL BEST** Exchange recommendations with your partner. Is your partner's recommendation convincing?

Personal Best Write a paragraph recommending yourself for one of the positions in exercise 6A. 101

UNIT 12 New discoveries

LANGUAGE present and future unreal conditions ■ phrasal verbs (2)

12A Must-have apps

1 A Read the descriptions of three apps. Match the phrasal verbs in **bold** with definitions a–c.

Best apps of the decade: our critics' picks

1Password — Always forgetting your password? *1Password* remembers all your log-in information for you and lets you **sign in** to different websites with just one password. Definitely worth a try.

CCleaner — Trying to **work out** a way to deal with the junk on your phone? Get *CCleaner* and delete all the files that may be making your phone slow. Highly recommended.

EVERNOTE — Can't find a pen and paper? *Evernote* helps you **note down** all kinds of things at home, work, and school. It's just like a notepad, so you can even label all your photos. A must-have.

a write down ____   b log in ____   c discover ____

B Are you familiar with these apps? In pairs, tell your partner about your top three apps.

Go to Vocabulary practice: phrasal verbs (2), page 157

2 A Read the social media comments. Do they refer to real or imaginary apps?

1. Wouldn't it be cool if they <u>invented</u> an app that could send some of your battery – wirelessly – to someone whose phone was running out of power?
   💬 5 ♡ 20 ⇄ 9

2. <u>I wish</u> there was an app that would go through my social-media feed and automatically delete all political discussions!
   💬 16 ♡ 40 ⇄ 12

3. <u>If only</u> there were an app that would let me back up my work phone conversations. Now that would be useful for legal reasons.
   💬 9 ♡ 14 ⇄ 3

4. <u>It's about time</u> they came up with an app to help me translate what my cat is trying to say! I mean, surely that's not impossible?
   💬 56 ♡ 73 ⇄ 25

5. To be honest, there are more important apps missing. <u>I'd rather</u> they created an app to hang up the phone whenever I got a call from a telemarketer!
   💬 13 ♡ 8 ⇄ 15

B In pairs, discuss which two apps you think would be the most popular. Why?

3 Read the comments in exercise 2A again and choose the correct options below. Then read the Grammar box.

1. In comment 1, *invented* has a *past / future* meaning.
2. The <u>underlined</u> expressions in 2–5 are used to talk about *real / imaginary* situations.
3. *Wish* and *if only* express the *same / different* ideas.
4. *Would rather* expresses a *preference / warning*.

102

present and future unreal conditions ■ phrasal verbs (2)   LANGUAGE   12A

Grammar: present and future unreal conditions

Second conditional:
If they invented a robot to clean my house, it would save me a lot of time.

wish and if only:
I wish there was/were someone that could help me!
If only my computer didn't have a virus.

It's about time:
It's about time they fixed the bugs in this app.

would rather:
I'd rather my son didn't spend so much time online.

Look! We use a past-tense verb to refer to present or future time in most unreal conditional sentences, but we use *would* or *could* to express future time after *wish* or *if only*:
Present: *If only my computer didn't have a virus* (but it does).
Future: *I wish they would invent an app to cook my dinner* (but they haven't yet).

Go to Grammar practice: present and future unreal conditions, page 134

4 A ▶ 12.3 **Pronunciation:** consonant-vowel linking Find two or three examples of consonant-vowel linking in the underlined part of each sentence.
1 <u>I wish I had a little more time</u> to spend with my family and friends.
2 <u>If only I could spend a week away</u> from home. I'm really stressed out.
3 <u>It's about time I went back</u> to the gym and lost a few pounds.
4 <u>I'd rather our English teacher didn't give us</u> so much homework every class!

B ▶ 12.3 Listen again and repeat. Which sentences are true for you?

5 Complete the blanks with the correct form of the verbs in the box.

| be   work   exist   have   invent   say   not waste |

What's a product that you wish ¹_____, but doesn't?   👤 Log in   🔍 Search

 A device designed to display how much water is being used during a shower. We ²_____ so much water if we had a device like that. **TomD**

 I have very cold feet – literally – and I often tell myself, "If only there ³_____ something I could wear to keep my feet warmer." Erm … electric socks maybe? **Ann87**

 It's about time they ⁴_____ a washer-dryer that could also fold clothes. **Madguy**

 I wish I ⁵_____ a gadget to erase people's memories – like in the movie *Men in Black*. So if I ever ⁶_____ something I regretted, I'd just have to push a button. **Luk4**

  Well, I'd rather they ⁷_____ out a way to block people – but not online! I mean, in real life! **Jennifer22**

6 Rewrite the sentences using the words in parentheses.
1 It's a shame cell-phone batteries die so quickly. (wish / last / longer)
   I wish cell-phone batteries lasted longer.
2 It's a shame "quality" tablets are so expensive. (wish / be / affordable)
3 Why do commercial sites have so many pop-ups? (if only / have / fewer)
4 Why is the weather in my country so cold? (rather / be / warmer)
5 I'm really impatient. (if only / be / patient) I'd like to be calmer. (wish / be)
6 I don't have a fast Internet connection. (about time / get / faster)

Go to Communication practice: Student A page 163, Student B page 169

7 Choose at least two topics to discuss in pairs. Use present and future unreal conditional sentences.
What would you change about your …

| personality? | routine? | neighborhood? | home? | career/studies? | country? |

Personal Best Add a social media comment to exercise 2A.

103

12 | SKILLS | READING predicting ■ adverbs and intended meaning

12B A robot revolution?

1 Look at the pictures on page 105. In pairs, discuss which jobs you think robots can learn to do better than humans.

2 Look at the title of the text. In pairs, discuss how you would answer the question. Then read paragraphs 1 and 2 to check if you were right.

🔧 Skill | predicting

Predicting helps you become actively involved in the reading process and increase your understanding of a text. You can use:
- your knowledge of the topic and text type to predict the kind of information that will be presented.
- the last sentence(s) of a paragraph to predict the content of the next one.
- linking words and adverbs to help you predict the rest of the sentence.

3 A Read the Skill box. Check (✓) the topics you think the text will discuss.

1 Why robots are taking human jobs ☐
2 The difficulties of teaching robots good manners ☐
3 Whether robots can increase productivity ☐
4 The importance of politeness in general ☐
5 Why it's important for robots to behave like humans ☐

B Read the rest of the text and check.

4 Read the text again. Predict the correct question, a or b, for the blanks in paragraphs 3 and 5. Then <u>underline</u> the answers in paragraphs 4 and 6.

Paragraph 3:
a Why would we want robots to mimic human behavior?
b What if robots become more polite than humans?
Paragraph 5:
a But should they be taught?
b But are they impossible to learn?

◀▶ Text builder | adverbs and intended meaning

Adverbs can help you understand a writer's intended meaning clearly. Often these are "comment adverbs."
Will robots take over the world? **Fortunately**, *the answer is no.* (I'm glad they won't.)
Apparently, *scientists are working on a new model.* (This is what I've heard.)
The XKX model is **surprisingly** *intelligent.* (I didn't expect it to be.)

5 Read the Text builder. Then look at the <u>underlined</u> adverbs in the text. Are the sentences below true (T) or false (F)?

The writer is:
1 very surprised that robots might be able to learn good manners. _____
2 sure that robots will learn how to say "please" and "thank you" at the right time. _____
3 surprised that some people think this research is a waste of time. _____
4 not sure whether it's possible to teach robots complex social rules. _____
5 happy that robots are not going to take over the world. _____

6 Discuss the questions in pairs.

1 Which jobs will robots never be able to do better then humans?
2 Why do some people want to develop the capabilities of robots?
3 Why are others resistant to this?

104

predicting ■ adverbs and intended meaning   READING   SKILLS   12B

"Please" and "thank you": can robots be taught how to be polite?

By Tom Goldberg, Staff Writer | December 28, 2018 11:30am ET

1 Imagine you were at an important meeting, and your cellphone rang. You would probably mute the phone or go outside to pick up the call. Now, imagine the call was answered by a robot. Obviously, without the kind of social awareness that humans possess, it would just automatically answer the call and disrupt the meeting. After all, robots can't learn human etiquette. Or can they?

2 [1]Shockingly, in the not-so-distant future they might be able to, thanks to a number of groundbreaking discoveries in the field of artificial intelligence (AI), which studies the "intelligence" of machines.

3 Scientists across the U.S. are working on complex formulas that they believe will allow machines to learn and interpret a large number of social rules. By analyzing tons of data on human interaction, they decided that robots could [2]theoretically learn, for example, how to say "please" and "thank you," respect personal space, move through crowds without bumping into people, or avoid interrupting them. This raises an important question, of course: _____?

4 Some people would [3]understandably dismiss these discoveries as a waste of time, but if "machine courtesy" is not relevant now, it might matter in the near future when robots are part of our everyday lives. So if you walked into a coffee shop and you were greeted by an automated barista, at the very least you'd expect it to say

"hello," serve you coffee, and thank you at the end. If it yelled at you or dropped your coffee, you'd probably look for another store – and get mad at robots in general. "If robots are rude, people will become even more resistant to artificial intelligence," says Marie Martin, one of the scientists studying the topic.

5 So far, the researchers have managed to create some concepts for this kind of machine learning, but there is still a long road ahead. For robots to learn "good manners" and apply them flexibly, beyond everyday business transactions, they would need to be taught a never-ending list of subtle social rules that humans take decades to pick up on, such as when it's appropriate to interrupt someone and how to have complex interactions with complete strangers. These "rules" are context-sensitive and may also vary from one culture to another. _____?

6 [4]Obviously, it's too soon to tell. Robots might never be able to display human-like behavior – at least not in our lifetimes. But one thing we can be sure of: while robots are busy saying "excuse me" and "thank you," [5]luckily we won't have to worry about them taking over the world!

Personal Best   Write a paragraph about one of the questions in exercise 6.   105

12 LANGUAGE — past unreal conditions ■ collocations with *come*, *do*, *go*, and *make*

12C Changes and regrets

1 Look at the pictures below. What differences are there between the two cars?

2 A Read the text and fill in the blanks with *come*, *do*, *go*, or *make*.

⚡ Going electric

Buying a first car is an exciting event in the lives of many young people. And before long, it may be a fully electric car. That's because in the near future many major cities are planning to ¹_____ away with both gasoline and diesel cars. It could happen fast, some experts say. By the year 2040, 90 percent of cars in the U.S., Canada, and Europe could be electric. And China may have as many as 60 million.

After all, cars replaced horses in a brief 10–15 years. If you had wanted a car in 1910, you might not have been able to afford one. Henry Ford's Model T cost the equivalent of $137,000. However, by 1921, when it had dropped to the equivalent of $35,000, a lot of people decided to ²_____ for it. And even if you still couldn't afford a car, it was easy to ride one of the new electric street cars.

You didn't have to ³_____ much effort at all to enjoy another new form of transportation!

Electric cars are still in the price range of the old Model T, but that may soon change. Lisa Farrow, a 25-year-old writer from Connecticut, bought her first electric car last year and had this to say: "If I'd bought this car sooner, I'd have more money. I wish I hadn't waited." That's because it can go as far as 180 miles on a single charge. "If only someone had told me electric cars were four-times more energy efficient," Lisa added.

Electric cars may be self-powered, too, before too long. Sending a car to pick up your groceries could be a dream that will ⁴_____ true in the very near future!

B In pairs, discuss if you would like to own an electric car. Why/Why not?

Go to Vocabulary practice: collocations with *come*, *do*, *go*, and *make*, page 157

3 ▶ 12.5 Listen to two friends talking about electric cars. Who thinks they are a good idea? Tom, Ann, or both of them?

4 A ▶ 12.5 Choose the correct options to complete the sentences. Listen again and check.
1. I wish I *waited* / *'d waited* a little bit longer before buying my car, too.
2. I might *buy* / *have bought* an electric car last month if I *knew* / *'d known* more about them.
3. If I *bought* / *'d bought* an electric car, I *was* / *'d be* able to save more.
4. If only I *read* / *'d read* this article sooner.

B In pairs, answer the questions about the sentences in exercise 4A. Then read the Grammar box.
1. What tense are the correct verbs in sentences 1 and 4?
2. Which sentence begins in the past, but ends in the present?
3. Which sentences only refer to the past?

past unreal conditions ■ collocations with *come*, *do*, *go*, and *make*   **LANGUAGE 12C**

Grammar: past unreal conditions

Third conditional:
If they **had bought** an electric car sooner, they **would have saved** money.

wish and *if only*:
I **wish** I **hadn't sold** my old motorbike.
If only I **had realized** sooner how much my life **would change**.

Mixed conditional:
If I **had bought** a house in the country last year, life **would be** better today.
If we **didn't have** three cars, we **would have moved** into a smaller place by now.

Go to **Grammar practice:** past unreal conditions, page 135

5 A ▶ 12.7 **Pronunciation:** stress in conditional sentences Listen to the sentences. Which <u>underlined</u> word in each sentence is stressed?

1 You could have texted me if you'd known you weren't coming.
2 It's a shame you couldn't go to the party. You would have enjoyed it!
3 If I'd gone to the mall last night, I might have seen your brother.
4 If I'd known it was your birthday, I would have bought you a present!

B ▶ 12.7 Listen again and repeat. In pairs, think of a response to each sentence.

6 A ▶ 12.8 Complete the texts with the correct affirmative or negative form of the verbs in the boxes. Listen and check.

Two people who regret their quick decisions

| be | buy | make | wait |

Lucy: Last year, I used all my savings to buy a motorcycle. Looking back, I wish I ¹_____ that decision so quickly. I like riding it a lot, but it gets really cold in the winter. If I ²_____ a little bit longer and saved a little more money, I ³_____ a car instead. And maybe I ⁴_____ so cold now every time I leave home!

| be | know | make | sell |

Ron: I know CDs are finished, but if only I ⁵_____ my collection of over 1,000 albums. Bad mistake! I'd been streaming my music for some time, so one day I decided I didn't need those albums anymore. Now I realize that some of them are not available online! If I ⁶_____ that at the time, I ⁷_____ a different decision, and I ⁸_____ able to listen to them today.

B Have you ever regretted a decision you made too quickly? What would be different now?

Go to **Communication practice:** Both students, page 173

7 In pairs, choose a topic. Start with *I wish* or *If only* and use third or mixed conditional sentences to explain what happened as a result.

Can you think of ...
1 something you wish you hadn't bought/sold?
2 a party you wish you hadn't been to?
3 a city you wish you'd visited sooner?
4 someone you wish you hadn't met?
5 someone you wish you'd met sooner?
6 something you wish you'd said when you had the chance?

Personal Best Write a paragraph about one of the topics in exercise 7.

107

12 SKILLS
SPEAKING talking about future trends ■ keeping a conversation going

12D Fads and trends

1 In pairs, discuss which of these technologies will still exist in 2025. Why do you think they will/won't last?

smartwatch   fitness tracker   smart glasses

2 ▶12.9 Watch or listen to the first part of *Talking Zone*. Which items in exercise 1 does Ben think will definitely last?

3 ▶12.9 Choose the correct options to complete the excerpts from the conversation. Watch or listen again and check.

Ben	You know, you should probably keep it – the new models are ¹*likely / unlikely* to get bigger as they get even smarter.
Abigail	You think so?
Ben	Oh, yeah. It's totally ²*conceivable / inconceivable* that smartwatches will replace smartphones.
Abigail	That is cool, especially when people are more concerned about health and fitness than ever before.
Ben	And the new models are amazing! There's no going back. All these wearable devices ³*aren't / are* bound to last.
Abigail	Really? I've never seen anyone wearing them.
Ben	Yeah, they're still relatively rare, so whether they'll become more popular or just vanish without a trace ⁴*is anyone's guess / is pretty clear*.

Conversation builder — talking about future trends

We can use a range of structures to talk about future trends and how probable we think they are.
3D printing **is likely to** *last.* (probable)
Robots **are bound to** *become more common.* (very probable)
It's conceivable that *"smart clothes" will become popular.* (possible)
Whether smartphones will last **is anyone's guess**. (not probable)

4 Read the Conversation builder. Which sentence shows that the speaker is not at all sure?

5 Rephrase opinions 1–4 with the words in parentheses. Then, in pairs, say if you agree or disagree.

In the next 10 years …
1 digital downloads will probably disappear. (bound to)
2 we probably won't find intelligent life on other planets. (likely to)
3 flying cars are a real possibility. (conceivable that)
4 who knows if robots will replace teachers. (anyone's guess)

talking about future trends ■ keeping a conversation going   **SPEAKING**   SKILLS **12D**

6 ▶ 12.10 Watch or listen to the second part of the show. Complete the sentences with one word.
1 Ben finds fidget spinners _____ and compares them to stress balls.
2 Many teachers think fidget spinners are distracting, so they are _____ in many schools.
3 Ben describes the Tamagotchi as an egg-shaped _____ .
4 Abigail had three Tamagotchies, and it was hard to stop them from _____ .
5 Ben used _____ so he would remember to feed his Tamagotchi.

7 ▶ 12.10 Number the sentences from Ben and Abigail's conversation in the order you hear them. Watch or listen again and check.
a ☐ **Abigail** I let the poor things die and moved on to the next fad, <u>whatever it was</u>.
b ☐ **Ben** <u>It's a bit like</u> those stress balls but it's more fun. Give it a try!
c ☐ **Abigail** Speaking of fads, <u>is that one of those</u>, what do you call them, fidget … ?
d ☐ **Ben** I sure did! You had to feed them <u>I don't know how many times</u> a day to keep them alive, right?
e ☐ **Abigail** Yeah, but <u>what exactly</u> do you do with it?
f ☐ **Ben** <u>You mean</u> the virtual pet? <u>The thing that looked like</u> an egg-shaped keychain?
g ☐ **Abigail** <u>That reminds me</u>, did you use to have a Tamagotchi at school?
h ☐ **Ben** Spinners? Pretty cool, huh?
i ☐ **Abigail** That's the one!

🔧 **Skill** keeping a conversation going

To keep a conversation going, it's important to keep the listener involved. You should:
• smile, nod, and use expressive intonation to show interest.
• introduce a new topic in a general way.
• ask for clarification.
• describe things the listener may be unfamiliar with.
• avoid unnecessary details and be vague, if necessary.

8 Read the Skill box. Then write the <u>underlined</u> phrases in exercise 7 in the correct column(s). Some phrases can go in more than one column.

ask for clarification	describe	introduce a new topic	be vague, if necessary

Go to Communication practice: Both students, page 173

9 A PREPARE In pairs, choose a current fad or trend. Use the ideas in the pictures below. Develop a conversation around it.

smartwatch

smart speaker

eggcutter

instant print camera

B PRACTICE Practice the conversation in pairs, keeping it going for at least one minute.

C PERSONAL BEST Listen to another pair's conversation. How successfully do they keep the conversation going?

Personal Best Write a paragraph about a fad or trend that you really like.

11 and 12 — REVIEW and PRACTICE

Grammar

1 Choose the correct options to complete the sentences.

1 I know a really funny joke, but you might *have to hear / have heard* it before.

2 If I *was / would be* older, I'd be earning a lot more money than I do. It's disgraceful!

3 I can't believe you walk up this hill every day! You must *be / have been* in very good shape.

4 I made a lot of mistakes when I was younger. I wish I *knew / had known* then what I know now.

5 John asked me to *meet / have met* him outside his office. I wonder what he wants.

6 I'd love to stay longer, but I have to go home. If only I *didn't have / wouldn't have* to go to work tomorrow!

7 Yvonne urged me *apply / to apply* for the job.

8 If my parents *hadn't moved / didn't move* to France when I was a child, I wouldn't be fluent in French now.

2 Use the words in parentheses to complete the sentences so they mean the same as the first sentence.

1 I don't think it's possible that Francis lied to me.
Francis _____ . (couldn't)

2 I wish we had talked about this yesterday.
It _____ good if _____ about this yesterday. (would)

3 My mother asked, "Did you do your homework?"
My mother asked me _____ . (whether)

4 His boss said, "You'll have to work on the weekend."
His boss _____ . (told)

5 You should have apologized to me before now.
_____ to me. (time)

6 I think you have a lot of money because you have an expensive sports car.
_____ because you have an expensive sports car. (must)

7 I'm certain they haven't found a cure for diabetes.
They _____ . (can't)

8 I really don't want him to bother me all the time.
I _____ . (wish)

9 "I made the chocolates myself."
She _____ . (explained)

10 You don't live near here, so I can't help you out.
_____ help you out. (lived)

3 Choose the correct options to complete the job reference.

Anton has been working with us for four years, and during that time, he has been a tremendous asset to the team. In fact, if it [1]*wasn't / isn't* for his hard work, we [2]*won't / wouldn't* be in such a strong position today. When he began his role here, I thought he must [3]*have worked / work* in a similar position before, but he explained that he [4]*didn't / hadn't*. He joined us at a very difficult time when everyone was under a lot of pressure, which [5]*can't / could* have been easy for him, but he didn't seem to have any problems picking up the job. He told us he [6]*was / will be* just a quick learner! Anton [7]*must / can* have a natural ability for predicting problems because he has saved us from difficult situations several times. On one occasion, he heard of our plans to restructure our organization, and he politely asked us if we [8]*considered / had considered* doing things in a different way. At first, we assured him that we [9]*were / are* experienced enough to know the best course of action, but Anton urged us [10]*to reconsider / reconsidering*. He was able to analyze the situation so effectively that we began to wonder if we [11]*might / must* be making a mistake. We took his advice and changed our plans. Looking back, if we [12]*didn't follow / hadn't followed* his advice, we [13]*would have / have* had serious problems a few months later. If we [14]*are / were* able to persuade Anton to stay we would, but, frankly, it's about time he [15]*would move / moved* to a bigger company where he can fulfill his potential.

Vocabulary

1 Circle the word or expression that is different. Explain why.

1 take a nap   oversleep   fall asleep   doze off

2 data   prove   gather   analyze

3 note down   sign in   write down   break down

4 geologist   psychology   economics   law

5 decision   experiment   agreement   conclusion

6 unimaginable   unsatisfactory   unacceptable   undesirable

REVIEW and PRACTICE 11 and 12

2 Match the words and expressions in the box with definitions 1–8.

> analyze   irresponsible   do your part
> evidence   uncontroversial   hypothesis
> illegal   go for something

1 against the law _____
2 unlikely to cause disagreement _____
3 not properly considering the consequences of your actions _____
4 look at something in detail _____
5 a proposed explanation based on limited information _____
6 try hard to get or achieve something _____
7 facts or information that show that something is true _____
8 help to achieve something _____

3 Choose the correct options to complete the sentences.

1 I was sad when the vacation ended, but all good things *go for / come to* an end.
2 Try not to worry about losing your phone. I'm sure it will *hang up / turn up*.
3 He must be very tired. Did you notice he was *yawning / snoring* throughout dinner?
4 You should have come to the soccer game with us yesterday. Nine goals! It was *unimpressive / unbelievable*!
5 It took a long time to work *out / through* the correct answer.
6 I'm afraid I didn't understand your essay. It really doesn't *make / have* sense.
7 I studied *psychology / psychologist* at college because I'm interested in the human mind.
8 As a visitor, you'll need to sign *in / on* when you arrive.

4 Complete the text with the words in the box.

> controversial   doing   through   came   carried   keep
> sleep-deprived   irresponsible   awake   done

Although scientists have always been interested in sleep, not much research has been [1]_____ out on what happens when someone stays [2]_____ for a long time. This is because [3]_____ experiments with [4]_____ people is very [5]_____ . Due to possible health problems, many scientists believe it is [6]_____ to [7]_____ someone awake for long periods. However, the record for the longest time spent staying awake is apparently 11 days! In 1964, Randy Gardner went [8]_____ this experience, and when the experiment [9]_____ to an end, he claimed it had not [10]_____ him any harm!

Personal Best

Lesson 11A
Use modal verbs to make three deductions about the people in your classroom.

Lesson 12A
Describe three present and future unreal situations. Explain the consequences of each one.

Lesson 11A
Name four things scientists commonly do.

Lesson 12A
Write six sentences using three phrasal verbs that have more than one meaning.

Lesson 11B
Write six sentences using three pairs of opposite adjectives.

Lesson 12B
Describe three things that have happened recently and comment on each one with an adverb.

Lesson 11C
Report four things that people have told or asked you recently.

Lesson 12C
Name three important past events and describe the consequences if they had not happened.

Lesson 11C
Describe your typical sleeping habits using sleep-related vocabulary.

Lesson 12C
Name two collocations for *make, do, go,* and *come* and write a sentence with each one.

Lesson 11D
Describe five classmates using at least two adjectives for each person.

Lesson 12D
Describe three trends and predict how these trends could change in the future.

111

GRAMMAR PRACTICE

1A Present forms; *like*, *as if*, and *as though*

 1.2

The Earth **goes** around the sun.
He **looks** great with a beard.
It **sounds as though** you're happy.
It's **as if** you**'re not listening**.
You**'re always making** quick decisions.

I **don't want** to talk to anyone.
I**'m feeling** more relaxed now.

Simple present with action or state verbs

We use the simple present with action or state verbs to talk about things that are always true and to talk about regular routines.

Every evening, I listen to music to relax.
I like to spend my free time with a good book.

State verbs include:
- Feelings: *like, love, hate, want, prefer, need*
- Thoughts and opinions: *know, believe, remember, forget, understand, think, feel, consider, realize, expect, agree, suppose, doubt, mean*
- States: *be, have* (possess), *exist, seem, appear, belong, own, matter*
- Senses: *taste, sound, look, feel, hear, smell*

Present continuous with action verbs

We use the present continuous to talk about things that are happening now and things that are temporary.

I'm coming! I'm on my way. NOT *I come! I'm on my way.*
You're working such long hours this week.

We can use the present continuous with *always* to talk about things that happen frequently, especially things that are annoying.

My parents are always criticizing me!   Why are you always interrupting her?

Some verbs, such as *think*, *have*, and *feel*, can be both action and state verbs, with different meanings. When they are action verbs, we use the present continuous, but when they are state verbs, we use the simple present.

I'm thinking about taking a course in communication skills. (the action of thinking = action verb)
I think everyone has a unique personal style. (an opinion = state verb)

Sense verbs with adjectives, nouns, and clauses

When we use sense verbs (*taste*, *sound*, *look*, *feel*, and *smell*), we usually use *like* before a noun, but *as if* or *as though* before a clause.

Those flowers smell wonderful! (adjective)
It looks like gold. (noun)
It feels as if you want us to break up. (clause)

In informal spoken English, we sometimes use *like* before a clause. We do not use *like* in more formal speech and writing. *As though* is a little more formal than *as if*.

It sounds like she's really mad at you. (informal)
It looks as if/as though we don't have the budget.

> **Look!** Adjectives, not adverbs, follow sense verbs.
> *That sounds wonderful.* NOT *That sounds wonderfully.*
> *You look really good in green.* NOT *You look really well in green.*

1 Complete the conversation with the correct form of the verbs in parentheses.

A ¹_____ you _____ (think) it's true that people ²_____ (have) different communication styles?
B Maybe. Some people ³_____ (speak) more slowly than others. And my mom ⁴_____ (use) her hands a lot.
A My mom ⁵_____ (be) a very good listener. But she ⁶_____ (like) talking to people too!
C Hey! We're in a library! I ⁷_____ (try) to concentrate!
A Sorry! We ⁸_____ (talk) about communication.
C It ⁹_____ (sound) interesting, but I ¹⁰_____ (hurry) to finish this essay!

2 Complete the sentences with *always* and the simple present or present continuous form of the verbs in parentheses.

1 You _____ (tell) me what to do! Let me decide for myself!
2 My mother _____ (give) me good advice when I have a problem.
3 Why _____ you _____ (copy) my homework? Don't you know that's called cheating?
4 My neighbor _____ (water) my plants when I'm away.
5 My boss _____ (arrive) at work on time.
6 Nancy's kids _____ (take) food out of our refrigerator without asking!

3 Choose the correct options to complete the sentences.

1 What a mess! It *looks as if / looks* a tornado has hit!
2 It *seems / is seeming* like a good idea to include Roberto on our team.
3 This sweater *feels / is feeling* so soft.
4 Dinner smells really *good / well*. What is it?
5 They *think / 're thinking* about getting a dog.
6 Please call an ambulance! I think this man *has / is having* a heart attack!
7 Your vacation sounds *as / like* an adventure!
8 I *live / 'm living* with my aunt and uncle this year.

◀ Go back to page 5

GRAMMAR PRACTICE

1C Narrative tenses

 1.10

I **rode** my bike every day last summer, and one day I **fell** and **hurt** myself.
When I **arrived**, people **were** already **having** lunch.
I **'d been** to Jim's house a few times before yesterday.
By the time I **got** to the party, Lori **had** already **left**.
I **'d been thinking** of breaking up, but Amy **decided** to do it first.

Simple past

We use the simple past to describe the main events in a narrative. These are completed actions in the past.

I opened the door to my house and found a cat inside! I didn't know what to do.

Past continuous

We use the past continuous to describe the background events in a narrative. We also use the past continuous to describe an action that was in progress when a completed action happened.

Lots of people were dancing at the party. (background event)
I was drinking my coffee when Amy came up and said hello. (action in progress)

We usually use the simple past with state verbs, but we can use the past continuous with verbs that can be both action and state verbs.

We liked our apartment, but we were thinking of selling it.

We often use *when* and *while* to connect past events.

When/While I was waiting for my brother, I got a phone call.

Look! *When* may mean "in the moment when" or "during the time when."
I was just finishing dinner when the bell rang. = in the moment when the bell rang.
When/While I was eating dinner, the bell rang. = during the time when I was eating dinner.

Past perfect

We use the past perfect to describe an action or state that happened before another action in the past.

I had just woken up when I started to feel sick.

We often connect past events with *by the time* or *before* where one verb is in the past perfect.

By the time I got to school, everyone had finished the exam.
Before the flight took off, we'd already been on the runway for two hours.

In conversation, when the sequence of events is clear, we can often use the past perfect or the simple past.

I had written/wrote to Bill, and soon after, I got an answer. (First, I wrote. Then I got an answer.)

Past perfect continuous

We use the past perfect continuous to describe the background events in a narrative.

It had been raining heavily for several hours.

We also use the past perfect continuous to describe an action that was in progress before another action happened.

My sister had been sleeping for only a few minutes when she heard a loud noise.
By the time I graduated, I'd been studying English for six years.

1 Choose the correct options to complete the sentences.

1 Jim *had waited / was waiting* for us when we arrived at the station.
2 We *'d been dying / 'd died* to see the new movie for weeks by the time we finally *had seen / saw* it.
3 Henry *had been feeling / felt* a little depressed, so he *decided / was deciding* to take a vacation.
4 I *was owning / owned* a great apartment in Italy, right by the sea.
5 *Had your brother not realized / Had your brother not been realizing* that it was an expensive restaurant?
6 While I *had talked / was talking* to some friends, someone *tapped / was tapping* me on the shoulder.
7 By the time Anna *joined / was joining* us for dinner, we *had eaten / ate* most of the food.
8 When I *met / was meeting* Mike in person, it *felt / was feeling* as if I *was knowing / had known* him my whole life!

2 Complete the conversation with past narrative tenses. Use the verbs in parentheses.

A You're not going to believe what [1]_____ (happen) to me a few days ago!
B What? [2]_____ (win) the lottery?
A No, but while I [3]_____ (wait) for the bus, I [4]_____ (meet) someone amazing. He [5]_____ (take) the same bus as me many times before, but I [6]_____ (not notice) him until then.
B So … ? Don't stop there!
A Well, I [7]_____ (stand) at the bus stop, and I [8]_____ (think) about my day at work. Then when I [9]_____ (turn) around, I [10]_____ (see) this really good-looking guy. He [11]_____ (try) to make eye contact and kept looking in my direction. He [12]_____ (seem) to want to talk to me.
B And now you're engaged!
A Well, not exactly! But yesterday, while I [13]_____ (walk) to the bus stop, he [14]_____ (come) up to me, and [15]_____ (ask) me out. He [16]_____ (wait) for ten minutes for me to walk by! And this time, I think it's going to be the real thing!

◀ Go back to page 9

GRAMMAR PRACTICE

2A Question patterns

> 🔊 2.4
> **Who took** this great photo?
> **Which** movie **did** you **see**?
> **Haven't** we **been** here before?
> You **like** museums, **don't** you?
> **Do** you **know why** he **didn't go**?
> **Could** you **tell** me **if** they**'re** here?

wh- subject and object questions

In subject questions, the question word or phrase (*who, what, how many, how much, which, what type of,* etc.) is the subject of the verb. We use the positive form of the verb, so in simple present and simple past tenses, we don't use *do/does/did*.

Who usually teaches this class?   What happened last week?

In many *wh-* questions, the question word or phrase is the object of the verb. In object questions, we use an auxiliary verb before the subject.

Who have you invited to your party?   What are you doing?

Negative questions

To form a negative question, we put a contracted negative form of the verb *be*, auxiliary, or modal verb before the subject.

Wasn't she the woman we met last week?   Don't you want to go out tonight?

We use a negative question when we think we know something, but we want to check.

Didn't he write several novels? = I think he wrote several novels. Is that right?

We also use negative questions to express surprise or to make a suggestion.

Haven't you been to this museum before? (surprise)
Shouldn't you start thinking about graduate school? (suggestion)

Tag questions

We can use a statement with a tag question when we think we know something, but we want to check. The intonation rises on the tag question.

You're from Spain, aren't you? ↗ = I think you're from Spain. Is that right?
He doesn't like art, does he? ↗ = I don't think he likes art. Is that right?

When we use a tag question as a conversation opener or to make a comment, the intonation falls on the tag question.

It's a hot day, isn't it? ↘ (conversation opener)
He's not very organized, is he? ↘ (comment)

With positive statements, we use a negative tag question. With negative statements, we use a positive tag question. The negative tag for *I am* is *aren't I*.

I'm usually right, aren't I?

Indirect questions

We ask an indirect *Yes/No* question with the following structure:

Yes/No question + *if* + subject + verb form + rest of sentence

Did they play yesterday? ⇨ *Could you tell me if they played yesterday?*

When we ask an indirect *wh-* question, we use the question word(s) instead of *if*.

How much will it cost? ⇨ *Could you tell me how much it will cost?*

> **Look!** In an indirect question, we cannot use the usual question word order.
> *Do you know where the box office is?* NOT ~~Do you know where is the box office?~~

1 Write *wh-* subject or object questions for the underlined answers.

1 <u>Bordalo</u> painted *Raccoon*.
   _____
2 I like <u>modern</u> art.
   _____
3 <u>About a hundred people</u> came to the concert.
   _____
4 The title of the painting is <u>The Kiss</u>.
   _____
5 <u>The Belvedere Museum in Vienna</u> has *The Kiss*.
   _____
6 <u>I was listening to music</u> when the phone rang.
   _____
7 Oh no! <u>Someone was hit by a car</u>.
   _____
8 I visited <u>my grandparents</u> on the weekend.
   _____

2 Complete the blanks to make a negative question or a tag question.

1 Graffiti is really good sometimes, _____ ?
2 _____ we been to this museum before?
3 You didn't notice the title of that painting, _____ ?
4 Modern art can be a real disappointment, _____ ?
5 _____ that the famous sculpture the *Fearless Girl*?
6 _____ Klimt have some problems before his gold phase?
7 I'm a pretty bad photographer, _____ ?
8 _____ you start studying? Your exam is tomorrow.

3 Complete the indirect questions for the statements.

1 Could you please tell me where _____ ?
   Yes, the Klimt exhibit is downstairs.
2 Do you know if _____ ?
   No, Kristan Visbal didn't make this sculpture. It's too traditional.
3 Could I ask you why _____ ?
   There's a lot of graffiti here because the city is encouraging street art.
4 Do you know how _____ ?
   Yes, you can get to the Guggenheim by taking the number 4 bus.
5 Could you explain how _____ ?
   I think Bordalo made this piece of art using garbage.

◀ Go back to page 13

2C Using linkers (1)

 2.9

Although I love music, I don't listen to it very often.
I don't like to cook. I love to eat, **though**!
I like movies a lot. **However**, I rarely go to see them.
Despite a lot of effort, I've never learned to speak French.
In spite of the fact that I play tennis regularly, I haven't improved.
In order to appreciate classical music, I bought a good set of headphones.
I threw out all my old books **so that** I could have more room at home.

Expressing contrast

We use *although*, *even though*, and *though* to link two contrasting thoughts. *Although* and *Even though* are a little more formal than *though*.

Even though/Although I hate to study, I have to do it every evening.
I hated my apartment. I loved the neighborhood, though.

Look! Be careful not to confuse *though* and *as though*.
It looks as though he's not here. NOT *It looks though he's not here.*

We also use *however* to express contrast. *However* is a slightly more formal way to say *but*. We do not use a comma before *however*; instead we start a new sentence.

I'm not too crazy about Thai food. However, I had it last night.
NOT *I'm not too crazy about Thai food, however, I had it last night.*

In spite of and *despite* have the same meaning as *although*, *even though*, and *though*. After *in spite of/despite*, we use a noun or the *-ing* form of a verb.

In spite of her success, she's very modest. (noun)
Despite having many problems, he finally finished college. (*-ing* form)

We put *not* before the *-ing* form of the verb to make it negative.

In spite of not having very good grades, I managed to get a job.

Use *the fact that* after *despite/in spite of* when a clause follows.

Despite the fact that I hate large crowds, I went out on New Year's Eve.
NOT *Despite I hate large concerts, I went out on New Year's Eve.*

Expressing purpose

(*In order*) *to* and *so* (*that*) both express a purpose. A clause beginning with *in order to* or *so that* is more formal than one beginning with *to* or *so*.

We've started a new program so that students can get extra training. (more formal)
I downloaded the song to see what everyone was talking about. (more informal)

We do not use *for* in a purpose clause with (*in order*) *to*.

I go to the gym every day to get some exercise. NOT *I go to the gym every day for to get some exercise.*

(*In order*) *to* is followed by the base form of a verb. *So* (*that*) is followed by a clause.

She works part-time to earn some money for her training.
I took a course so (that) I could learn more about history.

To make most purpose clauses negative, we use *not*, a negative auxiliary, or a negative modal verb. The negative form of *in order to* is *in order not to*.

I always play my music softly at home so I don't annoy my parents/in order not to annoy my parents.

GRAMMAR PRACTICE

1 Choose the correct options to complete the sentences.
   1 I almost never listen to music at home *in spite of / even though* I have a lot of good albums.
   2 The program was really difficult. *However, / Despite,* she never gave up.
   3 Swift talked her family into moving to Nashville *so / in order to* she could pursue her music.
   4 I like jazz. I really don't like folk music *although / though*.
   5 We set out early *in order not to / so that* miss the start of the concert.
   6 *In spite of / Although* having really musical parents, I didn't inherit their talent.

2 Rewrite the sentences. Correct the mistakes.
   1 Despite I don't know much about classical music, I love Beethoven.
   _____
   2 You need to be really determined for to be successful as a performer.
   _____
   3 My brother talked me into going to a rock concert however I didn't enjoy it.
   _____
   4 In spite of I take a course in the history of music, I still feel I don't know a lot about it.
   _____
   5 I love Adele. I never went to one of her concerts, even though.
   _____
   6 I gave up studying engineering that I could devote my time to music.
   _____

3 Write sentences that have the same meaning. Use the words in parentheses.
   1 I love going to concerts. I can't afford to go to many, though. (although)
   _____
   2 Even though she's very young, she's a very confident performer. (despite the fact that)
   _____
   3 I practiced swimming for three hours a day so I'd get on the team. (in order to)
   _____
   4 I really looked up to my older sister, but I didn't share her taste in clothes. (however)
   _____
   5 In spite of the fact that I'm home a lot, I never read. (even though)
   _____
   6 He waited in line for hours in order to buy a new cell phone. (so)
   _____

◀ Go back to page 17

115

GRAMMAR PRACTICE

3A Advice, expectation, and obligation

 3.2

They **should** charge people to park downtown.
I really **ought to** call my parents.
I **wouldn't** pay that price (if I were you).
We**'d better** hurry. The trains stop at midnight.
The train **is supposed to** arrive soon.
You **can't** use that entrance. You **have to** go around the block.
You**'re not allowed to** park there. You'll get a ticket!

Advice

We use *should* or *ought to* to give advice or make a suggestion.

Maybe you should/ought to try to do things differently.
You shouldn't expect to succeed instantly. It will take a lot of effort.

We also use *would* and *wouldn't* to give advice. The words "if I were you" are often implied.

I would stay somewhere else (if I were you). The service at this hotel is pretty bad.

Strong advice/warning

We use *had better* (*not*) to express strong advice or a warning. *Had better* is followed by the base form of the verb.

You'd better drive slowly tonight. The roads are very icy.
They'd better not play their music again tonight. I'll call the police!

In the first person, we can use *had better* to express a strong obligation.

I'd better renew my passport, or I won't be able to travel.

Expectation

We use *be supposed to* to express something that we're expected to do, but don't always do. In a negative sentence *not* goes after a form of *be*.

You're supposed to wait.   You're not supposed to be here.

Personal obligation

We use *should* or *ought to* to express a personal obligation.

I really should/ought to tell Dan I'm taking the trip with you.

External obligation/rules

We use *can* to express permission or talk about rules. We use the negative *can't* to express that permission hasn't been granted.

You can go to the front of the line, but you can't use your cell phone in here.

We can also use *be allowed to* to express permission. The negative expresses that permission hasn't been granted and is a little more formal than *can't*.

You're not allowed to/can't drive on the right in the UK!

We use *have to* to express external obligation and *don't have to* where no obligation is present. In American English, we use *must* only for very strong obligation or rules.

You have to pay by tomorrow, but you don't have to pay the full amount.
All passengers have to/must board through the door on the right.

> **Look!** We can use *prohibited* or *forbidden* to talk about rules in more formal or written English. *Taking photos in this exhibit is strictly prohibited/forbidden.*

1 Choose the correct options to complete the sentences.

1 We *'d better / 're supposed to* take a taxi, or we'll be late.
2 *You wouldn't / You're supposed to* take a basket or a shopping cart around the grocery store.
3 Perhaps we *ought to / have to* use the crosswalk, as it's a lot safer.
4 You *'d better not / don't have to* forget my books. They're due at the library today!
5 Are we *supposed to / allowed to* line up at the taxi stand?
6 You *can't / must* have insurance! It's strictly prohibited to drive without it.
7 You *can't / shouldn't* ride a motorcycle without a helmet. It's not allowed.
8 *We're not allowed to / We'd better not* play music now. We might wake up the baby.

2 Complete the sentences with the words in the box. Use the correct form. Add any words you need.

> allowed to   (not) have to   better not   ought to
> can't   supposed to   forbidden   have to

1 You _____ late or your father will be very angry.
2 You _____ put your password in to get into your account. You can't access it without it.
3 The use of barbecue grills inside the apartment is _____ .
4 I totally forgot I _____ be in a meeting later this afternoon. Maybe someone else can go.
5 Good news! They've changed the rules on calculators. Now we _____ use them on the economics exam.
6 You _____ play ball near the windows. You might break one!
7 We really _____ introduce Sam to our group. He's new here.
8 We _____ get up early tomorrow. It's a holiday!

◀ Go back to page 23

116

3C Phrasal verbs

 3.13

We **broke up** last week after the party.
I **threw out** my homework by mistake!
Katie **showed** her parents **around** her new apartment.
You dropped a fork. Please **pick** it **up** and put it in the sink.
You **take after** your mother. You're just like her!
If you had to **put up with** my boss, you'd quit, too.

This section gives you an overview of phrasal verbs and how they operate. See page 174 for a list of common phrasal verbs.

What are phrasal verbs?

A phrasal verb is a verb followed by words like *up*, *down*, *through*, *on*, and *off*. You may be able to guess the meaning from the main verb.

She **turned off** the light and went to sleep.
I **took** my girlfriend **out** for dinner last night.

However, most phrasal verbs have an idiomatic meaning, and the combination of the two words does not make the meaning clear.

I **came across** a really interesting article. (= found)

The best way to remember phrasal verbs is to learn them in context.

Without an object

These phrasal verbs are not followed by an object. The two parts of these verbs are never separated.

My daughter wants to be a doctor when she **grows up**.
What time should we **go back** tomorrow?

With an object (separable)

These phrasal verbs are followed by an object. In many cases, the object can go *after* or *between* the two parts of the phrasal verb. (Because the two parts can be separated, these verbs are called "separable.")

I wanted to **try** my new shoes **on**/**try on** my new shoes.

In some cases, the object can *only* be placed *between* the two parts of the phrasal verb.

This afternoon I'm going to **show** the tourists **around** the old town.

When the object of these verbs is a pronoun, it always goes *between* the two parts.

I bought you a new jacket. **Try** it **on**. NOT *Try on it*.

With an object (non-separable)

These phrasal verbs are followed by an object. The object can *only* be placed *after* the two parts of the phrasal verb.

You'd better **get on** the bus now! It's about to leave!

When the object of these verbs is a pronoun, it always goes after the two parts.

The questions aren't hard. I'll **go over** them with you later. NOT *I'll go them over*.

With three words (non-separable)

These phrasal verbs are followed by an object. The three parts of these phrasal verbs are never separated. When the object is a pronoun, it goes after the verb.

Do you **get along with** your sister?
He tried to cheat on the exam, but he didn't **get away with** it.

GRAMMAR PRACTICE

1 Complete the sentences with the correct form of the phrasal verbs in the box. You do not need one of them. Add any pronouns you need.

eat out	look for	look forward to
look up	put up with	take after
take off	talk into	turn down

1 I really don't know how much longer I can _____ my boss!
2 If you don't know a word, you can _____ .
3 I think my daughter really _____ her father.
4 I've been _____ the party all week.
5 Paul _____ going away last weekend, so I didn't finish my assignment.
6 I can't find my glasses! I _____ all day yesterday!
7 Our plane _____ on time and landed early.
8 Let's _____ tonight! I'm too tired to cook.

2 Rewrite the sentences. Correct the mistakes. Check (✓) the two sentences that are correct.

1 I love coffee. I could never do it without!
   _____
2 I thought I'd lost my wallet, but then it turned it up.
   _____
3 I came something really weird across. I don't know what it is.
   _____
4 Hey, there's no soap. I hope you didn't use up it!
   _____
5 Why isn't Joe with you? Did you break up with him?
   _____
6 I tried, but I couldn't come up any good ideas.
   _____
7 The course was so much work, but, in the end, it really paid it off.
   _____
8 John was offered a good job, but he turned it down.
   _____
9 I know you don't want to go, but we can't get it out of.
   _____
10 These math problems are hard. I can't figure out them!
   _____

◀ Go back to page 27

117

GRAMMAR PRACTICE

4A Subject-verb agreement

 4.5

Some of the **things** she said **were** very funny.
The **information** he gave me **was** very surprising.
One of you **is** lying!
Everyone finds it hard to meet new people.
A few of my friends **want** to go traveling together next year.
My family is very understanding.
My friends, as well as my mother, all **think** I should look for a new job.

Countable and uncountable nouns

Countable nouns can be singular or plural. When they are plural, they are followed by the plural form of a verb. Uncountable nouns are always singular and are followed by the singular form of a verb.

Your colleagues think you made the right decision. NOT *Your colleagues thinks you made the right decision.*
Your advice was very helpful. NOT *Your advices were very helpful.*

Indefinite pronouns

The indefinite pronouns *one*, *everyone*, *no one*, *someone*, and *anyone* are followed by a singular verb.

Everyone has been trying to help me find an apartment.
Does anyone want to go to the beach this weekend?

Each and *each of* are followed by a singular verb. However, *many* (*of*), *some* (*of*), *both* (*of*), *several* (*of*), and *a few* (*of*) are all followed by a plural verb.

Each neighborhood has its own play area for children.
Several of my friends have bought their own apartments recently.

In informal conversation, singular words like *everyone* and *everybody* are sometimes followed by the word *their* + a noun. However, in American English, this is not considered correct in writing.

Everyone disagrees with their parents at times. (spoken, informal)
Everybody asks his or her parents for money on occasion. (usually written)

Collective nouns

In American English, collective nouns are generally singular. (In British English, many collective nouns are frequently plural.)

My team is playing very well at the moment.
The government wants to employ more elementary school teachers.

Collective nouns referring to a group of individuals, however, are plural.

The police are stopping cars along the highway.
The Japanese are usually very polite.

Asides

When a sentence has a comment in the middle as an "aside," the verb always agrees with the subject of the sentence, not the noun in the aside. Asides often begin with inclusive phrases, like *as well as* or *in addition to*, or exclusive phrases, like *aside from* or *apart from*.

My sister, in addition to a lot of my friends, loves dancing. NOT *My sister, in addition to a lot of my friends, love dancing.*
All of my teachers, apart from just one, are planning to come to my wedding.
NOT *All of my teachers, apart from just one, is planning to come to my wedding.*

1 Choose the correct options to complete the sentences.
  1 Some of the information *was* / *were* very helpful.
  2 Everyone always *stands* / *stand* near the door when I try to get on the train.
  3 My boyfriend, as well as my friends, *thinks* / *think* people don't have any manners.
  4 Only one of us *doesn't* / *don't* have any pet peeves.
  5 In American English, we say "My family *gets* / *get* together every weekend."
  6 Some of my decisions *has* / *have* turned out OK.
  7 The police *believes* / *believe* that two people were involved in the robbery.
  8 The stores here, apart from one, *is* / *are* very expensive.

2 Read the text. Choose the correct options.

> **Life in the city – a pet peeve**
>
> Many pedestrians in Barcelona ¹*has* / *have* experienced nearly being knocked over by a bicyclist riding on the sidewalk. One of my friends ²*was* / *were* hit by a bike last year. Only a few of these riders ³*is* / *are* ever fined for this dangerous behavior. Even when bike riders use the street, some of them ⁴*don't* / *doesn't* stop at red lights, so a pedestrian ⁵*risks* / *risk* his or her life crossing the street. Of course, pedestrians also ⁶*needs* / *need* to follow the rules and not walk in bike lanes. Each of us ⁷*has* / *have* to do our part to make Barcelona a safer city. My advice ⁸*is* / *are* to look behind you frequently as you walk!

3 Read the text. Correct the eight mistakes.

> One of my pet peeves are tattoos. Almost everyone I know think tattoos are really beautiful, but I think they're ugly. Untattooed skin are much nicer. Some of my friends, as well as my sister, has wanted to have their tattoos removed, but the process are expensive and not always successful. No one think about this, though, in advance. One of my friends really don't want his tattoo with his ex-girlfriend's name anymore! Everyone need to think carefully before getting a tattoo!

◀ Go back to page 31

118

GRAMMAR PRACTICE

4C Perfect and past forms

▶ 4.9

Have you **been** here before?
We **haven't had** dinner yet.
I**'ve been looking** for a new job since the summer.
The kitchen's a mess because we**'ve been cooking**.
I**'ve wanted** to go for months.
There **has been** a bad accident on the highway.

Present perfect

We form the present perfect with *have/has* + past participle. We use it:

- to talk about past experiences in your life without saying when they happened.
  I've been to Mexico several times, but I've never been to Brazil.
- to talk about complete or incomplete past actions. We use *already*, *yet*, and *still*.
  They've already bought their mother a birthday present.
  I haven't spoken to Mike yet./I still haven't spoken to Mike.
- to talk about actions or states that start in the past and continue in the present, especially with *for* and *since*.
  Adam's worked here for 20 years/since 1998.
- to talk about past actions that have an effect on the present.
  I've left my job. Now I'm working as a freelance journalist.

Present perfect vs. simple past

We use the simple past:

- to talk about finished actions or states in the past.
  Simple past: *I lived in London for three years.* (But now I live in Paris.)
  Present perfect: *I've lived in London for three years.* (I still live there.)
- to talk about recent past actions:
  I bought a car recently.   I just handed in my essay.
- to talk about finished actions when we know when they happened.
  Simple past: *They saw the new Star Wars movie on Saturday.* (We know when.)
  Present perfect: *They've seen the new Star Wars movie.* (We don't know when.)

Present perfect continuous

We form the present perfect continuous with *have* + *been* + the *-ing* form of the verb. We use the present perfect continuous:

- to talk about longer or repeated actions that started in the past and continue in the present.
  We've been waiting for the bus for 45 minutes/since 1 p.m.
- to talk about a longer action in the past that has an effect on the present.
  I'm out of breath because I've been running.

Present perfect vs. present perfect continuous

We use the present perfect when the action is complete. We use the present perfect continuous when the action is still taking place.

I've written an essay. (The essay is finished.)
I've been writing an essay. (I'm still writing the essay.)

We can use both forms to talk about the duration of an action that starts in the past and continues in the present with verbs like *live*, *work* and *study*.
I've lived/been living here for ten years/since 2010.

We don't use the present perfect continuous with state verbs.
I've known Melanie for a long time. NOT *I've been knowing Melanie for a long time.*

1 Choose the correct options to complete the sentences.
 1 I've *preferred / been preferring* to bike to work for a couple of years.
 2 How long *did you live / have you lived* in New York before you *moved / have moved*?
 3 *We've been / We went* to the museum earlier today.
 4 It's the best movie *I've ever seen / I've ever been seeing*.
 5 *I've been sitting / I've sat* in this cold waiting room for three hours, and I'm still waiting!
 6 *They've been deciding / They've decided* to get married, so they're very excited and happy.

2 Complete the sentences with the correct form of the verbs in parentheses. There may be more than one answer.
 1 Tom _____ (have) a motorbike since he was 18.
 2 We _____ (think) of getting a dog since we moved here, but we're not sure if it's a good idea.
 3 _____ (you/take) this type of test before?
 4 I _____ (get up) early this morning, but I _____ (not finish) my paper yet.
 5 We _____ (live) here for the last two years.
 6 My sister _____ (work) hard in the garden, and now I think she should stop.

3 Choose the correct options to complete the conversations.
 1 A How long have you *known / been knowing* Jenny?
   B About four years, I guess.
 2 A When are you going to do your homework?
   B *I already did / I've already done* it.
 3 A Are you OK?
   B Yes, we're just a bit tired. *We've been helping / We help* a friend move.
 4 A *My dad never went / My dad's never been* to a Japanese restaurant, and he'd love to go to one.
   B Let's take him next week!
 5 A You look happy!
   B I am! *I just got / I've just been getting* some good news!

◀ Go back to page 35

119

GRAMMAR PRACTICE

5A so and such; so much/many, so little/few

 5.3

It's **so difficult** to change the way you eat.
There are **so many** different **ways** to protect our natural resources.
There are **so few** good **shows** on TV at the moment.
I have **so much homework** to do this week.
There is **so little money** to spend on recycling.
It was **such a relief** to go off my diet.
You have **such strange ideas**!
I found **such good information** online.

so

We use *so* before an adjective for emphasis.

It's so hard to have a conversation with my sister!

We use *so many* and *so few* before plural countable nouns.

There are so many good books on the environment.
There are so few days when I have time to cook.

We use *so much* and *so little* before uncountable nouns.

There's so much false information on the Internet these days.
I have so little time to do the things I want.

such

We use *such a/an* before singular countable nouns for emphasis.

Global warming is such a serious problem. NOT *Global warming is such serious problem.*
It makes such an enormous difference if you recycle.

We use *such* before plural countable nouns for emphasis.

They sell such nice products here! NOT *They sell such a nice products here.*
We've had such interesting discussions on so many issues.

We also use *such* before uncountable nouns.

My friends gave me such good advice. NOT *My friends gave me such a good advice.*
If you ever need a painter, Joe does such nice work.

> **Look!** *So* and *such* are often used in sentences that express cause and effect.
> *We've had such a dry summer (that) we may start to get forest fires.*
> *There's so much pollution (that) I can't breathe!*

1 Complete the conversation with *so*, *such*, *so much*, *so many*, *so little*, or *so few*.

A My neighbors are a problem again! They've been making [1]_____ noise that I haven't been able to sleep properly for days!
B There are [2]_____ people these days who are rude. Why do they have [3]_____ respect for others?
A I don't know, but it's [4]_____ a problem that I'm thinking of calling the manager. It makes me [5]_____ angry! I've already talked to my neighbors [6]_____ times, but they just ignore me.
B It must be [7]_____ frustrating.
A It sure is! And tiring. There are [8]_____ nights when I sleep well now.

2 Complete the sentences using the prompts and *so*, *such*, *so much*, *so many*, *so little* or *so few*.

1 almost no clean water
   There's _____ that we have to buy bottled water.
2 lots of benefits to a zero-impact month
   There are _____ that we're going to try it next month.
3 lots of friends on social media
   I keep in touch with _____ that I don't want to stop using it.
4 big problem with recycling
   We have _____ that we don't even try to do it.
5 enjoyable to bike to work
   It's _____ that I do it every morning.
6 a large amount of trash outside my door
   There's _____ that I've complained about it to the city.
7 easy ways to help the environment
   These are _____ that everyone can do them.
8 almost no paper bags in stores
   There are _____ that I bring my own from home.
9 good advice on energy-saving
   This is _____ that I'm going to follow it.
10 expensive to have a car
   It's _____ that I've decided not to get one.

◀ Go back to page 41

5C Future predictions

 5.12

In my opinion, public transportation **will improve** in the next ten years.
Won't many people **suffer** from the effects of climate change in the future?
We**'re going to have** much more extreme weather.
By 2050, we **will have invented** many new ways to save energy.
When the year ends, we **might not have made** much progress.
We**'ll** definitely **be living** in a different world twenty years from now!
Will we still **be working** when we're 100?

Future with *will*, *going to*, *may*, and *might*

We use *will* and *won't* to make predictions about the future, based on our personal opinions.

In my opinion, the planet will be very hot in 50 years.

We often use *Do you think … ?* to ask someone to make a prediction.

Do you think we'll be better at controlling our resources?

We use *be going to* to make predictions that we are sure about, based on something we can see or something that we know.

Look at all this trash. I'm positive we're going to have mice in our apartment!

We use the adverbs *probably* and *definitely* to make a prediction less or more certain. We use them after *will* but before *won't*.

They'll probably collect the trash later. It definitely won't be here tomorrow.
They're definitely not going to let this continue!

We use *may* and *might* to make predictions that we're less certain about.

It hasn't rained at all this month. I think we may/might not have enough water.

Look! To make a negative prediction with *will*, we normally use the negative form of *think*, followed by *will*.
I don't think we'll be much more aware. NOT ~~I think we won't be much more aware.~~

Future perfect

We form the future perfect with *will/won't + have* + the past participle of the main verb. We use the future perfect to predict events that will be completed before a certain point in the future.

By the year 2020, we will have given up non-electric cars.
In 50 years, pollution will have disappeared.
How long will you have lived here by 2020? NOT ~~How long will you live here by 2020?~~

We can also form the future perfect with *may* or *might* to express a possibility that we are less sure of. We sometimes use phrases like *I think* or *It seems that*.

I think by 2100 some of our lakes may have disappeared.
We might not have found other energy sources by then.

Future continuous

We form the future continuous with *will/won't + be* + the *-ing* form of the main verb. We use the future continuous to predict events that will be in progress at a certain point in the future.

In 50 years, we'll be living on a very hot planet!
We won't be getting a lot of help from the government.
Will people still be wasting so much water?

GRAMMAR PRACTICE

1 Choose the best options to complete the conversations.
  1 A I feel terrible!
    B I'm sure that you *will feel / may feel* better tomorrow.
  2 A I'm so worried about Molly.
    B I'm not. I think she *will have solved / might be solving* her problem at work by the time we see her again.
  3 A What are you doing this weekend?
    B I'm not sure. I *will go / may go* for a hike with some friends, but nothing's planned yet.
  4 A Do you know about this great app that monitors your energy use at home?
    B Yes! I'm already using it. In a year, I *will cut / will have cut* my energy use in half.
  5 A I hope they do something soon about people who throw gum in the street!
    B Me too. I read that they *will be getting / might have gotten* fines in the future.
  6 A Can I read your report?
    B It's not done yet. But I *might be finishing / might have finished* it by tomorrow.
  7 A The traffic's awful this morning! We're not moving at all!
    B I know! *I'm going to miss / I'll miss* my train!
  8 A Should we go shopping now?
    B Yes, good idea. The stores *probably won't / won't probably* be too crowded now.

2 Complete the sentences with *will* + a future perfect or future continuous form of the verbs in the box.

| work | not fly | rain | improve |
| get | increase | live | use |

  1 By the end of the century, forest fires _____ by 50 percent!
  2 It's raining again! By tomorrow, it _____ every day this week.
  3 If I don't start saving money now, I _____ even when I'm 70!
  4 I think many more people _____ solar energy in a few years.
  5 I hope that in the future, we _____ in more energy-efficient homes.
  6 With all this evidence, it's safe to say that climate change _____ a lot worse by 2050.
  7 I think healthcare _____ a lot by the time we're in our fifties.
  8 In my view, people _____ so much in the future.

◀ Go back to page 45

GRAMMAR PRACTICE

6A The habitual past

 6.2

I **used to love** rock music, but now I like reggae.
Did you **use to play** an instrument when you were young?
I **didn't use to play** soccer, but I **would go** to games.
I **used to spend** a lot of time at home. I **would watch** TV every afternoon.
My teachers **were always yelling** at me because I was late.
She'**d** often **go** running after school. She'**d** also **gone** running that evening.

used to and would

We use *used to* + infinitive to talk about states or habits that were true in the past but are not true now. Habits are repeated actions.

I used to hate classical music, but now I love it.   She used to go swimming every day.

In affirmative statements, *used* in *used to* ends with a *d*, just like other regular verbs in the simple past. *Use to* is incorrect.

We used to spend every evening outside in the summer. NOT *We use to spend every evening outside in the summer.*

We form negative statements and questions without a *d*, like other simple past verbs. We may also use *never used to* instead of *didn't use to*.

I didn't use to like classical music. NOT *I didn't used to like classical music.*
Did you use to live around here? NOT *Did you used to live around here?*
I never used to watch YouTube videos, but now I like them.

We often use a mixture of *used to* and *would* when we describe past habits. We start with *used to* and continue with *would*.

I used to do a lot of exercise when I was in high school. I would play tennis every weekend and go swimming three or four times a week.

We do not use *would* to describe states. Instead we use *used to* or the simple past.

I hated/used to hate vegetables when I was a kid. NOT *I would hate vegetables when I was a kid.*

Simple past

We may use either *used to* or the simple past when the habitual meaning is clear. We often use a mixture of *used to* and the simple past to describe past situations.

I didn't use to play any sports when I was younger. I hated sports.

We use the simple past, not *used to*, when we talk about single actions or say how many times something happened.

We went to Rio three times when I was young. NOT *We used to go to Rio three times when I was young.*

Past continuous with *always*

We can use the past continuous with *always* to show that something happened repeatedly, or to talk about things that were annoying.

I remember her well. She was always sitting outside when I went by.
I never had any privacy. My brother was always listening to my conversations.

would vs. had

When we talk about the past, the contraction *'d* may mean the habitual past *would* or the past perfect *had*. Be careful not to confuse them.

Every evening, we'd go for a swim in the lake. (= we would)
We'd just gotten out of the water when we saw my sister. (= we had)

1 Choose the correct options to complete the sentences.
   1 I *used to / would* love visiting my grandparents. They were such wonderful people.
   2 You're such a good tennis player. Did you *used / use* to play when you were younger?
   3 I *used to go / went* to Europe twice when I was in college, but I haven't been since.
   4 I *used to / would* know all my neighbors, but I don't now.
   5 My brother and I *were always arguing / were arguing* when we were younger.
   6 We *didn't used / didn't use* to go on vacation very often.
   7 My sister *used to / would* have a bike that she *rode / was riding* everywhere.
   8 My friends and I never *used / use* to play baseball after school because we had nowhere to play.

2 Rewrite the underlined words. Use a pronoun + *had* or *would*.
   1 Every day I'd _____ come home from school and play video games.
   2 I'd _____ forgotten how much fun it was to go fishing. We'd _____ go fishing all the time when I was a kid.
   3 I used to really enjoy reading, and I'd _____ read at least one book a week.
   4 My sister used to buy really weird clothes, and she'd _____ wear them to parties.
   5 We had no money for the bus home because we'd _____ spent all our money on ice cream.
   6 That summer my brother was going out with Teresa. He'd _____ met her in college and was crazy about her.

3 Complete the text with a form of *used to*, *would*, the simple past, or the past continuous with *always*, and the verbs in the box. There may be more than one answer.

   | complain   go (x2)   not listen |
   | love   make   stay   take |

   When I was a child, my family ¹_____ a trip every summer to the Shenandoah National Park in the state of Virginia. We ²_____ at a little cabin in the woods, and every day we ³_____ on long nature walks. My younger sister didn't enjoy them much, and she ⁴_____ that she was tired. However, my older sister and I ⁵_____ being outdoors all day. We ⁶_____ to the reports of bears because we didn't really think there were any! When we went to bed, we ⁷_____ sure we hadn't left any food around, though. We loved it so much that we ⁸_____ back there at least ten times.

◀ Go back to page 49

122

GRAMMAR PRACTICE

6C be used to and get used to

 6.7

I **wasn't used to making** my own decisions.
Now I **'m used to living** on my own.
I've slowly **gotten used to working** in an office.
Getting used to college life hasn't been easy.
Are you **getting used to not having** a car?

be used to

Be used to means "be accustomed to." We use *be used to* to express a state. *Be used to* is usually followed by the *-ing* form of a verb or a noun.

When I first started this job, I wasn't used to working on weekends.
Are you used to your new home?

When *be used to* is followed by a clause, use *the fact that*.

I'm just not used to the fact that I'm now responsible for my own rent.

Look! Be careful not to confuse *be used to* with the habitual past *used to*.
Are you used to getting up early? (= accustomed to)
No, I never used to get up before 10 a.m. until I got this job. (= habitual past)

The word *used* always has a *d* in *be used to*.

Is your sister used to driving around here? NOT *Is your sister use to driving around here?*

get used to

We use *get used to* to express a process. It means "become accustomed to." *Get used to* is usually followed by the *-ing* form or a noun.

I can't get used to being away from home.
I hope I'll get used to college.
You've always gotten used to everything before.

Get used to can also be followed by *the fact that* + a clause.

I'll never get used to the fact that I didn't get accepted to Harvard.

The subject of a sentence can also contain the *-ing* form of *get used to*.

Getting used to a big move has never been easy.

Look! Be careful not to confuse *get used to* with the habitual past *used to*.
I can't get used to living here.
NOT *I can't used to live here.*
Did you get used to things by the end of the year?
NOT *Did you use to things by the end of the year?*

1 Choose the correct options to complete the sentences.

1 I just can't *be used to / get used to* living alone. I don't know what I'm going to do.
2 I *used to / 'm used to* be nervous about flying, but slowly I *got used to / was used to* it.
3 *Are you use to / Are you used to* your new dorm? I hope you have nice roommates.
4 *Getting used to / Being used to* life in the U.S. was hard at first, but it's now easier.
5 My new job is an incredible amount of work, but *I'm being used / I'm getting used* to it slowly.
6 We *weren't used to / didn't use to* living in a city, so we found the move to Chicago hard.
7 I think my new dog *is finally used to / finally used to* me. I'm so happy I have him.
8 My parents couldn't get used to *that / the fact that* I was looking for my own apartment.

2 Complete the conversations with a form of *be used to* or *get used to*. There may be more than one answer.

1 A I'm a little worried. My daughter [1]_____ going to school by bus, and she doesn't want to leave home in the morning.
   B Oh, don't worry. She [2]_____ it soon, I'm sure. My son didn't like it at first, either, but he [3]_____ to it quite quickly.
2 A You know what? I [4]_____ being an adult yet.
   B Why do you say that?
   A I just can't [5]_____ having so much responsibility.
3 A So, [6]_____ living on your own at school now?
   B Well, I guess I could say I [7]_____ it little by little. I [8]_____ the food yet, though. It's awful!
4 A Your parents [9]_____ their new home, haven't they?
   B Yes, I think so. But they [10]_____ the new neighbors yet, who play music at all hours!

◀ Go back to page 53

123

GRAMMAR PRACTICE

7A Relative clauses; reduced and comment clauses

 7.2

They're the students **who had the party**.
This is the test **that I'm most worried about**.
Anyone **hoping to learn a language** needs to practice every day.
Anyone **chosen for the play** will be told shortly.
My history professor, **who was excellent,** retired last year.
I think I failed my exam, **which is really a disaster**!

Defining relative clauses

We use a defining relative clause to say which person, thing, or place we are talking about.

He's the person who/that told me about this course.
This is the book that/which I enjoyed so much.
They're the couple whose son was in the news last week.
That's the college where my sister went.

We can omit *who*, *that*, and *which* when the verbs in the main clause and the relative clause have different subjects. We can't omit the relative pronoun when it refers to the subject of the relative clause.

He is the man (who/that) I saw at the library.   She's the woman who teaches French.

Reduced relative clauses

We can reduce defining relative clauses that refer to the subject of the sentence. When the original clause is in the simple present, the verb changes to an *-ing* form.

Anyone wanting (= who wants) *to take the exam late needs to speak to me.*
Students waiting (= who are waiting) *to enter the lecture hall should move to the side.*

We can also reduce relative clauses in the passive when they refer to the subject of the sentence. The context determines whether the sentence refers to the present or past.

Assignments submitted (= which <u>were</u> submitted) <u>last month</u> *will be returned in April.*
The actors seen (= who <u>are</u> seen) *on the video you're watching <u>now</u> aren't professionals.*

To make a reduced relative clause negative, we put the word *not* before the verb.

Anyone not waiting (= who's not waiting) *in line, please take a seat.*

Non-defining relative clauses

A non-defining relative clause gives us extra information about something in the main clause. If we omit this clause, the sentence still makes sense. We add a comma before a non-defining clause.

This is my friend Barbara, who was in my math class last year.

A non-defining relative clause in the middle of a sentence is more common in writing.

This course, which is a requirement for psychology majors, is only in the morning.

> **Look!** Notice the difference in meaning between the sentences below.
> *The students who passed the exam received a certificate.* (= only some students passed)
> *The students, who passed the exam, received a certificate.* (= all the students passed)

Comment clauses

We can also use a non-defining relative clause to comment on another clause. Comment clauses are common in conversation.

I failed my biology exam, which my parents weren't too happy about.

---

1 Link the two sentences with a relative clause. Use commas where necessary.

1 I'd like to go to a school. I can study surf science there.
   I'd like to go to a school where I can study surf science.
2 That's the teacher. Her class on ethical hacking was excellent.
   That's the teacher _____.
3 I can't find my notes. I took them yesterday.
   I can't find my notes _____.
4 This is my brother's old cell phone. He gave it to me last month.
   This is my brother's old cell phone _____.
5 In one progressive school, some students skip class. They're not punished.
   In one progressive school, students _____ aren't punished.
6 The next module is compulsory. It includes creating a comic.
   The next module _____ is compulsory.

2 Rewrite the sentences with reduced relative clauses. Check (✓) the sentences that are passive.

1 Students who cheat on any exam will not graduate.
   Students cheating on any exam will not graduate.
2 Books that have been borrowed from the library must be returned by tomorrow.
   _____.
3 Those who want to take the test on Saturday, please come speak to me.
   _____.
4 Everyone who uses this lab has to be very careful with the equipment.
   _____.
5 Students who are sent away to school are often homesick.
   _____.
6 People who don't need foreign languages often don't study them.
   _____.

3 Choose the best comment clauses to complete the sentences.

1 My children hardly ever put their phones down, *which is really annoying / which is encouraging*.
2 I'm learning to ski, *which doesn't require any practice at all / which is a lot harder than I thought*.
3 Students arriving late can't take the exam, *which seems really unfair / which has increased traffic problems*.
4 They say "practice makes perfect," *which is definitely true / which doesn't apply to playing tennis*.
5 My neighbor was very noisy, *which isn't why we stayed / which is why we moved*.

◀ Go back to page 59

7C Present and future real conditions

 7.10

If I **get up** early, I **do** more during the day.
If you **search** online, you**'ll find** a lot of material.
Until I **try** something, I **won't say** I'm not good at it.
As long as you**'re** motivated, you can learn a new language.
Provided that this room **is** available, we**'ll meet** here next week.
Unless you **learn** to cook, you**'ll spend** a lot of money on food.
Even if you **don't like** the course at first, you might enjoy it later.

Zero and first conditionals

We use the zero conditional to talk about routines or situations that are generally true, including facts. We use the simple present in both the *if* clause and the main clause.

If students take their work seriously, they always do well.
When I listen to my favorite songs, I immediately start to relax.

We use the first conditional to talk about the result of a possible action. We form the *if* clause with *if* + simple present, and we form the main clause with *will* or a modal verb + base form, or an imperative.

They'll be late if they don't leave immediately.
If you come to the party on Saturday, you might meet someone.
If at first you don't succeed, try, try again. (proverb)

We can put either clause first with no change in meaning. However, if we put the main clause first, we don't use a comma between the two clauses.

You'll really like hiking if you give it a try.
If you look for an apartment, you'll find one.

Future time clauses

We use the simple present, not *will* + base form, after words and phrases like *when*, *until*, *before*, *after*, and *as soon as* when we are referring to the future.

I'll give you a call as soon as I get out of class.
She won't talk to him until he apologizes.

Alternatives to *if*

Several other words express conditions and are alternatives to *if*. We use the simple present after them to refer to the future.

As long as and *provided* (*that*) mean the same as *if* and can be followed by an affirmative or negative verb. *Provided* (*that*) is a little more formal than *as long as*.

As long as you know what you want, it's not hard to plan your future.
You'll do well on your finals provided (that) you don't wait until the last minute to study.

We can use *unless* to mean *if* + ... *not*.

Unless you work harder, you won't pass your exam. = *If you don't work harder, you won't pass your exam.*

Even if expresses a contrast and a condition and means *despite the possibility that*.

Even if you find English difficult, you'll definitely improve if you practice.
We can still go out to dinner even if you get home late.

GRAMMAR PRACTICE

1 Check (✓) the sentences that are correct. Correct the incorrect sentences.

 1 If you don't understand a word, look at the context. ____
 2 If I start my report now, I finish it this afternoon. ____
 3 We don't do much work if we study together in the same room. ____
 4 Before you will become a serious tennis player, you have to practice a lot. ____
 5 If you have some acting lessons, you'll become less self-conscious. ____
 6 You won't know if you like skiing until you'll try it. ____

2 Choose the correct options to complete the sentences.

 1 You can learn to play an instrument *even if / unless* you've never taken lessons before.
 2 *As long as / Unless* you practice, it's hard to improve your English.
 3 The course will begin on Monday, *provided / even if* there are enough students.
 4 She's planning to get a job *as soon as / as long as* she leaves school.
 5 I'm sure you'll do very well *unless / as long as* you keep working hard.
 6 They'll probably want to have a meal *when / until* they get here.

3 Rewrite the sentences with *as long as*, *even if*, or *unless*.

 1 Provided that I review my notes, I always do well on tests.
 _____
 2 Despite the possibility that you're not athletic, you can still enjoy learning a sport.
 _____
 3 If we don't give up social media, we'll never improve our social skills.
 _____
 4 I'll do my best to help you, provided that you tell me the truth.
 _____
 5 If I don't make a note of this, I'll forget it.
 _____
 6 I'm sure you'll have a great time despite the possibility that you don't have much money.
 _____

◀ Go back to page 63

125

GRAMMAR PRACTICE

8A Using linkers (2)

 8.2

Whereas most people sleep late on weekends, I get up early.
Some people like comedy shows, **while** others are really bored.
Unlike many of my friends at school, I'm not interested in technology.
I gave away my TV **as** I never watched it.
Because of the high rent, we've had to close our store.
I'm in much better shape **as a result of** my training program.
This is a very important decision. **Therefore**, we need to think about it carefully.

Expressing a contrast or comparison

We use a clause with *whereas* or *while* to express a contrast or comparison.

Most older people still watch TV, whereas younger people choose YouTube videos.
One of us wants to stay home on weekends, while the other likes to go out.

We can also use *whereas* and *while* to mean *although* or *in spite of the fact that*.

I haven't gone ice-skating in years, whereas I loved it when I was young.
While I don't really like spinach, I eat it sometimes.

We can also use *unlike* to express a comparison.

Unlike all the people I know, I hate shopping.

> **Look!** Be careful not to confuse the two meanings of *while*.
> *While I was watching TV, my phone rang.* (= when)
> *While I sometimes turn on the TV to relax, I usually read, instead.* (= whereas)

Expressing a reason

We use *since* and *as* to express a reason. They mean *because*.

Since I only read e-books, I've thrown out many of my paper books.
I'm going to forget about my friend Dave as he never calls me.

We also use *due to*, *because of*, and *as a result of* to express a reason. They are frequently followed by a noun.

Due to/Because of/As a result of illness, we had to cancel the concert.
We canceled the course due to/because of/as a result of lack of interest.

When *due to* is followed by a clause, we use *due to the fact that*. This is more formal than *because* or *since*.

The library closed due to the fact that it had no money. NOT *due to it had no money.*

We can also express a reason with *therefore* and *as a result*. *Therefore* is a little more formal than *so*.

This show is very popular. Therefore/As a result, other similar shows have been produced. = This show is very popular, so other similar shows have been produced.

We start a new sentence with *therefore*. We do not use a comma before it.

The heating system has broken down. Therefore, we have closed the school.
NOT *The heating system has broken down, therefore, we have closed the school.*

> **Look!** Be careful not to confuse the two meanings of *since*. *Since* can be followed by an *-ing* form of a verb only when it means *from the time when*.
> *Since moving/I moved here, I've made many new friends.* (= from the time when)
> *Since I live in New York, there's always a lot to do.* (= because)

1 Choose the linker in parentheses which means the same as the linker in the sentence.
   1 While (*Whereas / When*) I once wanted to become rich, now I'm not interested in money.
   2 Apartments outside the city are cheaper. As a result (*Unlike / Therefore*), many families are moving out.
   3 Since (*As / Therefore*) there are so many things to do, I have trouble making a decision.
   4 Netflix has been so popular due to (*as a result of / since*) viewers' desire for flexibility.
   5 Although (*Unlike / While*) having a dog has many advantages, it's also a lot of work.
   6 While (*When / Whereas*) I eat dinner, I sometimes watch the news.

2 Choose the correct options to complete the text.

> ¹*As / Whereas* moviegoers need to feel they're getting the most for their money, theaters are always looking for new ways to impress them. ²*While / Therefore*, the movie industry is borrowing ideas from the airline industry. Now movie seats may be assigned, ³*since / unlike* just a few years ago. In addition, they may have comfortable foot rests that pop up ⁴*while / whereas* you watch. ⁵*Due to the fact that / As a result of* watching a movie is a much more pleasant experience than it used to be, fewer people are complaining about the cost. They're even buying dinner at the theater ⁶*since / due to* an evening at the movies has become luxury entertainment!

3 Rewrite the sentences with words from the box that mean the same as the underlined words. Use each option once. Add any words you need.

> as a result   as /since   due to   therefore   while

   1 <u>Whereas</u> everyone used to watch programs on TV, now many of us watch them online.
   _____
   2 Sporting events attract large audiences. <u>Therefore</u>, many TV stations want to broadcast them.
   _____
   3 <u>Because of</u> new technology, DVDs have become a thing of the past.
   _____
   4 <u>Due to the fact that</u> there are so many shows, the audience for each one is small.
   _____
   5 News is always available online, <u>so</u> people don't watch the news on TV so much.
   _____

◀ Go back to page 67

8C -ing forms and infinitives

 8.8

Playing computer games can be hard to stop!
I **have trouble concentrating** sometimes!
I **encouraged** my son **to take** a vacation.
I **let** a friend **borrow** my computer.
I **remembered to turn off** my phone before class started.
I **remembered turning off** my phone, but it rang anyway.

We use the *-ing* form:
- after prepositions and certain verbs, including *avoid, enjoy, feel like, finish, hate, keep, like, love, (don't) mind, miss, prefer, recommend,* and *suggest*.
  We watched six episodes without stopping.   I suggest talking to a lawyer.
- as the subject of a sentence.
  Keeping up with technology is important to me.
- in expressions with a negative meaning, such as *There's no point, It's no use/good, I can't help, I have trouble, I have a hard time,* and *I have a problem*.
  I have trouble saving money.   It's no use talking to him.
- We put *not* before an *-ing* form to make a negative.
  I love not having to get up early on weekends.

We use the infinitive:
- after certain verbs, including *afford, agree, decide, expect, forget, help, hope, learn, need, offer, plan, promise, refuse, want, would like/love/hate/prefer*.
  I can't afford to buy any more clothes.
- after adjectives.
  It's hard to think about summer when it's so cold.
- to give a reason.
  I called my friend Sally to see if she could help me.
- We put *not* before an infinitive to make a negative.
  I promise not to be so critical of people in the future.

Infinitive vs. base form:
- With some verbs, we use the infinitive after the object. These verbs include *ask, encourage, expect, tell, want,* and *would like*.
  I want you to try to spend less time on the Internet.
- With *make* and *let*, we use the base form after the object. We can also use the base form after *help* + object.
  I made him put his phone away. NOT *I made him to put his phone away.*
  I let her see my photos.   She helped me finish my homework.

We use the *-ing* form or the infinitive:
- with *begin, continue,* and *start* with no change in meaning.
  I started playing/to play video games when I was very young.
- with *forget, remember, stop,* and *try* with a change in meaning.
  I forgot about inviting everyone to my house. = I forgot that I'd done something.
  I forgot to buy the groceries. = I forgot I needed to do something.
  I remember having a meal here. = I remember that I've done something.
  I remembered to turn off my phone. = I remembered I needed to do something.
  I stopped using social media. = I did not do something any more.
  I stopped to talk to them. = I paused in order to do something.
  I tried not having a TV. = I experimented with something.
  I tried to tell you. = I made an effort to do something.

GRAMMAR PRACTICE

1 Complete the sentences with the correct form of the verbs in parentheses.

  1 _____ (eat) a whole bar of chocolate made me realize I was out of control.
  2 I always have a hard time _____ (finish) my assignments on time.
  3 I really can't afford _____ (go) on vacation.
  4 We went to the mall _____ (do) something different for a change.
  5 It's really hard not _____ (cry) when I see a sad movie.
  6 I expected _____ (be) more surprised when my old boyfriend called.
  7 I recognized your face right away and remember _____ (see) you once before.
  8 Have you tried _____ (listen) to the radio? That might help you go to sleep.

2 Rewrite the sentences. Correct the mistakes. Some sentences have two mistakes.

  1 There's no point spend so much money on shoes.
  _____
  2 I'm looking forward to not have so much homework next semester.
  _____
  3 I don't mind not have a new phone, but I would like buy a new tablet.
  _____
  4 I asked my parents buy me a motorcycle, but they said no.
  _____
  5 Don't worry. I won't forget stop to pick up some milk.
  _____
  6 I really feel like see the movie, but I don't want go today.
  _____
  7 Joe made me to promise go to the doctor about my headaches.
  _____
  8 I stopped watch the news on TV a couple of years ago.
  _____

◀ Go back to page 71

127

GRAMMAR PRACTICE

9A Position of adverbs

 9.3

Luckily, I decided to change my lifestyle.
This book was **amazingly** helpful.
Our teacher **slowly** explained what we had to do.
I've **frequently** considered taking a break from school.
I explained my reasons very **carefully**.

Beginning of a sentence

Comment adverbs (*actually, amazingly, incredibly, luckily, obviously*) give the speaker's opinion and often modify the whole sentence. Therefore, they often go at the beginning of the sentence.

Actually, I'm very unhappy with my apartment right now and want to redesign it.
Amazingly, I got a full scholarship when I was in college.

Middle of a sentence

Comment adverbs can also give the speaker's opinion of an action or state. When they are used like this, they go in the middle of the sentence.

I've stupidly left home without any cash. *You're obviously artistic.*

Some adverbs of degree (*very, extremely, amazingly, incredibly*) modify adjectives and come before them.

She was amazingly talented. NOT *She was talented amazingly.*

Other adverbs of degree (*a lot, a little, a bit*) modify adjectives or verbs. When they modify adjectives, they come before them, but when they modify verbs, they come after them.

He's a bit talkative. (*a bit* modifies the adjective *talkative*)
She rested a little when she got home. (*a little* modifies the verb *rested*)

Adverbs of manner (*slowly, clearly, carefully, truly*) modify verbs and often go before the verb. We cannot place them between a verb and its object.

She carefully considered her decision. NOT *She considered carefully her decision.*

Adverbs of frequency modify verbs. They go before the main verb, but after the verb *be*.

He's always positive, and he never complains. NOT *he complains never.*

Adverbs of frequency go after an auxiliary verb.

I've often considered changing my lifestyle, but I haven't done anything about it.

Look! Some adverbs (*really, quite*) may be comment adverbs or adverbs of degree. The position of the adverb reflects the meaning.
It's really a fantastic opportunity to study here. (comment adverb)
It's a really great course, and I'm glad I signed up for it. (degree adverb)

End of a sentence

Adverbs of manner (*slowly, clearly, carefully*) may also go at the end of a sentence. Putting adverbs at the end of a sentence gives them more emphasis.

She entered the room suddenly.

An adverb of manner comes after an adverb of degree.

You're not talking very clearly. (degree + manner)

1 Check (✓) the sentences that are correct. Correct the position of the adverbs in the incorrect sentences.
   1 I've considered often changing my job. ____
   2 Incredibly, I got an A on my exam. I never expected it. ____
   3 The thief managed to steal quickly the car. ____
   4 He's shy a bit, and so he sometimes has trouble at work. ____
   5 It was very cold, but we didn't have any gloves. ____
   6 After the phone call, my friends left quickly. ____
   7 He was handsome extremely, but he wasn't a very nice person. ____
   8 I was able to relax a little when the plane landed. ____
   9 They don't know much English, so just pronounce clearly the words. ____
   10 The buses are late in the mornings, so I prefer usually to ride my bike to work. ____

2 Choose the correct options to complete the text.

¹*Incredibly / Obviously*, we'd all love to have a beautiful house, but it's ²*really / fortunately* difficult to find a house at a reasonable price. ³*Clearly / Amazingly*, a friend of mine offered to design one for me. I looked over ⁴*the plans carefully / carefully the plans*, and I could ⁵*imagine easily / easily imagine* myself in the house. I was ⁶*actually / extremely* lucky, and I ⁷*often thank / thank often* my friend for her design. It's a great place, and I ⁸*very / truly* love it!

3 Complete the conversations with the adverbs in parentheses in their correct positions.
   1 A Are you excited about going away to college? (very)
     B Well, I feel nervous (a bit), but I'm sure it will be OK.
   2 A You look like someone who's shy, but only at first. (a little)
     B I'd say that's very accurate. (amazingly)
   3 A I'm ready for the exam now. I've prepared for it. (carefully)
     B That's great! You work hard, don't you? (always)
   4 A I admire my uncle. (truly)
     B He's a sensitive person (really), and he's kind. (incredibly)

◀ Go back to page 77

9C Passives and causative *have*

▶ 9.12

The package **was delivered** two days ago.
Our proposal **is being considered** right now.
Before long, all our money **will have been spent**.
Your bike **could be stolen** if you don't lock it up.
The teacher **had us take** our books out.
I might **have my hair cut** this weekend.

Forming the passive

In active sentences, the focus is on the person that does the action. In passive sentences, the focus is on the action itself or on the thing that the action affects. We often use the passive if we don't know, or it's not important, who did the action.

Our office is being painted this week.

We can use *by* in a passive sentence to say who does an action. We often use *by* when the person who does the action is new information.

My sink was fixed by my neighbor. He's a plumber.

We form the passive with a form of the verb *be* + past participle. We can use the passive with most tenses and modal verbs.

	active	passive
simple present	They usually interview people here.	People are usually interviewed here.
simple past	They called him last night.	He was called last night.
present perfect	We've completed the project.	The project has been completed.
present continuous	A doctor is seeing him.	He's being seen by a doctor.
past continuous	She was cleaning the house.	The house was being cleaned.
past perfect	They'd arrested him by the time we arrived.	He'd been arrested by the time we arrived.
modal verbs	You can hire them for $25 a day.	They can be hired for $25 a day.
future perfect	She'll have fixed it by then.	It will have been fixed by then.

We form negatives and questions in the usual way with a form of the verb *be*.

It hasn't been washed. Has it been washed?

Look! The passive is not usually used in the perfect continuous tenses or with continuous or past modal verbs.
They've been keeping him in the hospital. NOT ~~He's been being kept in the hospital.~~
They might be calling you now. NOT ~~You might be being called now.~~

Causative *have*

A causative sentence may be active or passive. We form an active causative sentence with the verb *have* + object + base form.

They had us wait in line to enter the museum.

We form a passive causative with the verb *have* + object + past participle.

I'm having a swimming pool built. (= I'm having someone build a swimming pool.)

GRAMMAR PRACTICE

1 Rewrite the sentences with the passive.

1 The neighbors give candy to children on Halloween.
   _____
2 A police officer stopped me on my way home yesterday.
   _____
3 Eating too much junk food can damage your health.
   _____
4 Scientists might discover new forms of life by the start of the next century.
   _____
5 A nurse is examining my brother right now.
   _____
6 How many students did the college accept this year?
   _____
7 They won't have finished the new building by next month.
   _____
8 They were fixing my toilet when you called.
   _____
9 Someone has stolen my wallet!
   _____
10 Weather forecasters had warned people about the hurricane.
   _____

2 Complete the conversations with active or passive causative sentences. Use the verbs in parentheses. Add any words you need.

1 **A** Your hair's really long!
   B I know! I _____ this Saturday. (cut)
2 **A** I can't stay with you. Your shower doesn't work.
   B It's OK now. I _____ yesterday. (fix)
3 **A** What happened? You both look exhausted!
   B The instructor _____ lots of exercises for an hour! (do)
4 **A** Is this book a gift?
   B Yes. Could I please _____ ? (wrap)
5 **A** You have a lot of photos of you and your sister!
   B I know! She _____ a lot when we were on vacation. (take)
6 **A** I can't read very well these days.
   B I think you should _____ (test). Here's the name of my optician.

◀ Go back to page 81

GRAMMAR PRACTICE

10A Quantifiers

 10.3

A lot of people never think about saving money.
There are **quite a few** new ideas these days.
A great deal of patience is needed to succeed.
A few jobs are still available.
Not much money has been spent on our city.
Neither of these professions really appeals to me.

Large quantities

We use *a lot of* and *lots of* in positive statements before countable and uncountable nouns, and *a lot* without a noun.

I think there are lots of different possibilities at that company.
They spend a lot (of money).

An awful lot of means "very many" or "very much" and is used with both countable and uncountable nouns.

There's an awful lot of traffic today!

Quite a few and *a fair/large number of* mean "many." We use these expressions before countable nouns. We add *of* to *quite a few* before pronouns.

We've had quite a few applications in the last week.
A fair/large number of professions didn't exist 50 years ago.

The expressions *a great/good deal of*, *a fair/large amount of/plenty of* also mean "a lot of." We use them with uncountable nouns.

There's a fair amount of information on that topic.

Small quantities

We use *a few* before countable nouns. It means "a small number." We use *a little* before uncountable nouns. It means "a small quantity."

There are a few jobs I'm interested in, but not many.
Can you give me a little help with my résumé?

We use *not many* and *not much* in negative sentences. We use *not many* before countable nouns and *not much* before uncountable nouns.

I haven't had many interviews.   I haven't had much luck finding work.

We also use *few* and *little* (without *a*). They mean "not enough."

Few people have applied. I hope a few will show interest. NOT ~~I hope few will show interest.~~
There's little interest in this course. I hope we see a little enthusiasm. NOT ~~I hope we see little enthusiasm.~~

Both, all, neither, and none

We use *both* (*of*) with countable nouns when we refer to two things.

Both my bosses are very demanding. And both of them make me work late.

We use *all* (*of*) with countable and uncountable nouns to describe the full quantity of something.

All my friends have good jobs. In fact, all of them earn more than I do!

We use *neither* (*of*) with countable nouns and *none* (*of*) with countable or uncountable nouns when the quantity is zero. *Neither* takes a singular verb. *None* takes a singular verb in formal writing, and a plural verb at other times.

Neither of my brothers lives at home. And neither (of them) comes to visit very often.
None of the candidates was suitable.   None of my friends own a car.

130

1 Choose the correct options to complete the sentences.
  1 I received *little / a little* help when I started this job, so I felt quite unhappy.
  2 I think *few / a few* people will go on the hike Saturday, and I'm sure someone can give you a ride.
  3 My friends gave me *a fair number / a fair amount* of advice, but I didn't take any of it.
  4 Neither of my sisters *is / isn't* very helpful at home. I have to do everything!
  5 I have two bosses, and *all / both* of them have been giving me a hard time!
  6 I went to the library and found *quite a few / a good deal of* information.
  7 *Not much / Not many* free hours are needed to volunteer with us.
  8 We have so many choices because there are *quite a few / few* good jobs.
  9 *All / Few* of us like working here. No one dislikes it.
  10 There are a *great deal of / large amount of* things to choose from on this menu.

2 Read the text. Correct the eight mistakes.

A fair amount of young people starting their careers decide to work abroad. Little of them go in order to get away from home, but most go to take advantage of the large deal of opportunities available. I have two brothers, and all of them went to live in New York. They've made a little progress finding an apartment – in fact, none – and are still sleeping on friends' sofas, but not many time has gone by. They have lots stories to tell about their adventures. In fact, neither of them doesn't want to come home anytime soon!

◀ Go back to page 85

10C Comparison

 10.8

She spoke **more quietly than** I'd expected.
The more nervous I was, **the more** I forgot what to say.
The less I worried, **the more relaxed** I felt.
My most successful interview was the first.
He was **just as friendly as** I'd imagined.
It wasn't **quite as bad as** I'd thought it would be.

Comparatives

We use comparative adjectives + *than* to compare two things, people, or places.

With one-syllable adjectives, we add *-er*. With adjectives ending in *-y*, we change the *y* to *i* and add *-er*. For adjectives with more than two syllables, we use *more* or *less*.

Some application forms are easier to complete than others.
I think Jim is more intelligent than Peter.

We also use comparative forms of adverbs. We use *more* or *less* to form most of these.

He talked more excitedly than anyone else.

We can use *a bit*, *a little*, or *slightly* before a comparative to say there is a small difference, and *a lot*, *much*, or *far* to say there is a big difference.

He answered me a bit more rudely than I was expecting.
There are much more qualified candidates than me.

the ... the

We also use the structure *the ... the* to make comparisons. The comparisons may include nouns, adjectives, adverbs, or entire clauses or ideas, too.

The more interviews I have, the more confident I become. (noun, adjective)
The harder I try, the less frustrated I feel. (adverb, adjective)
The more we're prepared, the more we succeed. (clauses/ideas)

Superlatives

We use superlative adjectives to say that something is more or less than all the others in a group. With one-syllable adjectives, we put *the* in front and add *-est*. With two-syllable adjectives ending in *-y*, we change the *y* to *i* and add *-est*. With adjectives of more than two syllables, we use *the most* or *the least*.

The most enjoyable day was the one we spent together.
The least convincing argument was the one you gave!

Some adjectives have irregular comparative and superlative forms.

good – better – best   bad – worse – worst
far – farther/further – farthest/furthest

We can put *by far* before a superlative to make it stronger.

Biology is by far my worst subject.

We use the superlative with the present perfect + *ever* and *one of the* + plural noun.

That was one of the best jobs I've ever had!

as ... as

We use *as ... as* to say that two things are the same and *not (quite) as ... as* to say that two things are different. We can use *just* with *as ... as* to emphasize a similarity.

I was just as angry as he was!   The exam wasn't quite as hard as I expected.

GRAMMAR PRACTICE

1 Complete the second sentences so they mean the same as the first sentences.

1 The second interview wasn't as difficult as the first.
   The first interview was _____ the second.
2 The beginning of this movie isn't as good as the end.
   The end of this movie is _____ the beginning.
3 Eva behaved more calmly than the other candidates.
   Eva behaved _____ of all the candidates.
4 I was really happy, and my sister was happy, too.
   My sister was just _____ I was.
5 All the presentations were a lot more interesting than mine.
   By far _____ was mine.
6 The hotel was a little larger than we expected.
   The hotel wasn't quite _____ we expected.
7 If I don't work many hours, I don't make a lot of money.
   The _____ , the _____ money I make.
8 Lauren spoke much more quietly than Katie.
   Katie spoke _____ than Lauren.

2 Rewrite the sentences and correct the mistakes. Some sentences have more than one mistake.

1 The lovelyest flowers in the shop were most expensive.
  _____
2 More I do my job, more I enjoy it.
  _____
3 I have less classes this semester than my friends.
  _____
4 It was raining a lot heavily than I thought, so I got pretty wet.
  _____
5 The more exciting trip I've taken is when I went to Rome.
  _____
6 There are much fast players than me. I'm pretty slow!
  _____
7 Matt thinks more creative than the rest of us.
  _____
8 Last semester was one of the most happy times I've ever had.
  _____

◀ Go back to page 89

131

GRAMMAR PRACTICE

11A Present and past modals of deduction

> ▶ 11.5
> It **must have** an explanation. It really happened.
> It **can't be** true. I don't believe you.
> This **might not be** a new discovery. I think I read about it last year.
> Rick's in Chicago for the next week. He **must be visiting** his sister there.
> You **couldn't have seen** Katie. She didn't go to the party.
> Sue is still looking for a job. She **must not have gotten** the other one.

We use modals of deduction to talk about something when we don't know for sure if it's true, or if it was true.

Present modals of deduction

We use *must* + base form when we think something is true, based on logic.

You must be hungry. You haven't eaten anything all day. = I'm sure you're hungry.
He never wears jeans. He must not like them. = I'm sure that he doesn't like them.

We use *can't* or *couldn't* + base form when we are sure that something isn't true.

You can't/couldn't have the right address. The house is empty. = I'm sure you don't have the right address.

We use *might* or *might not* + base form when we think something is true, but we aren't sure.

David isn't at school. He might be sick, or he might not have any classes today. = It's possible that David is sick. It's possible that he doesn't have any classes today.

We also use *may* or *could* + base form when we think something is possible.

This restaurant's very popular, so it may be full.
I'm not sure when her birthday is. It could be next Saturday.

We often use the continuous form of the verb after modals of deduction when we talk about what we think is happening now.

Justin isn't in the living room. He must be watching TV in his bedroom.
Laurie might be getting ready in her room. I know she's going to a party later.

> **Look!** We never use *can* or contract *must not* to say what we think is or is not true. The word *mustn't* has a different meaning and expresses prohibition in British English.
> *Emma looks nervous. She might/could be afraid.* NOT *She can be afraid.*
> *That must not be the reason. It's not convincing.* NOT *That mustn't be the reason.*

Past modals of deduction

We use *must have* + the past participle when we are sure that something was true.

It must have been an alien. It didn't look human! = I'm sure it was an alien.

We use *can't have* or *couldn't have* + the past participle when we are sure something was not true.

The scientists can't/couldn't have found a new form of life. = I'm sure the scientists didn't find a new form of life.

We use *must not have* + the past participle when we think something was probably not true. We never contract *must not have*.

You must not have seen it. NOT *You mustn't have seen it.*

We use *could have, might have, might not have, may have* or *may not have* + the past participle when we think something was possibly true, but we aren't sure.

Adam isn't here yet. He could/might/may have gotten lost.
NOT *He can have gotten lost.*

1 Choose the correct options to complete the conversations.
   1 A Bill looks unhappy.
     B He *must not / mustn't* be very comfortable here. He doesn't know anyone.
   2 A Why isn't Hillary home yet?
     B I'm not sure. She *might / can't* have decided to work late. She was very busy.
   3 A There don't seem to be any buses today.
     B I think the drivers *can / could* be on strike.
   4 A I'm afraid this cake doesn't taste very good.
     B Hmm. You *couldn't follow / must not have followed* the recipe exactly.
   5 A Why isn't Sarah answering my question?
     B She *may not have heard / may not hear* you. It's noisy in here.
   6 A Great news. I got an A in chemistry!
     B You *must / might* have studied really hard. That course was so difficult!
   7 A Do you have any history books I could borrow?
     B I *might / can't* have one or two that I could lend you.
   8 A Paul has all their albums and goes to every concert.
     B He *could / must* really like them!

2 Rewrite the sentences using modals of deduction.

   1 I'm sure Sam ate all the cookies. I'm sure Joe didn't eat them.
   _____
   2 I'm sure that wasn't a magic trick. I'm sure it was real.
   _____
   3 I think I've passed, but I'm not sure. It's possible I've failed.
   _____
   4 Maybe John's sleeping. He's definitely not working.
   _____
   5 I'm not sure that noise is our dog. Maybe it's a burglar!
   _____
   6 It's not possible for you to be 40! I'm sure you're 30!
   _____
   7 I'm sure Kumiko missed her flight. I'm pretty sure she didn't set her alarm.
   _____
   8 I'm sure that they're traveling back today. It's possible that they're back already.
   _____

◀ Go back to page 95

11C Reported speech patterns

 11.13

I **said that I took it easy** on the weekends.
She **didn't mention that she would be** away.
Phil **didn't admit that he was sleeping** badly.
Rob **asked if I could recommend** a restaurant.
The doctor **asked me when I had started** feeling sick.
Several people **told us to get** our tickets early.
My sister **urged me not to stay** in a job I didn't like.

Reported statements

We use reported speech to say what someone said. We use verbs such as *say*, *tell*, *explain*, *admit*, *mention*, and *report*. In reported speech, we usually change the tense of the verbs.

- simple present ⇨ simple past
  "I live near the school." ⇨ *He said (that) he lived near the school.*
- simple past ⇨ past perfect
  "I failed my exam." ⇨ *She admitted (that) she had failed her exam.*
- present perfect continuous ⇨ past perfect continuous
  "I've been studying art." ⇨ *Sarah explained (that) she'd been studying art.*

Say is followed by (*that*) + a clause. *Tell* is followed by an object + (*that*) + a clause. *Explain*, *admit*, *mention*, and *report* may be followed by *to* + object + (*that*) + a clause.
Jeff said he was coming. NOT ~~Jeff said me he was coming.~~
Sarah told me (that) they might be late. NOT ~~Sarah told (that) they might be late.~~
I explained (to him that) I couldn't go. NOT ~~I explained him (that) I couldn't go.~~

The modal verbs *can*, *will*, and *may* also change in reported speech. The modal verbs *could*, *would*, *might* and *should* don't change in reported speech:
"I can't swim." ⇨ *Mark said (that) he couldn't swim.*
"We could meet you at six." ⇨ *Anna said (that) they could meet us at six.*

The tense usually does not change if the statement expresses something that is still true.
"I want to talk to you after class." ⇨ *Bob said (that) he wants to talk to me after class.*

Reported questions

We report a *Yes/No* question with the following structure: subject + *asked* + (object) + *if/whether* + subject + positive verb form + rest of sentence.
"Do you want your sweater?" ⇨ *She asked (me) if/whether I wanted my sweater.*

We report *wh-* questions with the question word(s) instead of *if/whether*.
"Which class are you in?" ⇨ *He asked (us) which class we were in.*

Look! We often need to change pronouns and words referring to time and place, if the sentence is reported on a different day or in a different place.
"I saw my uncle yesterday." ⇨ *He said he had seen his uncle the day before.*
"I'll wait for you here." ⇨ *He said he'd wait for us there.*

Reported commands

We report a command with the following structure: subject + verb + object + infinitive with (*not*) *to*.
We use verbs such as *tell*, *instruct*, *order*, *remind*, *forbid*, and *urge* to give commands.
"Read as much as possible." ⇨ *Our teacher urged us to read as much as possible.*
"Don't tell anyone." ⇨ *He forbid me to tell anyone./He told me not to tell anyone.*

---

1 Complete the sentences with reported speech.
  1 "I'm worried about my test."
    Nancy told me _____.
  2 "Which neighborhood do you live in?"
    The police officer asked us _____.
  3 "Cook the vegetables at a high temperature."
    Jake instructed me _____.
  4 "Take some sun cream on your hike tomorrow."
    My mother reminded me _____.
  5 "I'll be taking part in a sleep study."
    Ben mentioned _____.
  6 "Could you explain the assignment again, please?"
    I asked her _____.
  7 "I haven't been sleeping very well."
    Jane told her doctor _____.
  8 "Many places have a rainy season."
    Mark said _____.
  9 "Don't drive so fast."
    Ellie told me _____.
  10 "Are you going away during the summer?"
    She asked me _____?

2 Rewrite the conversation with the verbs in parentheses and reported speech.

  Jo My sister's in trouble at school. [1](say)
      Jo said her sister was in trouble at school.
  Ed Oh, what happened? [2](ask)
      _____
  Jo She's been skipping school a lot. [3](explain)
      _____
  Ed Really? Does she have problems at school? [4](ask)
      _____
  Jo Yes, some other kids have been mean to her. [5](admit)
      _____
  Ed What are your parents doing about it? [6](ask)
      _____
  Jo They've told her teachers. [7](answer)
      _____
  Ed Will the teachers talk to the other kids? [8](ask)
      _____
  Jo Yes, they will. I hope they can stop them from being mean. [9](say)
      _____
  Ed Well, don't worry. [10](tell) And talk to your sister as much as possible. [11](urge)
      _____
  Jo Sure. I'm spending tomorrow with her. [12](tell)
      _____

◀ Go back to page 99   133

GRAMMAR PRACTICE

12A Present and future unreal conditions

> ▶ 12.2
> If I **had** a robot to clean my house, I**'d be** very happy.
> I **wish there was** a better solution.
> **If only** the roads **weren't** so busy.
> **It's about time** we **looked** for a bigger apartment.
> I**'d rather** my daughter **spent** more time on her homework.

Second conditional

We use the second conditional to talk about unreal or unlikely conditions in the present or future and their consequences. We form the *if* clause with *if* + simple past, and we form the main clause with *would* + base form.

I'd take a really long vacation if I won the lottery. (unreal; I won't win the lottery)
If we didn't have a TV, we'd read more. (unlikely; we are going to keep our TV)

We can use *might* instead of *would* when the result isn't certain.

If they sold their business, they might be happier.

We can use *could* instead of *would* to talk about an ability in the future.

If I had more money, I could afford more clothes.

With the verb *be*, we often use *were* instead of *was* in more formal speech and writing in the *if* clause with *I*, *he*, *she* and *it*. We always use *were* in the phrase *If I were you* ... to give advice.

If John were here, he'd help you.   *If I were you, I'd tell your manager.*

> **Look!** Don't use *would* in the *if* clause.
> *If it were cooler, I'd go for a run.* NOT ~~If it would be cooler, I'd go for a run.~~

wish and if only

We use *wish* or *if only* to express a desire for a change that is unlikely. We use *wish* or *if only* + simple past to say we want something in the present to be different.

We all wish we were more talented. = we want to be more talented
If only my girlfriend didn't live so far away! = I want my girlfriend to live near me

We can also use *would* after *wish* and *if only* to talk about repeated actions.

I wish he cleaned up/would clean up more often! = I want him to clean up more often.
If only she didn't ask/wouldn't ask so many questions! = I want her not to ask so many questions.

We use *I wish* and *If only* + *would* or *could* to say we want something in the future to be different.

I wish they would improve our public transportation.
If only we could take a vacation next year.

It's (about) time

We use *It's (about) time* + simple past to express a wish for something to happen in the present. *It's about time* is more emphatic than *it's time*.

It's about time you got a new phone. = You really need a new phone.

would rather

We use *would rather* + simple past to say we would prefer somebody to do something, now or in the future. We usually contract *would* in informal speech or writing.

I'd rather he didn't interrupt me all the time. It's annoying!

1 Link the ideas in the two sentences with second conditionals. You may need to change some words.

1 I don't have a good computer. It's not easy to do my work.
   If I had a good computer, it would be easier to do my work.
2 We don't have a car. We could do more with one.
   _____
3 The shower doesn't turn off automatically. We waste so much water.
   _____
4 I don't wear glasses. That's why I have trouble reading.
   _____
5 I'm not you. You could invent an app to make decisions for people.
   _____
6 I don't have an automatic vacuum cleaner. I have to vacuum all the time!
   _____

2 Choose the correct options to complete the sentences.

1 *I wish I had / If I had* a phone that answered all my calls.
2 If only I *would / could* have a personal shopping assistant!
3 I wish you *might iron / would iron* my clothes for me!
4 *I'd rather you left / It's time you left* a little bit later.
5 If only we *have / had* a stove that cooked our dinner!
6 It's about time we *would get / got* a dishwasher.

3 Complete the conversations. Use the cues in parentheses. Add any words you need.

1 A My car won't start. This is the third time this week! (new car)
   B *If only you could buy a new car.*
2 A I can't understand our biology teacher. He's so confusing. (explain fully)
   B I know. I wish _____ .
3 A I don't have a computer. Can I use yours? (go to library)
   B Well, actually, I'd rather _____ .
4 A There are too many people at this party! (leave)
   B It's about time _____ .
5 A I can't pass my exams. Why not? (study more)
   B If I _____ .
6 A Does your job pay you enough? Mine doesn't. (earn)
   B We all wish _____ .

◀ Go back to page 103

12C Past unreal conditions

 12.6

If **I'd bought** an apartment earlier, it **would have been** a lot cheaper.
I **wish** I**'d called** my brother sooner. Now he's not home.
If only I **hadn't bought** this phone. It broke after two weeks!
If the bus **had come** earlier, I**'d be** home now.
If he **weren't** such a bad driver, he **wouldn't have had** the accident.

Third conditional

We use the third conditional to talk about unreal conditions in the past and their consequences.

If I'd had more money, I would have bought a car. = I didn't have more money, so I didn't buy a car.
If he hadn't been in such a hurry, he wouldn't have forgotten his keys. = He was in a hurry, so he forgot his keys.

We form the *if* clause with *if* + past perfect. We form the main clause with *would have* + past participle. *Had* in the *if* clause is frequently contracted.

If I'd (had) known you were in town, I would have made time to see you.

We use *might/may have* instead of *would have* when the consequences weren't certain.

If I hadn't arrived late for the interview, I might have gotten the job.

We use *could have* instead of *would have* to talk about hypothetical abilities in the past.

If my car hadn't broken down, I could have taken you to the airport yesterday.

wish and if only

We use *wish* and *if only* + past perfect to say that we want something in the past to have been different.

I wish I hadn't bought this book. It's awful!
If only she'd been more careful, she wouldn't have fallen.

If only expresses a slightly stronger regret than *wish*.

We wish we'd gotten our plane tickets sooner. Now prices have gone up!
If only we'd gotten our plane tickets sooner. Now they're double the price!

Look! Don't use *would have* after *wish* and *if only*.
They wish/If only they'd gotten up earlier. NOT ~~They wish/If only they would have gotten up earlier.~~

Mixed conditional

We can use a mixed conditional to describe an unreal condition in the past and a present consequence. We form the *if* clause with *if* + past perfect, and the main clause with *would* + base form.

If Sam and Jane hadn't given up so fast, they'd both have jobs now.
If I'd learned to swim as a child, I'd be a much better swimmer now.

We can also use a mixed conditional to describe an unreal condition in the present and a consequence in the past. We form the *if* clause with *if* + simple past, and the main clause with *would have* + past participle.

If my family was/were rich, I would have gone to different schools.
If Tom wanted a girlfriend, he would have found one by now.

GRAMMAR PRACTICE

1 Write sentences with the third conditional that link the two sentences.
  1 I read this article. I found out about this type of car.
     If I hadn't read this article, I wouldn't have found out about this type of car.
  2 My parents didn't have a lot of money. They didn't go on vacation every year.
     _____
  3 Lisa didn't enjoy school. She didn't go to college.
     _____
  4 My aunt worked in the theater. She met a fair number of famous actors.
     _____
  5 James didn't get Anna's phone number. He didn't ask her on a date.
     _____

2 Complete the conversations with the correct form of the verbs in the box.

   get   listen   love   not say   not stay   think

  1 A Did you pass your exam?
    B No, I didn't. I wish I _____ out all night the night before!
  2 A Did you and Al have a good time?
    B No, we had a terrible fight! If only I _____ to you before our trip.
  3 A It's such a shame you didn't come to the concert.
    B If only I'd known about it! I _____ to come!
  4 A Why is Rachel annoyed with you?
    B I told her I didn't like her boyfriend. I wish I _____ anything!
  5 A The traffic's bad! We're not going to get there in time.
    B Yes, I wish we _____ about that before we left.
  6 A Shelley finally went to the doctor, and now she's in the hospital.
    B If only she'd gone to the doctor earlier, she _____ so sick.

3 Write sentences with mixed conditionals that link the two sentences.
  1 I met Joana. I'm married now.
     If I hadn't met Joana, I wouldn't be married now.
  2 He studied science in school. He's an engineer now.
     _____
  3 We're not rich. We didn't take an expensive vacation.
     _____
  4 I love technology. I bought a new phone last week.
     _____
  5 We bought a robot to clean the apartment. We have more free time now.
     _____

◀ Go back to page 107

VOCABULARY PRACTICE

1A Body language and communication

1 ▶ 1.1 Match sentences 1–12 with pictures a–l. Listen and check.

1 Come here! **Give** me **a hug**!
2 When I asked him the way to the restaurant, he just **shrugged** his **shoulders**.
3 No one can hear me unless I **raise** my **voice**!
4 When we saw Mike **waving** at us, he **winked**, so we knew he had a secret.
5 She **tapped** me **on the shoulder** to get my attention.
6 When he asked her if she wanted coffee she **nodded** and said, "Yes, please."
7 I'm **shaking** my **head** because I don't know the answer.
8 We just **shook hands** because we don't know each other very well.
9 When I visit my mother, I always **kiss** her **on the cheek**.
10 That man is **staring** at me from across the room. He's trying to **make eye contact**.
11 I was **gazing** at the stars last night. They were beautiful.
12 I could tell she was annoyed with me because she was **frowning**.

a

b

c

d

e

f

g

h

i

j

k

l

2 Complete the sentences with the expressions in the box. Use the correct verb tenses and make any other necessary changes.

> shake hands   raise your voice   shrug your shoulders   tap someone on the shoulder
> nod   shake your head   wave   give someone a hug

1 I asked Ann where her dad was, but she just _____ – it was obvious she didn't know.
2 As a little boy, I always used to kiss my parents good night and _____ before I went to bed.
3 When she asked Keith if he agreed, he didn't say anything. He just _____ his head up and down.
4 In the business world, you can tell a lot about someone's character simply by how the person _____ with you.
5 When my mother told me the news, I said, "No way!" and _____ from side to side.
6 He was standing with his back to me, so I _____ .
7 "_____ good-bye to Grandpa, Lucy," my mother said.
8 There's no microphone, so the audience won't be able to hear you unless you _____ .

136 ◀ Go back to page 4

VOCABULARY PRACTICE

1B Compound adjectives

1 ▶ 1.4 Put the words in the box in the correct categories. Listen and check.

> far-reaching   forward-thinking   highly respected   life-changing   middle-aged
> open-minded   record-breaking   slow-moving   time-consuming   well-educated

adjective/adverb + present participle	adjective/adverb/noun + past/participle	noun + adjective/present participle
good-looking	old-fashioned self-centered	world-famous

2 Complete the sentences with the correct options.

1 That dress is very *old-fashioned* / *middle-aged*. It's totally out of style compared to your other clothes!
2 It's really *slow-moving* / *time-consuming* to do my homework. I'm not good at math.
3 When I meet new people, I always try to be *open-minded* / *well educated*, even when I don't think I like them.
4 My manager is very *forward-thinking* / *record-breaking* – he has some very innovative ideas.

5 People who are *highly respected* / *self-centered* only consider what is important for them.
6 A *world-famous* / *far-reaching* novelist spoke at our school yesterday, but I'd never heard of him.
7 When Emily was over 50, she made a *life-changing* / *middle-aged* decision and moved to China.
8 His decision to leave his job had *far-reaching* / *forward-thinking* consequences for his family.

◀ Go back to page 6

1C Expectations

1 ▶ 1.8 What do sentences 1–10 mean? Choose the correct option, a or b. Listen and check.

1 I **can't wait** to meet her. I won't **get a second chance**.
   a I'm really looking forward to meeting her.
   b I might meet her one day, but not now.
2 I was **hoping for** something better.
   a I was pleased.
   b I wasn't pleased.
3 His performance really **impressed** me.
   a I thought it was very good.
   b I didn't think it was very good.
4 She **made a good** first **impression on** me.
   a Before I got to know her well, I liked her.
   b After I got to know her well, I liked her.
5 My brother says he can't **live without** his cell phone.
   a He doesn't mind not having it with him.
   b He hates not having it with him.
6 The experiment was a **failure** because we **failed to** follow instructions.
   a It worked.
   b It didn't work.
7 I **expected** the food to be better, but had to **lower my expectations**.
   a It was as good as I'd hoped.
   b It wasn't as good as I'd hoped.
8 The service **met my expectations**.
   a It was what I expected.
   b It wasn't what I expected.
9 The play **was a success**.
   a People liked it.
   b People didn't like it.
10 The movie **was** such **a disappointment** to my mother.
   a She expected it to be better.
   b She expected it to be worse.

2 ▶ 1.9 Notice the forms of the nouns and verbs. Complete the chart with words from exercise 1. Listen and check.

verb	noun
disappoint	
	failure
succeed	
	expectation
impress	

3 Complete the review with the correct form of the words in the box.

> impress   expect   wait   succeed   hope   disappoint   fail

Commercially speaking, the band's last album was a big ^{1}_____ , as it sold millions of copies. But, to me, it was a huge ^{2}_____ and ^{3}_____ to meet my ^{4}_____ . This time, though, I'm ^{5}_____ for something much better, and I think the new album will be great. I just heard the first single from the album on the radio, and it made a good first ^{6}_____ on me. I can't ^{7}_____ to hear the whole album, which comes out next month.

◀ Go back to page 8

137

VOCABULARY PRACTICE

2A Adjective suffixes

1 ▶ 2.1 Put the adjective forms of the words in the box in the correct column. Listen and check.

ambition (n)   end (n)   attract (v)   memory (n)   home (n)   adventure (n)
option (n)   break (n)   power (n)   faith (n)   impress (v)   accident (n)

-able	-al	-ful	-ive	-ous	-less
desirable	controversial	colorful	aggressive	cautious	harmless
reasonable	conventional	cheerful	decisive	ridiculous	painless
washable	_____	dreadful	effective	_____	useless
_____	_____	painful	_____	_____	_____
_____		useful	_____		
		_____			
		_____			

2 Complete the discussion-forum messages with adjectives from exercise 1.

WHAT'S YOUR IDEAL PARTNER LIKE?

Amy27 My ideal partner is [1]a_____ and likes to try new things, visit exotic places, do extreme sports – that sort of thing. I tend to be a [2]c_____ person, who plans everything carefully and avoids taking risks, so I need someone who's the opposite of me. Perhaps I should date a skydiving instructor – that way I'd have some [3]m_____ experiences I'd never forget!

LauraZ Tough question, but, above all, he should be [4]c_____ and positive. You know, someone who makes me laugh and who's fun to be around. Oh, and being [5]f_____ is important, too, of course. I don't want my boyfriend to go out with anyone else! I also like people who are [6]d_____ and know what they want.

Adam3X I want her to surprise me from time to time – I'm tired of people with [7]c_____ attitudes, values, and tastes. I also like people who can make me think. You know, I enjoy discussing [8]c_____ topics, and I like it when my partner and I disagree on things. Oh, and I hope we meet by accident. I don't want to find love on a dating app.

Jas82 I've been married for eleven years, and my husband and I have a great relationship. He has most of the qualities I find [9]d_____ in a partner: He's fair and [10]r_____, and always makes logical decisions. And he wants to be successful, which is great.

Micky44 My ideal partner? Easy – my wife, Gloria. I really admire her. She's a very talented artist, with an [11]i_____ body of work for a young person. Her paintings are really [12]c_____. Surprisingly, she's not [13]a_____, but she's been very successful for someone her age.

138 ◀ Go back to page 12

VOCABULARY PRACTICE

2C Phrasal verbs (1)

1 ▶ 2.7 Read the text and match phrasal verbs 1–10 with definitions a–j. Listen and check.

FOUR secrets to success

1 **DON'T GIVE UP.** One of the reasons why I really ¹**look up to** people like J.K. Rowling, Michael Jordan, and Madonna is that they never give up. J.K. Rowling, for example, was ²**turned down** by several different publishers before Harry Potter became a worldwide phenomenon.

2 **BE PERSUASIVE.** Change can be scary. If you have a new idea, people will sometimes try to discourage you, and say your idea is "crazy" or "not practical." They're just trying to ³**get out of** accepting that change can actually be good. Don't ⁴**give in** and say, "Yes, you're right." Instead, try to find a way to ⁵**talk** them **into** seeing the benefits of your idea.

3 **PAY ATTENTION TO DETAIL.** Steve Jobs had a reputation for being a tough boss. People say he valued punctuality and used to get upset if people ⁶**showed up** late for work. But, more importantly, Jobs was obsessed with perfection, and he wouldn't accept mistakes or ⁷**put up with** negativity.

4 **LOOK FOR SIMPLE SOLUTIONS.** Bill Gates once said that one of the biggest obstacles to success is too much complexity. Throughout his career, he has always tried to ⁸**figure out** simple ways to solve complicated problems, and his efforts ⁹**paid off**: Microsoft Windows is still popular after all these years, and most computer users can't ¹⁰**do without** it.

a persuade or convince someone ____
b admire and respect someone ____
c bring good results; be worth the effort ____
d accept or tolerate something unpleasant ____
e arrive or appear somewhere ____
f refuse an offer or opportunity ____
g stop arguing; admit defeat ____
h finally understand or solve a problem ____
i manage without something ____
j avoid doing something ____

2 ▶ 2.8 Complete the sentences with the correct particles. Listen and check.

| across   after   off   out   up   with |

1 The game was **called** ____ because of the rain.

2 Bernie really **takes** ____ his father.

3 Lucy **came** ____ a briefcase full of money.

4 The tickets **sold** ____ within hours.

5 Helen **came up** ____ a great idea.

6 Someone **used** ____ all the toothpaste.

3 Choose the correct phrasal verbs from exercises 1 and 2 to complete the sentences.

1 Paul wanted to make a cake, but he realized he'd *sold out / used up* all the eggs in the fridge.
2 Calvin lost his job, so he had to learn to *do without / give in* many of the luxuries he was used to.
3 When I *come across / figure out* a word in English I've never seen before, I try to guess what it means.
4 One week before the wedding, Nina realized she didn't love Mike anymore, so the wedding was *paid off / called off*.
5 I *do without / take after* my mother more than my father.
6 Sandra *came up with / put up with* a great suggestion, which everybody liked.
7 The party was a huge success. More than a hundred people *turned down / showed up*.
8 I didn't want to get a dog, but my children eventually *talked me into / got out of* it.

◀ Go back to page 16

139

VOCABULARY PRACTICE

3A Urban places and problems

1   3.1 Match the words in the boxes with pictures 1–16. Listen and check.

| business district   city hall   courthouse   harbor   high-rise building   industrial area   residential area   taxi stand |

1 _____

2 _____

3 _____

4 _____

5 _____

6 _____

7 _____

8 _____

| vandalism   lack of parking   waste disposal   poverty   smog   (traffic) congestion   homlessness   overcrowding |

9 _____

10 _____

11 _____

12 _____

13 _____

14 _____

15 _____

16 _____

2   Complete two news stories with words from exercise 1.

A group of 100 people protested in front of [1]_____ this evening and demanded to speak to the mayor. The city was planning to tear down over 20 houses in one of the city's oldest [2]_____ and build a 70-story [3]_____ instead. The event was peaceful, with no signs of violence or [4]_____ .

A recent survey has shown that workers in the city's downtown [5]_____ think [6]_____ is the number one problem, as they are "shocked" by the number of people living on the streets. [7]_____ came second because of the number of cars, which increase commuting time. And [8]_____ was third as it often takes over half an hour to find a space.

140   ◀ Go back to page 23

VOCABULARY PRACTICE

3B Easily confused words

1A ▶ 3.6 Do you know these pairs of words? Listen and repeat.

1 actual / current _____	**a** not dangerous
2 affect / effect _____	**b** keep away from
3 annoyed / disgusted _____	**c** be important
4 argue / discuss _____	**d** a change that's the result of something
5 avoid / prevent _____	**e** select something from among different options
6 choose / elect _____	**f** understand clearly or become fully aware
7 claim / pretend _____	**g** a little angry or irritated
8 disappoint / deceive _____	**h** state that something is true
9 matter / mind _____	**i** easily able to understand someone's feelings
10 notice / realize _____	**j** talk about something with other people
11 safe / sure _____	**k** fail to fulfill hopes or expectations
12 sensible / sensitive _____	**l** real, existing in fact

B ▶ 3.7 Match one of the words in each pair 1–12 with its definition a–l. Listen and check.

2 Complete the sentences with the correct form of a word from exercise 1.

1 My children _____ with me all the time and never do what I tell them.

2 Sue was very _____ when she wasn't accepted by Harvard.

3 Marty is a very _____ person and always thinks about others.

4 Even though I always _____ eating sweets, I can't seem to lose weight!

5 Wilber Jones was _____ governor although the vote was very close.

6 The robber _____ to be my neighbor, and that's why I opened the door.

7 We were all very _____ by the awful accident.

8 That's not true! The _____ reason I didn't come is that I was sick.

◀ Go back to page 24

4A Personality and behavior

1A ▶ 4.1 Read the sentences. Then match the adjectives in **bold** in sentences 1–12 with definitions a–l. Listen and check.

1 How **thoughtful** of George to send me a get-well card! _____

2 Britney can be so **bossy**! She's always telling everyone what to do. _____

3 A **clumsy** waiter spilled juice all over Rick's new shirt. _____

4 My boss is extremely **unreasonable** and seems to enjoy saying no to us. _____

5 You've made your brother cry again! Why do you have to be so **mean** to him? _____

6 Julia can be really **stubborn**. It's really hard to get her to change her mind. _____

7 Stella married a **charming**, good-looking man in his mid-thirties. _____

8 I wonder why my father has been so **bad-tempered** recently. He's always yelling at people. _____

9 When I'm stressed out, I like watching **silly** movies on Netflix – nothing too complex or thought-provoking, you know. _____

10 My son is first in his class, but he's not **arrogant**. He says he's just like everyone else, not better than the others. _____

11 Sue seems very **enthusiastic** about her new job. I've never seen her happier. _____

12 Neil is 18, but he's not **responsible** enough to have a car yet. I'm afraid he'll have an accident. _____

a superior
b mature
c unkind
d passionate
e difficult to influence
f friendly and likeable
g unfair
h easily annoyed or made angry
i careless
j controlling
k kind and considerate
l not serious or important; ridiculous

B In pairs, discuss which of the adjectives in exercise 1A are usually positive.

2 ▶ 4.2 Complete the expressions in **bold** with the correct form of the verbs in the box. Listen and check.

get   stand   upset   forgive   boast   drive   take   praise   encourage   take

1 Bob wasn't the one who came up with the original idea, but he still _____ **credit for** his colleague's work at last week's meeting.

2 Lucy's teacher said her term paper was fantastic. He really _____ her **for** her achievement, and even _____ her **to** start a Ph.D. next year.

3 Ron really _____ **on** my **nerves**. I can't stand his attitude. Yesterday he embarrassed me, and I'll never _____ him **for** doing that.

4 Gary's new at the company, so his boss makes lots of unreasonable requests and _____ **advantage of** him.

5 Claire and Sophie can't be roommates because Claire loves cats, while Sophie **can't** _____ them. She says cats _____ her **crazy**.

6 Julio sometimes _____ people **by** constantly talking about how rich he is. Nobody likes the way he keeps _____ **about** his wealth.

◀ Go back to page 30

141

VOCABULARY PRACTICE

4C Word families

1 ▶ 4.8 Complete the chart with the words *adjective*, *noun*, and *verb*. Notice the common suffixes. Listen and check.

1 _____	2 _____	3 _____
achieve	achieve**ment**	achiev**able**
create	creativ**ity**	creat**ive**
consider	consider**ation**	consider**ate**
criticize	critic**ism**	critic**al**
persuade	persua**sion**	persuas**ive**
rely	reliab**ility**	reli**able**
risk	risk	risk**y**
succeed	success	success**ful**

2 Complete the text with the adjective or noun form of the verbs in parentheses.

How to meet deadlines

To be [1]_____ (succeed) at school or at work, you have to be hard-working, smart, and [2]_____ (create). But [3]_____ (rely) is also important, and so is meeting deadlines. Here are a few things you should take into [4]_____ (consider):

- First of all, put your deadlines on your calendar. Trusting your memory can be [5]_____ (risk)!
- Sometimes deadlines may not be [6]_____ (achieve). If so, consider asking for an extension, even if you have to be a little [7]_____ (persuade).
- If you find yourself procrastinating, maybe you're afraid of people's [8]_____ (criticize) of your work. Remember: Nobody's perfect!

◀ Go back to page 34

5A The environment

1A ▶ 5.1 Match the highlighted words with pictures 1–6. Listen and check.

Studies have shown that because of ¹**climate change**, ²**heat waves** have become much more common across the globe. When a heat wave occurs during a drought, the situation is even worse, since the lack of rain can contribute to wildfires, too.

We need to reduce ³**energy consumption** because our use of ⁴**fossil fuels**, such as coal and oil, is negatively affecting the planet. These fuels increase the amount of ⁵**carbon dioxide** (CO₂) in the atmosphere, which makes the planet warmer. Governments worldwide have been trying to encourage people to use ⁶**environmentally friendly** sources of power such as solar energy and to buy ⁷**energy-efficient** household appliances.

Life in our oceans is disappearing fast, and the most ⁸**endangered species** include birds, turtles, fish, and dolphins. Plastic bags litter our seas and are extremely dangerous to marine wildlife. Recent estimates suggest that nearly 200 species are at risk because they eat these bags and other kinds of litter. Another problem, of course, is toxic waste, which contains dangerous chemicals and sometimes even radioactive material.

B ▶ 5.2 Match the **bold** words 1–8 in the text with definitions a–h. Listen and check.

a periods of unusually hot weather ____
b a type of animal or plant that might disappear soon ____
c using only a small amount of gas or electricity ____
d the gas formed when people burn carbon ____
e not having a negative effect on the environment ____
f a long-term change in the planet's weather because of human activity ____
g fuels that form in the earth from dead plants or animals ____
h the amount of gas and electricity we use ____

2 Complete the sentences with words from the text in exercise 1.

1 When they're young, kids should be taught not to _____ the streets.
2 _____, as the name implies, comes from the sun.
3 Although we don't like to admit it, _____ around the world has been caused by our own carelessness.
4 We took a trip to Australia and saw some beautiful _____ on the Great Barrier Reef.
5 Environmental groups help to make sure _____ don't disappear completely.
6 _____ lightbulbs are a little more expensive, but they use less power.
7 Burning _____ releases _____ into the atmosphere, which causes global warming.
8 It hasn't rained since May, and we are experiencing the worst _____ in decades.

1 _____

2 _____

3 _____

4 _____

5 _____

6 _____

◀ Go back to page 40

VOCABULARY PRACTICE

5B Moods

1A ▶ 5.5 Which adjectives in the box describe positive moods (+) and which ones negative moods (−)? Listen and check.

| down | dynamic | energetic | enthusiastic | grumpy | lethargic |
| miserable | motivated | optimistic | pessimistic | | |

B Match the ten adjectives with the pictures below.

2 ▶ 5.6 Complete the conversations with words from exercise 1 and the box below. Use each word only once. Listen and check.

| desperate | distressing | eager | exhausting | passionate | positive |

1   A It's e_____ to have to shovel snow. I get so tired!
    B I wouldn't be very e_____ to do that, either.
2   A Almost no one around here cares about climate change. I find that so d_____ .
    B We need some new d_____ leaders who can make us feel more m_____ .
3   A I'm not sure what's wrong with me today. I feel g_____ and l_____ – you know, just kind of d_____ in general.
    B That's because it's the shortest day of the year. It's hard to feel e_____ and e_____ when it gets dark at 4:30 p.m.!
4   A Is there anything you're really p_____ about – you know, something that excites you that you really care about?
    B Not really. I feel p_____ about the world these days! Thinking about the future makes me feel m_____ !
5   A Why are you so d_____ to find a new job?
    B I really want to feel p_____ about work again.

◀ Go back to page 42

5C Adjective prefixes

1A ▶ 5.10 Complete the chart with the prefixes in the box. Listen and check.

| dis- | im- | in- | un- | il- | ir- | mis- |

1 _____	2 _____	3 _____	4 _____	5 _____	6 _____	7 _____
polite	appearing	fortunate	accurate	leading	legal	responsible
patient	organized	suitable	effective	pronounced	logical	relevant
mature	honest	available	visible	spelled	legible	regular
probable	satisfied	expected	formal			

B Which prefix is used with adjectives that begin with *r*? And with *l*?

2 Complete the sentences with words from exercise 1A.
1 It's really _____ that Ron failed his final exam. Now he'll have to repeat the course.
2 I'm getting a little _____ with my son. He still hasn't cleaned up his room!
3 In English, a _____ word can sometimes be very hard to understand because there are so many words that sound alike.
4 The bus schedule was completely _____ and had the wrong times. I missed the last bus home!
5 I think it's just so _____ to borrow money from friends and not pay them back.
6 I'm really worried about all the _____ wildlife. We're going to have more endangered species soon.
7 Your call can't be that important. It's really _____ to talk on your cell phone at the dinner table.
8 Plastic bags are _____ for recycling and have to be thrown away, but I don't really understand why.
9 What are you going to wear to the party? I think it's pretty casual and _____ .
10 In my city, littering is _____ . If they catch you, you get a big fine!
11 Some of what we learn in school is just so _____ and will never help us get jobs!
12 My ten-year-old son is still too _____ to understand the value of money.
13 This is the coldest winter ever, so how can the planet be getting warmer? It's completely _____ !
14 I can't find energy-efficient bulbs in any of the hardware stores. They're totally _____ at the moment.

◀ Go back to page 44

143

VOCABULARY PRACTICE

6A Expressions with *time*

1 6.1 Match the words in **bold** 1–14 with their definitions a–n. Listen and check.

WHAT'S YOUR BAD HABIT?

¹**From time to time**, I get really nervous and bite my nails during tests. What can I do? (Luke, London)

I have cheese twice a day, for both breakfast and dinner. It's ²**only a matter of time** before my cholesterol goes up. (Emily, Manchester)

I ³**waste** a lot of **time** reading readers' comments when I read the newspaper online. I don't know why! (Tomiko, New York)

I never seem to finish my exams because I keep going over my answers. Maybe if I ⁴**time myself** while taking practice exams it will help. (Roberta, Toronto)

I always eat too quickly! My mother was always saying, "⁵**Take your time**. Where's the fire?" (Mike, Boston)

I like to ⁶**pass the time** just looking out the window. I know I should be doing my homework, instead! (Peter, Seattle)

I'm almost never ⁷**on time** in the morning. And so I'm never ⁸**in time for** my first class! (María, Puerto Rico)

I'm always telling my sister to run so we can get to the bus stop ⁹**in no time**. And then, of course, we wait and wait while I tell her the bus is coming ¹⁰**any time now**. (Julie, San Francisco)

¹¹**For some time**, I've been playing computer games every night until two or three in the morning. I always feel exhausted when I'm at work! (Tom, Melbourne)

When I was a teenager I always used to listen to rap music. ¹²**At the time**, it really got on my dad's nerves. (Matt, Oxford)

My husband says I never ¹³**make time** for him. I suppose I should go to the soccer game with him occasionally. (Sara, Madrid)

Our city has been demolishing old movie theaters ¹⁴**one at a time**. It's so sad. (Joe, Sydney)

a don't hurry _____
b occasionally _____
c for quite a long period of time _____
d very soon _____
e early enough for something _____
f certain to happen at some point in the near future _____
g fast _____
h in those days _____
i on schedule _____
j don't use time well _____
k spend time _____
l one by one _____
m measure how long I take to do something _____
n reorganize your time for something/someone _____

2 Complete the sentences with the correct form of an expression with *time* from exercise 1.

1 A Are you ready for the marathon?
   B Yes, I _____ today, and I ran 20 km. in just over two hours!
2 A I'm not ready. I still have to take a shower!
   B _____ . We don't have to be there until 7:30.
3 A Tom's been late to work a lot. He's going to lose his job!
   B I know. It's _____ before his boss fires him.
4 A How's your grandmother?
   B A little better, thanks. She can't go out, but she _____ watching TV.
5 A Hey, Joe. Are you busy? Can I come in?
   B Sure. In fact, you're just _____ some hot chocolate!
6 A My little brother is always _____ playing video games.
   B Well, he's only 12. I'm sure he'll develop other interests.
7 A Where did you and your wife meet?
   B In Paris in 1998. We were both teaching at the university _____ .
8 A So, do you know your neighbors well?
   B Yes, we do. We have them over for dinner _____ .

144

◀ Go back to page 48

VOCABULARY PRACTICE

6C Expressions with prepositions

1 ▶ 6.4 Complete the sentences with the prepositions in the box. Pay attention to the adjectives in **bold**. Listen and check.

> about   of   to   with

1 I'm **addicted** _____ coffee, and I don't think I'll ever be able to give it up.
2 I'm going to work next year instead of starting college, and I'm very **comfortable** _____ my decision.
3 I don't know why people are **suspicious** _____ me. I'm a very nice person!
4 Young people today seem to think they're **entitled** _____ high salaries, even if they have no experience.
5 I'm so **anxious** _____ my exam tomorrow. I really hope I don't fail.
6 We're all very **concerned** _____ the high cost of living here. We might have to move.
7 Most millennials are **obsessed** _____ technology. It's a problem!
8 I'm really **fed up** _____ the term "generation gap." I feel I'm a lot like my parents.
9 Sarah was late for the concert because she was **confused** _____ the time. She thought it started at 8 p.m.
10 I'm **sympathetic** _____ my boyfriend's need for attention, but he's driving me crazy!

2 ▶ 6.5 Read Marcy's e-mail and her friend Laura's response. Complete them with the prepositions in the box. Listen and check.

> about   against   for   in   of   on   to

Hi Laura,
I was accepted into a theater program this summer, but I'm not sure if I should go! The main [1]**advantage** _____ going is that it will be an incredible experience, but the [2]**disadvantage** _____ attending the program is the expense. Maybe there will be the [3]**possibility** _____ getting a scholarship.
I don't want to [4]**insist** _____ any help with the program fees, though. They might not [5]**approve** _____ that.
Anyway, what's your [6]**reaction** _____ all of this? Please answer soon!
Love,
Marcy

Hi Marcy,
Wow! We all want to [7]**congratulate** you _____ your exciting news! I'd really [8]**advise** you _____ saying no. It's a wonderful opportunity! They can't [9]**criticize** you _____ being worried about the cost, or [10]**accuse** you _____ not being interested. I think you should explain everything honestly. I'm sure they **believe** [11]_____ their work and will [12]**care** _____ your situation.
Love,
Laura

◀ Go back to page 52

7A Collocations with *attend, get, make,* and *submit*

1 ▶ 7.1 Complete the collocations with *attend, get, make,* and *submit*. Listen and check.

1 _____ an application, a paper, a proposal, a report
2 _____ college, classes, a lecture, a conference
3 _____ a big difference, matters worse, the most out of, a living
4 _____ something across, ahead, hold of somebody/something, somebody's attention

2 Complete the sentences with collocations from exercise 1.

1 My grandfather used to _____ by working as a bus driver.
2 You have to take risks if you want to _____ and succeed in business.
3 I _____ last night that was so popular I had to stand up! The speaker was great.
4 Thelma would be a very good politician. She's a very convincing speaker, and she's so good at _____ her message _____ .
5 There are so many places I'd like to see when I go to Italy next summer. I've decided to rent a car so I can _____ of my stay.
6 I'm going to _____ to start a school newspaper to the principal. I hope she won't think the budget's too high.
7 I was already an hour late, and, to _____ , I got stuck in the elevator!
8 I _____ on the west coast – at UCLA, in fact. That's how I have so many friends in Los Angeles.
9 I'm not sure where I'll end up going to college, but I'm going to _____ to Harvard.
10 Maybe Teresa is away. I tried calling her at least five times, but I couldn't _____ her.

◀ Go back to page 58

145

VOCABULARY PRACTICE

7B Ability

1 ▶ 7.4 Complete the paragraphs with the correct form of the expressions in the boxes, making sure the entire paragraph is logical. Use each expression only once. There may be more than one correct answer. Listen and check.

| be capable of   can't seem to   have a talent for   be pretty/reasonably successful at   struggle to/with |

Not everyone ¹_____ learning foreign languages. Some people really ²_____ them and ³_____ remember anything they've learned. But, with motivation and practice, even they can ⁴_____ mastering a language. With enough effort, everyone ⁵_____ learning!

| find it hard to   succeed at   be pretty good/bad at   fail to   can't quite manage to |

Some of us ⁶_____ sports. We ⁷_____ keep up with our teammates and may ⁸_____ win even a single game. But even if we ⁹_____ hit the ball very far or do a high jump, we can all find a sport we're able to ¹⁰_____ . Some don't require strength or endurance at all!

◀ Go back to page 60

7C Mind and memory

1 ▶ 7.8 Which option, a or b, provides the correct interpretation? Listen and check.

1 I tried to remember his name, but **my mind went blank**.
  a I'm glad I didn't have to ask him.
  b In the end, I had to ask him.
2 **Keep in mind** that you won't be allowed in the theater after the performance begins.
  a So please don't be late.
  b But you can arrive late.
3 It never **crossed my mind** that Maria had learned English as a foreign language.
  a She sounds like a native speaker.
  b She's not very fluent.

4 I'm seeing *The Lion King* tomorrow with my nephew. I'm not into musicals, but I'll try to **keep an open mind**.
  a I'm sure I'll hate it.
  b Maybe I'll be pleasantly surprised.
5 At first I thought Jack was unfriendly, but I've **changed my mind**.
  a He's really nice.
  b He's really rude.
6 I can't **make up my mind** which suit I like better.
  a Definitely the blue one.
  b Maybe the blue one.

2 Complete each sentence with the correct form of a verb from exercise 1. You may have to change the tense.

1 So you're not joining us for dinner? What a shame! But text me if you _____ your mind, OK?
2 My mind always _____ blank when I'm speaking in public. I don't know why I get so nervous!
3 I might spend New Year's Eve in London, but I haven't _____ up my mind yet.
4 If you want to invite Ann for dinner, _____ in mind that she's a vegetarian.

3 ▶ 7.9 For 1–6, complete the second sentence so that it means the same as the first, using the words and expressions in the box. Listen and check.

| boost your memory   have a good/bad memory   learn something by heart   memorable   recall   remind |

1 I memorize irregular verbs, so I never have to look them up.
  I _____ , and now I never have to look them up.
2 Please don't let me forget to water the plants.
  Please _____ me to water the plants.
3 They say fish oil can improve your memory.
  They say fish oil can _____ .

4 You won't forget this experience.
  This will be a _____ experience.
5 I haven't forgotten my wedding day. I remember it perfectly.
  I can still _____ my wedding day perfectly.
6 I never seem to be able to remember people's names.
  I've always _____ for people's names.

146

◀ Go back to page 62

VOCABULARY PRACTICE

8A The media

1 ▶ 8.1 Match words 1–15 in the box with definitions a–o. Listen and check.

1 breaking news 2 the headlines 3 host 4 mass media 5 stream 6 subscription services 7 tabloid 8 viewer 9 ad 10 audience 11 broadcast 12 follow 13 network 14 on the air 15 the press

a the main types of communication like television, radio, and newspapers ____
b recently received information about an event or story that is currently occurring or developing ____
c the titles at the top of newspaper articles or the most important items of news on TV or the radio ____
d a person who watches TV or a movie ____
e send or receive audio or video data that can be played continuously over the Internet ____
f a newspaper with a popular style and sensational stories ____
g a person who presents a radio or television program ____
h programs, series, or movies that customers who pay a fee can watch on their television sets ____
i journalists or newspapers viewed collectively ____
j take an active interest in or support someone on social media ____
k transmit or send a radio or television show or program ____
l being shown or heard now on television or radio ____
m a group of TV stations that connect to present the same programs in different locations ____
n an abbreviation or short form of the word *advertisement* ____
o the people who watch or listen to a television or radio program ____

2 Choose the correct options to complete the paragraph.

What are my media habits? An interesting question. Well, first of all, I like to follow ¹*breaking news / mass media* as it develops. And I enjoy watching ²*tabloids / networks* I know because I usually trust them. I also like to watch programs that attract a lot of ³*viewers / the press* so I can discuss them later with people. When a popular show is ⁴*followed / on the air*, I turn it on right away. The only problem is that I really can't stand a lot of ⁵*headlines / ads*, so these days, I prefer to ⁶*stream / broadcast* the programs I like. There's no need to even download them!

3 Complete the reactions to the evening news, choosing the best option.

A *What did you think of the news last night?*
B *I thought it was …*
1 clearly *fair / biased* against the government. You could tell that the journalist didn't like the president.
2 completely *accurate / sensational*. All of the information was correct.
3 balanced and *objective / inaccurate*. It presented both points of view. I've always felt this channel was fair.
4 emotional and *sensational / biased*, almost like a tabloid. I agreed with its interpretation of events, but it was so exaggerated!
5 really *sensational / fair*. It was based on facts, rather than opinions, and presented the news as it was happening.

◀ Go back to page 66

VOCABULARY PRACTICE

8C Expressions with *at*, *for*, *in*, and *on*

1 ▶ 8.5 Match the expressions in **bold** in sentences 1–12 with definitions a–l. Listen and check.

1 Everything happened **at once**. I moved, got a job, and got married, all in May! _____
2 Bob was determined to win **at all costs**, and nothing could stop him. _____
3 It would be nice if, just **for once**, you could help me with the dishes! _____
4 We have shortened and adapted the text **for the sake of** simplicity. _____
5 Glenn is so deeply **in debt** and desperate for money that he's selling his car. _____
6 If Mom finds out I only got a D on the test, I'm **in trouble**! _____
7 I suggest we meet **on a regular basis** to discuss your progress. _____
8 The teacher proudly accepted the award **on behalf of** the whole class. _____
9 I was really **in doubt** and couldn't decide which apartment to buy. _____
10 When Bill lost his job, he was **at risk** of becoming homeless. _____
11 We go out for Thai food **once in a while**, but it's a little too spicy for me. _____
12 The police officer was **on duty**, so he was wearing a uniform. _____

a despite the effort needed
b for the purpose or in the interest of
c immediately, at the same time
d often or frequently
e in a situation where you might be punished or blamed
f on only one occasion
g in place of or as a representative of
h working at that moment
i in danger
j occasionally, from time to time
k unsure about something
l the state of owing money

2 Complete the sentences with expressions from exercise 1.

1 Her bike is too close to the cars. She's _____ of being hit!
2 He's _____ because he doesn't know which suit to buy.
3 I can't go and have coffee. I'm _____ right now at work.
4 I'm really _____ – I've just broken a really expensive ornament!
5 I don't see Cindy very often, just _____ .
6 Can't Henry be quiet _____ ! I'm trying to do my homework.
7 I can't pay my rent this month as I'm so badly _____ .
8 They have to stay friends _____ . I hope they start talking to each other soon.

3 ▶ 8.6 Complete the texts with the expressions in the box. Listen and check.

| for a change   on average   for sure   at first   at least   on top of   in control   for no reason |

Last night my girlfriend seemed upset ¹_____ . When I asked her what was wrong, she said, "Nothing." ²_____ , I just thought she was in a bad mood, but when I checked my Facebook page, I realized that it was her birthday yesterday. I'd completely forgotten! And ³_____ that, she told me she'd taken the day off work yesterday so we could celebrate it together. Well, ⁴_____ I won't forget it next year – I've already written it in my work diary and set an alarm on my phone to remind me!

I didn't know ⁵_____ , but I'd always thought that women lived longer than men. So last weekend I went online, and, according to the government website, ⁶_____ , women live between five and seven years longer than men. I thought that my husband and I were rather out of shape, so I suggested to him that we should do more to be ⁷_____ of our health. So yesterday, instead of just watching TV after dinner, we decided to go for a long walk ⁸_____ . I feel so much more energetic today!

◀ Go back to page 70

VOCABULARY PRACTICE

9A Collocations with *have* and *take*

1 ▶ 9.1 Read the quotes and match the **bold** collocations 1–8 with definitions a–h. Listen and check.

1 A person's self-esteem **has nothing to do with** how she looks. (Halle Berry)

2 When you're a celebrity, people think they know you, but they **don't have a clue**. (Willie Aames)

3 When I'm down, I talk to myself a lot. I look crazy because I'm constantly **having an argument with** myself. (Serena Williams)

4 I love cooking and **having friends over** for dinner, so a beautiful table to sit around is a must. (Ella Woodward)

5 Nowadays I'm not even sure if newspapers **take into account** whether a person is a good writer. (Bob Schieffer)

6 I look at life as a one-time opportunity, and you have to **take pleasure in** each moment, even if it is very problematic. (Ori Gersht)

7 Comedy is free therapy. And if it's done well, the audience and the comic **take turns** being the doctor as well as the patient. (Maysoon Zayid)

8 You've got to **take responsibility for** your actions. (Richard DeVos)

a invite someone to your house ____
b consider something when you make a decision ____
c do something alternately with another person ____
d have no idea about something (informal) ____
e have no connection to someone or something ____
f get happiness and enjoyment from something ____
g disagree with someone about something angrily ____
h have a moral obligation or be accountable for something ____

2 ▶ 9.2 Complete the mind maps with *have* or *take*. Listen and check.

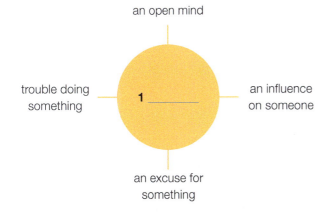

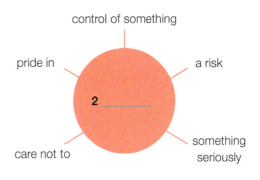

3 Complete the sentences with expressions from exercises 1 and 2. You may need to change the form of the verb.

1 I _____ with my sister, and now she won't even talk to me.
2 This is entirely my decision, and it _____ you, so I'll _____ it if it goes wrong.
3 We're planning a surprise birthday party for Hannah, and she _____ what's going on!
4 I arrived really late, so I entered the room quietly and _____ wake up my roommate.
5 When planning lessons, teachers should _____ students' ages _____ .
6 Sorry I'm late. I _____ finding somewhere to park.
7 I love to bake, and I really _____ making delicious desserts everyone enjoys.
8 At home, my father usually makes dinner, and my mother and I _____ washing the dishes.
9 Don't _____ everything Jane says so _____ . She's just joking!
10 I was sick in bed, so I _____ a perfect _____ not going to the party.

◀ Go back to page 76

149

VOCABULARY PRACTICE

9B Colors

1 ▶ 9.5 Match the colors in the box with pictures 1–16. Listen and check.

| blueish-green bronze dark blue gold lavender light blue maroon multicolored |
| pinkish-orange reddish ruby silver teal turquoise violet yellowish-brown |

2 Put the colors in the correct category. Which two colors can go in two categories?

metals	gems	single color	shade of a single color	combination of colors
_____	_____	_____	_____	_____
_____	_____	_____	_____	_____
_____	_____	_____	_____	_____
		_____	_____	
		_____		

3 Complete the sentences with the correct color.

150　　　　　　　　　　　　　　　　　　　　　　　　　　　◀ Go back to page 78

VOCABULARY PRACTICE

9C Dimensions and weight

1 ▶ 9.9 Study the chart. Then choose the correct options to complete sentences 1–8.

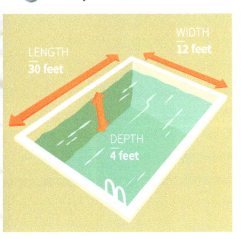
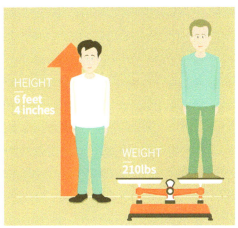

noun	adjective	verb
depth	deep	deepen
length	long	lengthen
width	wide	widen
height	high/tall	heighten
shortness	short	shorten
weight	(heavy)	weigh

1 As of Friday morning, 30% of the state was covered in snow, with an average *deep / depth* of 3.4 inches.

2 The roof of the local police station has collapsed under the *weigh / weight* of heavy snow.

3 If you're driving, be aware that roads can be extremely slippery when wet, which will *length / lengthen* the time it takes to stop.

4 The *short / shortness* of winter is the result of climate change, a trend that will continue.

5 For the first time in decades, the snow in south London and in the suburbs was one foot *deep / deepen*.

6 There is a higher incidence of forest fires in many places around the world, and the *length / long* of the fire season has increased significantly.

7 In this article, meteorologist John Elliot answers a tricky question – just how much does snow *weigh / weight*?

8 After the storm, the city had to spend a fortune on snow removal to clear streets that aren't *wide / width* enough for two cars to pass each other.

2 ▶ 9.10 Study the chart. Then complete sentences 1–5.

linear measure	capacity	weight
1 inch = 2.54 centimeters	1 gallon = 3.8 liters	1 ounce = 28.3 grams
1 foot = 0.3 meters	1 pint = 0.5 liters	1 pound = 0.45 kilograms
1 mile = 1.6 kilometers	1 quart = 0.9 liters	1 ton = 907 kilograms

1 John traveled 500 *miles* and João traveled 700 kilometers, so John traveled further.
2 Ann bought two _____ of milk, and Ana bought two liters of milk, so Ana bought more milk.
3 Paul weighs 170 _____, and Pablo weighs 90 kilograms, so Pablo weighs more.
4 Alice is 5 feet 2 _____, and Alicia is 1.75 meters tall, so Alicia is taller.
5 Carl bought half a _____ of cheese, and Carlos bought 250 grams, so Carl bought more cheese.

3 Complete the sentences logically using words from the box.

high   deep   long   tall   wide

1 The pool is only three feet _____, so you can go in even if you don't know how to swim.
2 I am nearly seven feet _____, which means everyone in my family is shorter than me.
3 For a wheelchair to go comfortably through a doorway, it must be 32 inches _____.
4 The Danyang-Kunshan Grand Bridge in China is over 100 miles _____, so it can take more than an hour to cross.
5 My bed is about three feet _____, so I have to use a stool to climb into it.

◀ Go back to page 80

VOCABULARY PRACTICE

10A Trends and business

1 ▶ 10.1 Write the words in the box below the correct graphs 1–3. Listen and check.

decline (n, v)   decrease (n, v)   drop (n, v)   fall (n, v)   grow (v)   growth (n)   increase (n, v)   remain stable (v)   rise (n, v)

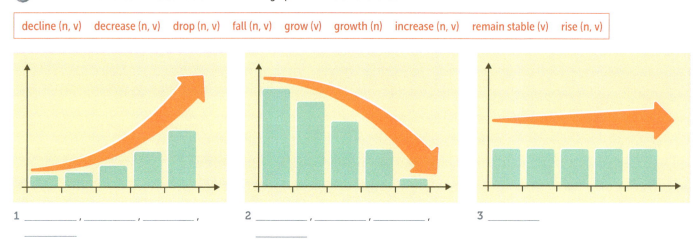

1 _____, _____, _____, _____

2 _____, _____, _____, _____

3 _____

2 Complete the sentences with the correct forms of the words in exercise 1. There may be more than one answer, but try to use each noun or verb only once.

GOOD NEWS FROM AROUND THE WORLD

1 Since the mid-1990s, violent crime in the UK ⬇ _____ by two-thirds.
2 Global average life expectancy ⬆ _____ by five years between 2000 and 2015, the fastest ⬆ _____ since the 1960s.
3 Since 1991, there's been a ⬇ _____ in cancer deaths in the U.S. by 25%.
4 A new report from the European Union said that between 1990 and 2016, the economy ⬆ _____ by 53%.
5 Since 2001, there's been a(n) ⬆ _____ in the number of people with access to electricity to nearly 1.2 billion.
6 A number of studies have shown that bullying in American schools ⬇ _____ slowly, but steadily, year after year.
7 The snow leopard is no longer an endangered species, and populations ⊖ _____ in the past few years.
8 In 2017, there was a ⬇ _____ in UK carbon emissions to the lowest level since the 19th century.

3 ▶ 10.2 Read a company's e-mail to its employees. Complete the sentences with the correct form of the words in the box. Listen and check.

verbs	nouns
launch go out of business manufacture raise provide set up	branch chain main office entrepreneur

Eight reasons why it's been a great year! We have:

- increased sales by 10%, while some of our competitors ¹_____ due to low sales;
- ²_____ a brand new website, which our customers love;
- ³_____ a committee to study ways to attract young ⁴_____ with creative ideas;
- opened a new factory to ⁵_____ our products;
- spent more on training so we can ⁶_____ quality services to our customers;
- acquired a ⁷_____ of stores in multiple locations around the country;
- found innovative ways to ⁸_____ money so we can open a new ⁹_____ ;
- moved our ¹⁰_____ to a more modern and spacious building.

◀ Go back to page 84

152

VOCABULARY PRACTICE

10C Word pairs

1 ▶ 10.5 Read the text. Match the expressions in **bold** 1–5 with definitions a–e. Listen and check.

Working from home: is it right for you?

We hear ¹**over and over** that working from home is the way of the future and that traditional offices will disappear one day. But there are a number of ²**pros and cons** to consider before you set up a home office. These are the advantages:
- There is no commute, so you will save time and money. But remember that ³**now and then** you might have to attend meetings or visit customers.
- There is more flexibility. If you're becoming ⁴**sick and tired** of a 9 to 5 working day, you will enjoy having a home office.
- You can do more work at home. ⁵**By and large**, you can use your time more effectively because you won't have any interruptions.

a in general _____
b occasionally _____
c fed up with _____
d advantages and disadvantages _____
e repeatedly _____

2 ▶ 10.6 Try to guess the meaning of the expressions in the box. Then complete the rest of the text with the correct expressions. Listen and check.

little by little   once or twice   side by side   sooner or later   peace and quiet   ups and downs   each and every

And these are the disadvantages:
- You have to be organized ¹_____ day of the week, without exception. It's OK to take breaks ²_____ a day, but longer ones shouldn't become a habit.
- It can be lonely. In the beginning, you will enjoy the ³_____ of a noise-free environment, but ⁴_____ the day may come when you'll start missing being with your coworkers.
- It's easier to get to know people when you work in an office. When you work ⁵_____ , in the same physical space, day in day out, ⁶_____ you become friends and may start to socialize after work.

So, in sum, think about your personality and what's important to you. For most people, working at home is a positive experience. You may have some ⁷_____ , but you'll probably end up enjoying it.

◀ Go back to page 88

153

VOCABULARY PRACTICE

11A Science

1A ▶ 11.1 Order tips a–d in the most logical way. Listen and check.

> How to **have** a scientific **breakthrough** – the four necessary steps:
>
> a ☐ **Analyze** the **evidence**. Does it **prove** your **theory**?
> b ☐ **Identify** a **problem** and **make a hypothesis**.
> c ☐ Try to **reach** a **conclusion**. Then **publish** the **results**.
> d ☐ **Carry out research** to investigate it.
>   **Do experiments**, if necessary, and **gather** as much **data** as you can.

B ▶ 11.2 Complete the collocations with the words in the box. Listen and check.

> an agreement   information   a hypothesis   a study

You can:
1 **prove** a theory, information, and _____ .
2 **reach** a conclusion, a decision, and _____ .
3 **carry out** research, an experiment, and _____ .
4 **gather** data, evidence, and _____ .

2 Read the text and complete collocations 1–8 with verbs from exercise 1. You may need to change the form of the verb.

Last year, Dr. Rose Silverstein, from our university, [1] _____ a series of **experiments** to investigate the effect of background music on shopping behavior. She wanted to [2] _____ the **hypothesis** she had started to research earlier: that everything from music volume to tempo could influence how consumers spend money. Dr. Silverstein spent six months interviewing customers and [3] _____ **data**, and she has [4] _____ some fascinating **conclusions**. She plans to [5] _____ the **results** next month. Apparently, loud and upbeat music tends to encourage customers to shop faster and spend less. She needs to [6] _____ the **evidence** a bit more, but she may [7] have _____ a scientific **breakthrough**. At the very least, she has [8] _____ **a problem** that has concerned many store owners.

3 ▶ 11.3 Complete the chart, using a dictionary if necessary. Listen and check. Then complete sentences 1–5 with words from the chart.

field	person
psychology	_____
_____	economist
the law	_____
_____	archeologist
geology	_____

1 My brother studied _____ in college and now he works for the Treasury Department as an _____ .
2 _____ is a fascinating topic and helps people who are anxious or depressed. But there aren't enough trained _____ .
3 If you don't obey _____ , you might find that you need a good _____ !
4 I went on a tour of an ancient Roman city over the weekend, led by a well-known _____ . It was so fascinating I was sorry I hadn't studied _____ .
5 _____ is an important field that teaches us how to use our natural resources effectively. In fact, our government needs to hire more _____ .

◀ Go back to page 94

VOCABULARY PRACTICE

11B Opposite adjectives

1 ▶ 11.7 Complete the chart with the opposite of the adjectives below. Listen and check.

positive	negative
1 _____	unacceptable
2 believable	_____
3 controversial	_____
4 _____	undesirable
5 imaginable	_____
6 _____	unimpressive
7 legal	_____
8 responsible	_____
9 _____	unsatisfactory

2 Match sentences 1–6 with pictures a–f. Then complete the sentences with an adjective from exercise 1.

1 Sam's behavior in class is completely _____ . He needs to sit down and focus on his work. ____
2 Laurie is a very _____ young woman, and her company is lucky to have such a dedicated worker. ____
3 There's another community meeting tonight about the new housing development. In my view, it's totally _____ . ____
4 I don't think you can park there now. It's only _____ after 5:30 p.m.. ____
5 A lot of what we read in the news these days isn't very _____ . ____
6 I found the lecture _____ and, to be honest, I don't remember much of it. ____

◀ Go back to page 96

VOCABULARY PRACTICE

11C Sleep

1 ▶ 11.11 Match sentences 1–5 with pictures a–e. Listen and check.
 1 The lesson was so boring that I began to **yawn**. ____
 2 At 11:30 last night, my son **sleepwalked** downstairs and came into the kitchen! ____
 3 My mother **snores** really loudly, and it **keeps** my father **awake** most nights. ____
 4 The dog lay down in front of the fire and **fell asleep**. ____
 5 Alfred texted his boss to apologize when he realized he'd **overslept** again. ____

2 ▶ 11.12 Read the text and match the words in **bold** 1–6 with definitions a–f. Listen and check.

> Feeling ¹**sleepy** at work is a common occurrence. According to a recent study, of the Americans who sleep an average of six hours a night, 45% say they feel very tired at least three times a week. When you're ²**sleep-deprived**, it can be difficult to concentrate and get things done at work. Unfortunately, most people can't ³**take a nap** at the office, so when they feel like they're starting to ⁴**doze off** at work, they drink coffee to help them ⁵**stay awake**. However, most of the people taking part in the survey say they ⁶**sleep in** on Saturday and Sunday mornings.

 a not to fall asleep ____
 b fall asleep lightly ____
 c sleep for a short time during the day ____
 d sleep longer than usual on purpose ____
 e not getting enough sleep ____
 f ready to fall asleep ____

3 Complete the sentences with words from exercises 1 and 2. You may need to change the verb forms.
 1 It was a nice hotel, but the street noise _____ me _____ all night.
 2 Every day my grandmother _____ right after lunch. She says it's the secret to a long life.
 3 Harry opened his mouth and _____ loudly in the middle of the lecture. I thought it was really rude of him.
 4 Unless I drink a large cup of coffee first thing in the morning, I have trouble _____ during the day.
 5 My husband _____ , so I have to sleep with earplugs.
 6 When my grandpa's watching TV, he sometimes _____ for a few minutes and then suddenly wakes up again.
 7 As soon as we set off in the car, the baby stopped crying and _____ .
 8 I was half an hour late for work this morning because I _____ .

◀ Go back to page 98

VOCABULARY PRACTICE

12A Phrasal verbs (2)

1 ▶ 12.1 Complete the list of features below with the correct form of the phrasal verbs in the boxes. Listen and check.

> back up   break down   work out   go through   hang up   note down
> run into   run out of   set up   sign in   turn down   turn up

Features of a perfect phone

- a way to automatically [1]_____ if I get an annoying call from a telemarketer;
- an easier way to [2]_____ songs and videos so I never lose them – better than the existing "cloud services";
- an alarm if someone tries to unlock my phone and [3]_____ my messages when I'm not looking;
- a lifetime warranty so I can get a free replacement if I [4]_____ a technical problem and the phone [5]_____ ;
- an app that [6]_____ important information when you talk to it – and doesn't misunderstand what you say;
- an app that [7]_____ who is calling you when you don't recognize the number;
- a way for me to increase the volume by simply saying, "[8]_____ the music"… and lower it by saying, "[9]_____ the music" – without touching the screen;
- better password managers so I can [10]_____ to all my accounts more easily;
- a faster way to [11]_____ a brand-new phone as soon as I leave the store – without having to go online;
- and last but not least: better battery life! I'm tired of [12]_____ battery in the middle of the day.

2A Read sentences 1–6 and choose the correct definition for each phrasal verb in **bold**, a or b.

1 Jill lost her job, so she's **going through** a difficult time right now.
  a experience something hard
  b examine something carefully
2 Let's **set up** a meeting for Monday so we can try to come to a final decision.
  a arrange or organize something
  b get something ready for use
3 I **ran into** an old friend at the shopping mall.
  a meet somebody by chance
  b experience a problem
4 Joe, could you **turn down** the air conditioning, please? It's a bit cold.
  a refuse an offer or request
  b reduce the amount of heat, light, or sound
5 The money I thought I'd lost **turned up** under my bed!
  a be found after being lost
  b increase the amount of heat, light, or sound
6 When you write an essay, you should **back up** your main points with facts.
  a support with information
  b make a copy of digital information

B Do any phrasal verbs in exercise 2A have the same meaning as those in exercise 1?

◀ Go back to page 102

12C Collocations with *come*, *do*, *go*, and *make*

1 ▶ 12.4 Complete the sentences with the words in the boxes. Listen and check.

> along   out   to an end   true

1 The new album is **coming** _____ in July. I can't wait to hear it.
2 I'd always dreamed of appearing in a Broadway show, and last month my dream **came** _____ .
3 An opportunity like this doesn't **come** _____ every day. You should definitely take it!
4 After three long months, the work has finally **come** _____ .

> harm   the minimum   your part   away with

5 The government should have **done** _____ these useless regulations years ago.
6 A good teacher can help you learn, but you've got to **do** _____ as well.
7 My brother didn't do much work when he was in college. He just **did** _____ to pass his exams.
8 We've **done** a lot of _____ to the environment without realizing how serious the problem is.

> ahead   for   into detail   over

9 If you really want this job, what are you waiting for? Just **go** _____ it!
10 The government has **gone** _____ with plans to build a new airport.
11 At the end of the lesson, the teacher **went** _____ the main points again to make sure everyone had understood.
12 The newspaper article **went** _____ great _____ about the governor's views.

> a point   sense   an effort   a living

13 I wish my father would **make** _____ to get along with my boyfriend.
14 My grandfather **made** _____ by selling cars at the local dealership.
15 Jack **made** _____ good _____ during the debate, which really made me stop and think.
16 You're not **making** _____ , Ann. What exactly are you trying to say?

◀ Go back to page 106

157

COMMUNICATION PRACTICE

1C Student A

1 Think of a hobby or interest that was a disappointment to you. Listen to Student B's questions.

2 Ask Student B questions 1–8 about a disappointing place.
   1 What was the place?
   2 When did you go there?
   3 How did you get there?
   4 Who were you with?
   5 Had you been looking forward to going there?
   6 Had you been saving money so you could go?
   7 Why did it fail to impress you?
   8 Will you give the place a second chance?

2A Student A

1 Look at the chart about the artist David Hockney. Answer Student B's questions.

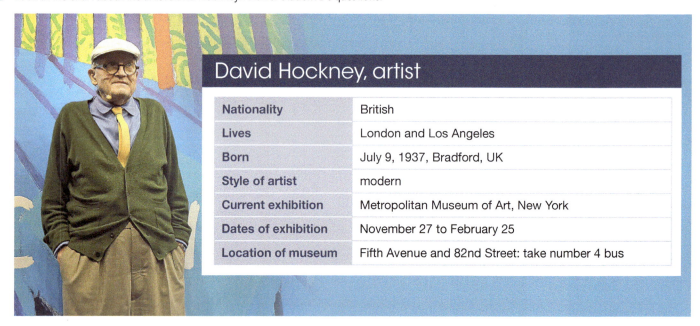

David Hockney, artist	
Nationality	British
Lives	London and Los Angeles
Born	July 9, 1937, Bradford, UK
Style of artist	modern
Current exhibition	Metropolitan Museum of Art, New York
Dates of exhibition	November 27 to February 25
Location of museum	Fifth Avenue and 82nd Street: take number 4 bus

2 Ask Student B questions about the singer Adele to complete the chart. Use a variety of question patterns to show how much you already know about her.

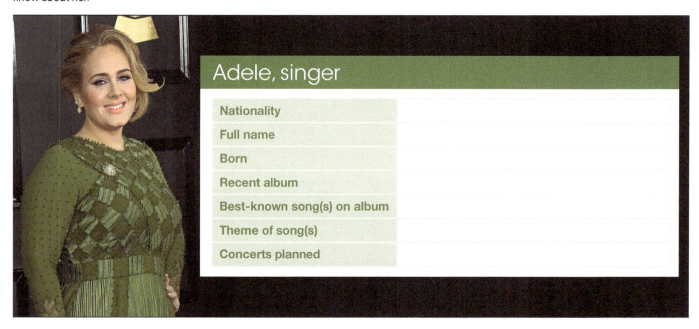

Adele, singer	
Nationality	
Full name	
Born	
Recent album	
Best-known song(s) on album	
Theme of song(s)	
Concerts planned	

COMMUNICATION PRACTICE

2D Student A

1 Describe the movie *Jurassic World: Fallen Kingdom* to Student B. Follow the steps below.

Jurassic World: Fallen Kingdom

The movie is set in the future, four years after the Jurassic World amusement park closes. It takes place on the island of Isla Nubar and is about a mission to save the dinosaurs from a volcanic eruption that threatens life on Earth. Directed by J. A. Bayona, the cast includes Chris Pratt, Bryce Dallas Howard, and Jeff Goldblum. If you really enjoyed the original *Jurassic World*, you'll love this movie also.

1 Say when or where the movie takes place.
2 Briefly describe the plot.
3 Mention the cast or director.
4 Give your overall impressions.

2 Listen to Student B describe the movie *The Predator*. Respond by saying whether you'd like to see it.

3C Student A

1 Think about how you would answer questions 1–6 about your family. Then ask your partner the questions about his/her family. Take notes on the answers.

FAMILY QUESTIONNAIRE

1 Who do you take after physically? And in personality?
2 Who do you look up to and admire the most?
3 What do you usually look forward to doing most with your family?
4 Did you ever try to get away with something as a child but you got caught?
5 If someone in your family doesn't want to do something, do you try to talk him/her into it?
6 Is there something your mother/father/brother/sister can't do without?

2 Compare your answers to all 12 questions. Can you find three similarities and three differences between your families?

4A Student A

1 Read sentence beginnings 1–6 to Student B. He/She will complete them. Decide together if the sentences are correct.

1 Most of the interesting people I know ...
2 Everyone in my class ...
3 The advice that my parents have given me ...
4 The government these days ...
5 A lot of people, including myself, ...
6 Only a few young people ...

2 Choose two of the sentences to discuss in more detail. Ask follow-up questions.

4C Student A

1 Think about these topics and make notes. Then tell Student B about each topic and answer his/her questions.

1 something creative that you enjoyed when you were a child
2 an exotic or unusual food that you've eaten
3 something you've been learning and have been successful at
4 someone you've known for a long time who's very persuasive
5 something you've been saving for and are hoping to buy

2 Listen to Student B. Ask follow-up questions to find out more.

159

COMMUNICATION PRACTICE

4D Student A

1 Choose one of the pictures and describe a memorable experience around it. Follow the steps below.

  1 Create suspense and describe your reaction to the experience.
  2 Respond to Student B and finish describing the experience.

2 Listen to Student B describe a memorable experience. Be sure to do the following.

  1 Guess how the story will continue and show surprise.
  2 Show empathy or happiness, as necessary.

6A Student A

1 Complete sentences 1–5. Make three statements true and two false. Then read them to Student B, who will try and guess which are true and which are false.

When I was a child …
1 I lived in a _____ near _____ .
2 I would spend hours watching _____ .
3 I never used to eat _____ , which made my _____ angry.
4 In school, I used to be good at _____ .
5 I would _____ (your own idea) _____ .

2 Student B will read five sentences about himself/herself. Three of the statements are true and two are false. Guess which are true and which are false. How many answers did you guess correctly?

6C Student A

1 Look at the photo of Lyall, a young man from Madison, Wisconsin, and read the text. Then answer Student B's questions about Lyall's experience.

So, I've been here in Madrid for a few months now. My Spanish is still pretty basic, but I'm slowly getting used to speaking it. I love the food, and now I'm used to drinking *café con leche* every morning and eating a Spanish tortilla (a kind of potato omelette). It's the best! Some things are harder to get used to – my apartment is tiny! I used to live in a big house, so I don't think I'll ever get used to living in a closet! And they drive so fast – I'm definitely not used to that yet, and I worry when I cross the street. Luckily, I don't drive – I take the subway. I've learned the different train lines, so I'm used to getting around the city. The subway is a great way to travel, but it can take a while to get from one place to another. I'm still getting used to that.

2 Look at Student B's photo of Betty, a young woman from Taiwan. Ask questions about her experience of living in Montreal, using prompts 1–6.

1 how she likes the weather
2 if it's difficult communicating in French
3 how she likes living in a big city
4 if it's hard being away from her family
5 how she finds the Canadian people
6 how she likes the food

COMMUNICATION PRACTICE

6D Student A

1 You and Student B are planning a vacation together. Mention problems 1–4 to Student B.

  1 "The direct flights are so expensive!"
  2 "What if it rains? What will we do to pass the time?"
  3 "Should we rent an apartment on Airbnb? Hotels are really expensive there!"
  4 "Maybe we should take a vacation closer to home!"

2 You and Student B are hoping to move. Suggest a neighborhood. He/She will mention different problems. Respond using the skills below.

  1 Make a point.
  2 Suggest alternatives.
  3 Ask for clarification.
  4 Challenge Student B to keep thinking.

7A Student A

1 Complete part of an e-mail from a college student. Try to be creative with the relative clauses.

> School is going pretty well, but I have a lot of work. I have to submit a long report on Monday, which _____ . And I have trouble with lectures containing _____ and classes having _____ . The good news, though, is that I passed _____ , which _____ .
> As for this summer, my parents suggested I get a job working _____ , one that would give me experience in _____ . It's not a bad idea, but I've been thinking of _____ , which _____ !
> Can you give me some advice on these things?

2 Imagine you're the college student in exercise 1. Summarize what you wrote for Student B. He/She will give you advice.

3 Listen to Student B, a recent college graduate. Give him/her advice.

8A Student A

1 Read the text carefully. Then cover it and tell Student B about it in your own words. Try to use the linkers.

Vinyl's back – but who's buying it?

After disappearing from the market for many years, vinyl records (or LPs) have become popular again, and sales have been going up steadily since 2008. As a result, more and more artists are releasing their new albums on vinyl. Interestingly, while most people think only older adults buy LPs, in some locations, vinyl sales are very high with those under 30, too. Perhaps these younger music fans love the sound and feel of a physical object, which, unlike Spotify, is more personal. Also, the renewed interest in LPs is partly due to their availability, as they are becoming easier and easier to find.

2 Now listen to Student B tell you the story behind this photo. Do you personally think Polaroid is a success story?

8C Student A

1 Ask Student B questions 1–5. Listen to each response and then tell him/her your own responses.

  1 Do you still go to the movies?
  2 Do you check your phone as soon as you wake up?
  3 Are you planning to attend a live concert this year?
  4 When you watch a movie in English, do you read the subtitles?
  5 Do you lend books to friends?

2 Listen to Student B's questions. Give a true response, choosing one of the two options.

  1 Yes, I spend some time … / No, I've stopped …
  2 Sure, I wouldn't mind … / No, I'd have a hard time …
  3 Yes, … are fun. / No, I'm not into …
  4 Yes, it's important … / No, there's no point …
  5 Yes, I used to have fun … / No, I was tired of …

161

COMMUNICATION PRACTICE

8D Student A

1 Comment on these annoying situations to Student B and explain why you feel the way you do. Express doubt if necessary.

1 companies that make mistakes in your telephone or electricity bill
2 restaurants that make you wait a long time before taking your order
3 drivers who park too close to your car
4 dog owners who don't clean up after their pets

2 Student B will comment on some annoying situations. React to his/her explanations.

9A Student A

1 Listen to Student B describe his/her neighborhood. At the end, write down the eight adverbs you heard. Is each one a comment adverb or an adverb of degree, frequency, or manner?

2 Tell Student B about your plans for next year. Check his/her adverbs, using the key below.

> Personally, I don't plan to go to graduate school. Realistically, I don't think it's a worthwhile expense, and actually, I think you can get a good job without a graduate degree. Also, it's unusually hard to get into some graduate schools, and the entrance exam is really difficult. I think I can do well in the work world without an MA. Things frequently change at companies, and they're always looking for new people.
>
> **Key:**
> *personally*, *realistically*, *actually*: comment adverbs
> *unusually*, *really*: adverbs of degree
> *frequently*, *always*: adverbs of frequency
> *well*: adverb of manner

9C Student A

1 Read the text carefully. Then cover it and tell Student B about it in your own words. Include passives and causative *have* structures.

> I have a teacher who makes us work so hard I can rarely go out. We're often assigned homework at the last minute. So far this year, we've been given over 20 unexpected tasks to do. One time, a student was even sent home because she came to class without her homework. My teacher also has us do extra exercises on Friday, so we frequently have to stay late. And since he says we have plenty of free time, he has us do longer projects on the weekend, too!

2 Listen to Student B's problem. What advice can you give to help him/her deal with this situation?

10A Student A

1 Read each trivia question to Student B twice, once with each option. The answers are below.

2 Listen to Student B. How many answers can you guess?

🌢 Rainy day quiz

1 *Not many / Quite a few* people know that Elvis Presley really had blond hair. It was dyed black.
2 *Few / Quite a few* people know that the world has 24 time zones, and some are only 30 to 45 minutes apart.
3 Bill Gates's teachers had *not many / a lot of* reasons to suspect that he had written a computer program scheduling classes for himself with students he liked.
4 *A fair number of / Few* people know Martin Luther King Jr. was a *Star Trek* fan.
5 Children's book author Dr. Seuss wrote *Green Eggs and Ham* with *quite a few / not many* words for young children – only 50 in all!

Answers: 1 Not many   2 Few   3 not many   4 Few   5 not many

162

COMMUNICATION PRACTICE

10D Student A

1 Imagine you're upset because you didn't get onto a program you'd applied to. Tell Student B about it.

2 Listen to Student B's problem. React after each sentence and be as supportive as you can.
   1 Show sympathy.
   2 Show the positive side of the problem.
   3 Make a suggestion.
   4 Try to cheer your partner up.

11A Student A

1 Read the mystery slowly to Student B. At the end, give him/her five tries to solve the mystery.

> In two villages in northern Kazakhstan – in Central Asia, south of Russia – people of all ages were suffering from a strange illness. They would fall asleep suddenly, even while they were walking, and would wake up with memory loss, headaches, and a weak feeling. Sometimes they slept for as long as six hours, but when they woke up, they remembered nothing and didn't know they had fallen asleep. Children sometimes claimed that they had seen horses with wings or were sure there were snakes in their beds. Even pets got the strange illness and fell asleep without warning. There were many explanations, and some thought the villagers (and even the pets) probably had psychological problems. Others were sure the problem was nearby mines that had closed years before. *Something* was entering the atmosphere. What could it be?
>
> **Solution**: The old mines were releasing carbon dioxide, and so people weren't getting enough oxygen. They've now moved to different villages.

2 Listen to Student B tell you a mystery. When he/she pauses, ask questions to try to figure out the answer. At the end, Student B will give you five tries to solve the mystery.

I think he must have been someone else the man knew.

12A Student A

1 Imagine you are in each of these situations. Tell Student B at least two things you might wish for, using unreal conditional sentences. He/She has to guess each situation.

I wish they'd answer the phone. And I'd rather ...

2 Listen to Student B, who's having an unpleasant experience. Guess the situation.

163

COMMUNICATION PRACTICE

1C Student B

1 Ask Student A questions 1–8 about a disappointing hobby or interest.

1 What was your hobby or interest?
2 When did you start it?
3 Where did you practice it?
4 How did you pay for it?
5 Had you ever tried it before?
6 Had you been saving money to do it?
7 Why didn't it meet your expectations?
8 Will you give the hobby or interest a second chance?

2 Think of a place you've visited that was a disappointment to you. Listen to Student A's questions.

2A Student B

1 Ask Student A questions about the artist David Hockney to complete the chart. Use a variety of question patterns to show how much you already know about him.

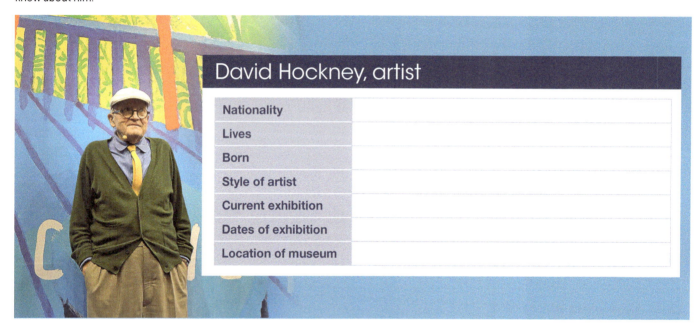

David Hockney, artist

Nationality	
Lives	
Born	
Style of artist	
Current exhibition	
Dates of exhibition	
Location of museum	

2 Look at the chart about the singer Adele. Answer Student A's questions.

Adele, singer

Nationality	British
Full name	Adele Laurie Blue Adkins
Born	May 5, 1988, London, UK
Recent album	25
Best-known song(s) on album	"Hello"
Theme of song(s)	a couple that broke up
Concerts planned	none

COMMUNICATION PRACTICE

2D Student B

1 Listen to Student A describe the movie *Jurassic World: Fallen Kingdom*. Respond by saying whether you'd like to see it.

2 Describe the movie *The Predator* to Student A. Follow the steps below.

The Predator

A long-awaited sequel to the 1987 sci-fi hit *Predator* is set between 1990 and 2010. Directed by Shane Black, the cast includes Jacob Tremblay, Sterling K. Brown, and Yvonne Strahovski. The movie is about a group of men who are stuck in a jungle with a monster that attacks them one by one. You'll be biting your nails from start to finish. It's very suspenseful!

1 Say when or where the movie takes place.
2 Briefly describe the plot.

3 Mention the cast or director.
4 Give your overall impressions.

3C Student B

1 Think about how you would answer questions 1–6 about your family. Then ask your partner the questions about his/her family. Take notes on the answers.

── FAMILY QUESTIONNAIRE ──

1 Who do you get along best/worst with in your family?
2 When you were little, who looked after you when you came home from school?
3 In your family, do you always use leftover food up, or do you throw it out?
4 Do you keep a lot of mementos from childhood that you really should throw out?
5 Do you have any relatives who have ever called a wedding off? What happened?
6 If you're invited to a family event and you really don't want to go, how do you get out of it?

2 Compare your answers to all 12 questions. Can you find three similarities and three differences between your families?

4A Student B

1 Read sentence beginnings 1–6 to Student A. He/She will complete them. Decide together if the sentences are correct.

1 One of the most talented people I can think of …
2 Anyone who doesn't want to go to college …
3 A lot of information you find on social media …

4 The police where I live …
5 All of my friends, except …
6 Only some of the people I know …

2 Choose two of the sentences to discuss in more detail. Ask follow-up questions.

4C Student B

1 Listen to Student A. Ask follow-up questions to find out more.

2 Think about these topics and make notes. Then tell Student A about each topic and answer his/her questions.

1 something exciting that you did last year
2 a personal possession you've lost that you really miss
3 something you've achieved that you're really proud of
4 someone you've always admired and who you rely on
5 an activity you've been doing a lot lately, which may be a little risky

165

COMMUNICATION PRACTICE

4D Student B

1 Listen to Student A describe a memorable experience. Be sure to do the following.
   1 Guess how the story will continue and show surprise.
   2 Show empathy or happiness, as necessary.

2 Choose one of the pictures and describe a memorable experience around it. Follow the steps below.

   1 Create suspense and describe your reaction to the experience.
   2 Respond to Student A and finish describing the experience.

6A Student B

1 Student A will read five sentences about himself/herself. Three of the statements are true and two are false. Guess which are true and which are false. How many answers did you guess correctly?

2 Complete sentences 1–5. Make three statements true and two false. Then read them to Student A, who will try and guess which are true and which are false.

When I was a child …
1 I used to like drinking _____ .
2 I would spend hours playing _____ with my _____ .
3 In school, I didn't use to do well in _____ .
4 I used to be really _____ and _____ .
5 I would _____ (your own idea) _____ .

6C Student B

1 Look at Student A's photo of Lyall, a young man from Madison, Wisconsin. Ask questions about his experience of living in Madrid, using prompts 1–6.

   1 if he's having difficulty with the language
   2 how he likes the food
   3 how he likes living in a small apartment
   4 if the traffic is a problem
   5 if it's easy to get around Madrid
   6 what he thinks of the subway

2 Look at the photo of Betty, a young woman from Taiwan, and read the text. Then answer Student A's questions about Betty's experience.

Well, here I am in Montreal, and it's snowing for the first time. It's beautiful, but very cold! I'll never get used to this weather. Everything here is in English and French, but for me that's not a problem. My father is French, and I'm used to speaking the language. I come from a small town in southern Taiwan, and Montreal seems large by comparison, but I guess I'm slowly getting used to living in a big city. It's very hard being away from my family, though, especially my mom. I don't think I'll ever get used to it. But the Canadians are really nice and friendly, and I find them funny, now that I've gotten used to their sense of humor. What else? Oh, the food. It's good, but they eat so much. I'm not used to eating such big portions of everything.

COMMUNICATION PRACTICE

6D Student B

1 You and Student A are planning a vacation together. Suggest a place to go. He/She will mention different problems. Respond using the skills below.

1 Make a point.
2 Suggest alternatives.
3 Ask for clarification.
4 Challenge Student A to keep thinking.

2 You and Student A are hoping to move. Mention problems 1–4 to Student A.

1 "Some apartments in that area aren't very nice!"
2 "And the rent may not be any less than we're paying now."
3 "The neighborhood isn't very close to school, either."
4 "Maybe we shouldn't move after all!"

7A Student B

1 Listen to Student A, a college student. Give him/her advice.

2 Complete part of an e-mail from a recent college graduate. Try to be creative with the relative clauses.

> Well, I've graduated! But now I want a job offering _____ , and that's not easy to find. There are things I miss, as well. I was really into _____ in college, which _____ . And I used to enjoy _____ , which _____ . The good thing, though, is that I have some friends living across the street who _____ . But my parents say I have to _____ , which _____ ! Can you give me some advice on these things?

3 Imagine you're the college graduate. Summarize what you wrote for Student A. He/She will give you advice.

8A Student B

1 Listen to Student A tell you the story behind this photo. Do you personally think LPs are a success story?

2 Read the text carefully. Then cover it and tell Student A about it in your own words. Try to use the linkers.

Polaroid – the return of an old favorite?

When the first Polaroid camera was invented in 1945, it changed photography completely because of one unique feature: the ability to print photos instantly. However, when digital cameras were launched in the 1990s, all photos became "instant," and, therefore, by the turn of the century, Polaroid cameras had almost disappeared. But today, Polaroid is back, as young people want to experience photography the way their grandparents did, holding a photo in their hands. So whereas other 20th century companies have disappeared, Polaroid may be here to stay.

8C Student B

1 Listen to Student A's questions. Give a true response, choosing one of the two options.

1 Yes, I enjoy … / No, I've stopped …
2 Yes, it's hard not … / No, I try not …
3 Yes, I'm looking forward to … / No, I don't expect …
4 Yes, I can't help … / No, I avoid …
5 Yes, I don't have a problem … / No, I refuse …

2 Ask Student A questions 1–5. Listen to each response and then tell him/her your own responses.

1 Do you still watch regular TV shows?
2 Could you spend a whole day without talking to anyone?
3 Do you like seeing musicals?
4 Do you limit the amount of time you spend on social media?
5 Do you miss any friends you've lost touch with?

167

COMMUNICATION PRACTICE

8D Student B

1. Student A will comment on some annoying situations. React to his/her explanations.

2. Comment on these annoying situations to Student A and explain why you feel the way you do. Express doubt if necessary.
   1. companies that offer to call you back, but never do
   2. restaurants that have run out of most of the specials on the menu
   3. drivers who keep going when a traffic light turns red
   4. dog owners who don't keep their pets on a leash

9A Student B

1. Tell Student A about your neighborhood. Check his/her adverbs, using the key below.

   > <u>Fortunately</u>, my neighborhood hasn't gotten more expensive because I'm <u>very</u> happy there. <u>Ideally</u>, the rent won't go up at all during the next few years. It's <u>extremely</u> convenient, and I can get to work really <u>rapidly</u>. I <u>usually</u> go by car, but I take the traffic into account, and I'm careful not to drive in bad weather. I don't drive <u>well</u> in the snow. In fact, you could say, I drive really <u>badly</u>! I'm originally from Florida, so I'm not at all used to the snow up here in Maine.

   Key:
   fortunately, ideally: comment adverbs *usually*: adverb of frequency
   extremely, very: adverbs of degree *rapidly, well, badly*: adverbs of manner

2. Listen to Student A talk about his/her plans for next year. At the end, write down the eight adverbs you heard. Is each one a comment adverb or an adverb of degree, frequency, or manner?

9C Student B

1. Listen to Student A's problem. What advice can you give to help him/her deal with this situation?

2. Read the text carefully. Then cover it and tell Student A about it in your own words. Include passives and causative *have* structures.

   > I have a boss who has us work such long hours that I can never take a vacation. We're frequently given extra work before national holidays. In addition, he often has us take work home on the weekends. A friend of mine was fired for not showing up on Monday with a finished assignment. And my boss has already made me miss three important family events. We're yelled at if we complain, so we can't say anything!

10A Student B

1. Listen to Student A. How many answers can you guess?

2. Read each trivia question to Student A twice, once with each option. The answers are below.

   ### Rainy day quiz
   1. U.S. President Theodore Roosevelt read *few / quite a few* books as president, one a day, in fact.
   2. Two U.S. capital cities, Austin, Texas and Boston, Massachusetts have names that rhyme. *Both are / Neither is* spelled differently.
   3. *Few / A lot of* people are aware that Buzz Aldrin, who walked on the moon, actually wrote a rap song called "The rocket experience" 40 years later.
   4. There's *little / a fair amount of* information about the fact that right-handed people supposedly live up to nine years longer than left-handed people!
   5. There's *a fair amount / not much* that doesn't interest a four-year-old. They ask around 450 questions a day.

   Answers: 1 quite a few 2 Both are 3 Few 4 little 5 not much

COMMUNICATION PRACTICE

10D Student B

1. Listen to Student A's problem. React after each sentence and be as supportive as you can.
   1. Show sympathy.
   2. Show the positive side of the problem.
   3. Make a suggestion.
   4. Try to cheer your partner up.

2. Imagine you're upset because there was a mistake with your vacation reservation and the company has canceled it. Tell Student A about it.

11A Student B

1. Listen to Student A tell you a mystery. When he/she pauses, ask questions to try to figure out the answer. At the end, Student A will give you five tries to solve the mystery.

   Well, it might have been something in the water.

2. Read the mystery slowly to Student A. At the end, give him/her five tries to solve the mystery.

   In a nursing home outside Edinburgh, Scotland, an elderly man had just died. There was nothing unusual about this as he hadn't been in good health. But when a doctor was called to complete the necessary paperwork, she noticed something strange. The man had two dates of birth and three last names. He had no passport or birth certificate to prove his identity, but he had told the staff he once lived in Italy, which seemed strange, too. Eventually, the police discovered that he had been born in Italy and had to leave when he was 21. One of the three names really was his. Another one belonged to a woman he had once shared a house with. But why did he leave Italy? And why did he have so many names? Was he a criminal? Or could there be another reason his identity was a secret?

   Solution: He had escaped from Italy during World War II and already had a fake name when he became a British citizen in 1948. Having learned young that his safety depended on a fake identity, he was most comfortable keeping one (or two) fake names.

12A Student B

1. Listen to Student A, who's having an unpleasant experience. Guess the situation.
2. Imagine you are in each of these situations. Tell Student A two things you might wish for, using unreal conditional sentences. He/She has to guess each situation.

If only they'd tell us ... And it's about time ...

COMMUNICATION PRACTICE

1A Both students

Look at pictures a–f and discuss the questions for each one.

1 Where do you think the people are? Is the situation formal or informal?
2 What does it look as if they're doing?
3 Would the behavior be appropriate in your country? Why/Why not?
4 What advice would you give a visitor to your country about gestures and body language?

2C Both students

True or false? In teams, take the Oldies' Trivia Quiz. Then check your answers on page 173.

Oldies' Trivia Quiz

1. Despite the fact that it wasn't a new song, "Candle in the Wind" by Elton John was re-released in 1997 with some new lyrics in memory of Diana, Princess of Wales.
2. In spite of the rain, Woodstock, one of the most famous music festivals ever, took place over three days in 1968.
3. Although they usually sang in English, the 1970s group Abba was from Switzerland.
4. Bruce Springsteen is called "The Boss" because he was in charge of collecting the money so he could distribute it to the other band members.
5. In spite of the fact that he didn't write the song, Barry Manilow had a number 1 hit in 1976 called "I write the songs."
6. The British group The Clash borrowed a World War II phrase so they could name the song "London Calling." The original phrase was "America, this is London calling."
7. The famous nightclub, Copacabana, is in New York City. However, it was named after a neighborhood in Rio de Janeiro.
8. The line "I want to wake up in the city that doesn't sleep" is by Frank Sinatra and is about Los Angeles.

COMMUNICATION PRACTICE

3A Both students

1 Work in pairs. Look at the situations in pictures a–h. Make positive or negative sentences using the prompts in the box. How many sentences can you make for each picture?

> supposed to   should   be allowed to   'd better   have to   can   ought to

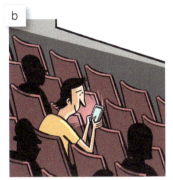

2 Which pair made the most sentences?

5A Both students

1 Complete the questionnaire with your own opinions. Don't show your partner.

What do you think? This is what our readers said:	Agree	Disagree
1 There's been such an increase in vegetarianism. I might well try it.		
2 There are so many endangered species. It makes me depressed.		
3 There are so few electric cars, but they're really fantastic.		
4 It's such a good idea to save rainwater for household tasks.		
5 Environmental groups do such vital work. I'm going to join one.		
6 There's so little organic food available, and it's far too expensive.		
7 Recycling is such a waste of time. It takes me ages to sort my garbage.		
8 The planet is in serious danger. There's so little time left to save it.		
9 Switching to energy-efficient light bulbs is such good advice.		
10 So many people are living to be 100. It must be due to changes in diet.		

2 Share your answers. Do you have similar opinions on health and the environment? How many of the questions did you answer in the same way?

COMMUNICATION PRACTICE

5C Both students

1 Complete the survey to predict your future. Don't show your partner your answers. On a scale of 1 (low) to 5 (high), how bright does your future look?

> 1 What new skill will you have learned to do by this time next year?
>
> 2 Will you have started a new job or changed jobs a year from now?
>
> 3 How will you be spending your leisure time six months from now?
>
> 4 Where will you be living in five years? Who will you be living with?
>
> 5 Will you be spending more or less money six months from now?
>
> 6 What important events will have taken place in the world two years from now?
>
> 7 By this time next year, will you have given anything up?
>
> 8 How much exercise will you be getting five years from now?

2 Take turns sharing your predictions. Which of you is more optimistic about the future?

7C Both students

1 Practice the mini-conversations in pairs. Extend each conversation to four or five lines.

1 A Could I borrow your car on the weekend?
  B Yes, as long as …
2 A Can you help me with the gardening on Sunday?
  B Sure. I'll help you even if …
3 A Can I borrow your laptop next week?
  B Yes, OK, provided that …

4 A Could you feed my cat while I'm on vacation?
  B Of course, unless I …
5 A Could you lend me your bicycle tomorrow?
  B That should be fine, as long as …
6 A Can you babysit the children tomorrow evening?
  B Yes, of course, unless …

2 Change roles and practice the conversations again with new outcomes.

10C Both students

1 Discuss the topics below in pairs. Give each other advice and use comparative structures where possible.

1 When speaking in public, …
  a is it better to have lots of detailed notes or just a few prompts?
  b how much should you practice?
  c what are some things you should never do?
2 When meeting someone who's older than you for the first time, …
  a do you need to use more formal language?
  b should you shake hands?
  c is it important to be careful what topics you talk about?

3 The day before an exam, …
  a how important is it to get a good night's sleep?
  b should you do most of your studying on the last day?
  c what can you do to make yourself feel less nervous?
4 On the first day of class, …
  a should you introduce yourself to everyone on the first day?
  b how can you improve your memory and learn everyone's name?
  c is it OK to ask the teacher lots of questions?

2 What's the most useful piece of advice your partner gave you?

COMMUNICATION PRACTICE

11C Both students

1 Interview your partner about these various sleep experiences.

   1 Have you ever dozed off at school or work, even for a minute?
   2 Does anyone in your family snore?
   3 Do you like to sleep in on the weekends?
   4 Have you ever overslept and arrived late for work/class?
   5 Do you have trouble falling asleep when you're angry or upset?
   6 Do you know anyone who sleepwalks?
   7 Have you ever felt sleep-deprived?
   8 Can you stay awake at night if you need to? How do you manage it?

2 Listen to your partner. Then find a new pair and report your conversation to him/her.

   Carlos admitted that he had dozed off a few times at work.

12C Both students

1 Imagine you regret something you did (or didn't do) in each of the situations below. What would have happened if you had made a different decision? Make notes.

   1 You saw a great apartment that was reasonably priced, but you turned it down because you thought you'd find something even better.
   2 You had a chance to study in New York for a year, but decided it was too expensive and too far away from your family and friends.
   3 You forgot it was your boyfriend's/girlfriend's birthday yesterday. He/She won't answer your calls or reply to your texts.
   4 You decided to work for a year before going to college, but when you finally applied to the college you had chosen, they didn't accept you.
   5 You moved because you accepted a job in a new town, but your new boss turned out to be awful.
   6 You didn't invite a cousin to your wedding because you didn't think he/she would come. Now your cousin isn't talking to you.

2 Share ideas with your partner. Then decide on a solution to each problem together.

12D Both students

Discuss the statements below in pairs. Try to keep the conversation going for a few minutes for each one.

   1 Desktop PCs are bound to disappear at some point.
   2 It's conceivable that electric cars will replace conventional cars completely.
   3 Robots aren't likely to be able to think or feel like humans at any point soon.
   4 Whether we'll be able to travel to Mars is anyone's guess.
   5 It's conceivable that drones will deliver all of our mail in the future.
   6 It's likely that most people will be vegetarian in 100 years.

2C Answers

1 1 T; 2 F: It took place in 1969; 3 F: They were from Sweden; 4 T; 5 T; 6 T; 7 T; 8 F: It is about New York.

173

Phrasal verbs

Phrasal verb	Meaning
back up sb/sth	support sb; save sth
break down	stop working
break out	start suddenly (war, fire, disease)
break up	end a relationship
burn out	become exhausted through overwork
call off sth	cancel
carry out	conduct an experiment (plan)
catch on	become popular
catch up (on sth)	get information; do sth there wasn't time for
cheer up (sb)	make happier
come across	find
come back (to sth)	return (to sth)
come together	join
come up	arise (an issue)
come up with	invent
deal with sth	take action; accept sth
do without sth	manage without
drift apart	separate without actively trying to
figure out sth	understand with careful thought
fit in	be socially compatible (in harmony with)
get on (along) with	have a good relationship
get out of (doing sth)	avoid doing sth
give away sth	give something no longer needed
give in	surrender
go back (a long way)	return; know each other a long time
go through sth	experience sth difficult
grow up	spend one's childhood
hang out	spend time together
hang up	end a phone call
hang sth up	put sth on a hook (hanger)
have sb over	invite sb to your house
hit (it) off	get along very well
hold sb back	prevent sb from moving ahead (succeeding)
let sb down	disappoint

Phrasal verb	Meaning
live up to	fulfill
look after	take care of
look down on sb	think one is better or more important
look forward to sth	anticipate; be happy about
look out for sb	watch (protect)
look up to sb	admire (respect)
make up	become friendly after an argument
mess up sth	spoil (do sth badly)
miss out	lose an opportunity
note down sth	write sth to not forget it
pay sb back	repay a loan
pay off	be worthwhile
put up with sth	accept without complaining
reach out (to sb)	contact; show interest in
run out of sth	not have enough
sell out	sell the last one and have no more of
set up sth	establish; prepare for use
settle down	make a home with sb
show up	appear
stand out	be better; be easy to see
talk sb into	convince (persuade)
take after sb	be similar to a family member
take off	not go to work; succeed
tell sb off	reprimand (scold)
think over sth	consider
think up sth	invent; think of a new idea
throw out	discard (get rid of)
try out sth	use sth to see if you like it
turn up	appear
turn up sth	raise (the volume)
turn down sth	lower (the volume); refuse
turn out	happen (have a certain result)
use up sth	finish (use completely)
work out	exercise; end successfully

Irregular verbs

Base form	Past simple	Past participle
arise	arose	arisen
awake	awoke	awoken
bear	bore	born
beat	beat	beaten
bend	bent	beaten
bet	bet	bet
bleed	bled	bled
blow	blew	blown
broadcast	broadcast	broadcast
burn	burned/burnt	burned/burnt
burst	burst	burst
catch	caught	caught
creep	crept	crept
cut	cut	cut
deal	dealt	dealt
dig	dug	dug
feed	fed	fed
fight	fought	fought
flee	fled	fled
forbid	forbade	forbidden
forecast	forecast	forecast
forgive	forgave	forgiven
freeze	froze	frozen
hang	hung	hung
hit	hit	hit
hurt	hurt	hurt
kneel	knelt/kneeled	knelt/kneeled
lead	led	led
leap	leaped/leapt	leaped/leapt
lend	lent	lent
mean	meant	meant

Base form	Past simple	Past participle
mistake	mistook	mistaken
overhear	overheard	overheard
oversleep	overslept	overslept
seek	sought	sought
set	set	set
shake	shook	shaken
shoot	shot	shot
show	showed	shown
shrink	shrank	shrunk
shut	shut	shut
sink	sank	sunk
sleep	slept	slept
slide	slid	slid
spin	spun	spun
split	split	split
spill	spilled/spilt	spilled/spilt
spread	spread	spread
spring	sprang	sprung
stick	stuck	stuck
sting	stung	stung
strike	struck	struck
swear	swore	sworn
sweep	swept	swept
tread	trod	trodden/trod
undertake	undertook	undertaken
undo	undid	undone
upset	upset	upset
weep	wept	wept
wind	wound	wound
withdraw	withdrew	withdrawn
withstand	withstood	withstood

Ⓡ Richmond

58 St Aldates
Oxford
OX1 1ST
United Kingdom

ISBN: 978-84-668-2101-8
CP: 642706
© Richmond / Santillana Global S.L. 2019

All rights reserved. No part of this book may be reproduced, stored in a retrieval system or transmitted in any form by any means, electronic, mechanical, photocopying, recording or otherwise, without the prior permission in writing of the Publisher.

Publishing Director: Deborah Tricker
Publisher: Simone Foster
Media Publisher: Sue Ashcroft
Content Developer: Deborah Goldblatt
Editors: Debra Emmett, Jamie Bowman, Shannon O'Neill
Design Manager: Lorna Heaslip
Cover Design: This Ain't Rock'n'Roll, London
Design & Layout: Lorna Heaslip, emc Design Ltd
Photo Researcher: Magdalena Mayo
Talking Zone video: Bagley Wood Productions
Audio Production: John Marshall Media
App Development: The Distance

We would also like to thank the following people for their valuable contribution to writing and developing the material:
James Styring, Jake Hughes, Brigit Viney, Diarmuid Carter (video script writer), Belen Fernandez (App Project Manager), Rob Sved (App Content Creator)

We would like to thank all those who have given their kind permission to reproduce material for this book:

Illustrators: Beach-o-matic Ltd; Victor Beuran c/o Astound Inc.; Roger Harris c/o NB Illustration; Guillaume Gennet c/o Lemonade; Julia Scheele

Photos:
D. Lezama; V. Atmán; 123RF; AGILEBITS INC.; ALAMY/Moviestore collection Ltd, Photofusion Picture Library, seewhatmitchsee, Everette Collection Inc, RosalreneBetancourt 6, ZUMA Press, Inc., Steve Moss, RosalreneBetancourt 9, Martin Parker, Moviestore Collection Ltd, Jeff Greenberg, Mr Pics, Hemis, RosalreneBetancourt 7, Collection Christophel, Magdalena Mayo, Radharc Images, Game Shots, urbanbuzz, NetPhotos, Image Source, CandyAppleRed Images, Art Directors & TRIP, RosalreneBetancourt 3, Chris Willson, Education & Exploration 2; COLIN BEAVAN; EVERNOTE; FERDI RIZKIYANTO; GETTY IMAGES SALES SPAIN/Flashpop, WALTER ZERLA, BSIP/UIG, hoozone, ImagesBazaar, Dmitry Ageev, Tolimir, By LTCE, Newton Daly, sturti, alxpin, AndreyPopov, Tainar, pinkomelet, jaochainoi, CasarsaGuru, izusek, Paul Morigi, Astarot, chepkoelena, DenBoma, Svtist, YangYin, MachineHeadz, ilbusca, bymuratdeniz, FS-Stock, CarmenMurillo, JGalione, Rouzes, Thinkstock, Tom Merton, RUSS ROHDE, Peter Cade, CoisaX, Maskot, AnaBGD, Adam Berry, thall, mrgao, istock/Thinkstock, Roberto Westbrook, omgimages, kali9, jacoblund, isitsharp, pixdeluxe, roundhill, tommaso79, Jose Luis Pelaez Inc, Chema Alba, Detailfoto, M.M. Sweet, acilo, Placebo365, flashfilm, SensorSpot, Richard I'Anson, Nikada, gradyreese, gregobagel, Westend61, MileA, Stockbyte, AngiePhotos, Jon Hicks, Felix Wirth, Hero Images, Matt Dutile, dszc, JangoBeat, PetrePlesea, Sam Edwards, franckreporter, hanapon1002,

mediaphotos, Dan MacMedan, Walter Bibikow, Goodshoot, Jaunty Junto, Kieran Stone, CHBD, PeopleImages, , Prasit photo, Ben Gabbe, A330Pilot, ferrantraite, Bernhard Lang, FOX, Caspar Benson, Daniel Ingold, Dougal Waters, ronnybas, Barcroft Media, Anadolu Agency, richiesd, SIphotography, Peathegee Inc, quavondo, Patrick Orton, Michael Blann, funstock, Florin Prunoiu, Jemal Countess, PhonlamaiPhoto, Sigrid Gombert, Thomas Barwick, Thomas Bullock, Mark Mainz/BC, James Devaney, jackscoldsweat, Comstock Images, Emir Memedovski, Gabriela Tulian, LWA/Dann Tardif, Photos.com Plus, cirano83, BahadirTanriover, Deborah Harrison, Dennis Macdonald, TravisPhotoWorks, blackestockphoto, David Paul Morris, Fancy/Veer/Corbis, GraphicaArtis, Fredrik Skold, Fred Stein Archive, Hannelore Foerster, MacFormat Magazine, Oleksiy Maksymenko, BG008/Bauer-Griffin, Fitria Ramli / EyeEm, RichLegg, Kantapat Phutthamkul, Gareth Cattermole/TAS, Maximilian Stock Ltd., Michael Ochs Archives, Photos.com/Thinkstock, Science Photo Library, Patchareeporn Sakoolchai; GREENPEACE; I. PREYSLER; ISTOCKPHOTO/Getty Images Sales Spain, monkeybusinessimages, Joel Carillet, cindygoff; PIRIFORM; SHUTTERSTOCK/Linda Bestwick, Mike Kuhlman, Giovanni G, Dima Moroz, kibri_ho; SOUTHWEST NEWSSWNS; WWF INTERNATIONAL; Chris Griffiths; Iwan Baan; ARCHIVO SANTILLANA

Cover Photo: GETTY IMAGES SALES SPAIN/Martin Dimitrov

Texts:
p15 Text adapted from article 'Dear Juliet: the fans who write to Shakespeare's heroine' by John Hooper, 19 May 2010, *The Guardian*, Copyright Guardian News & Media 2017, reprinted by permission.

p87 Text adapted from article 'Why starting a business at 19 was one of the best decisions I've ever made' by Chris Griffiths, 17 September 2013, published in *The Globe and Mail*, reprinted by permission of the author.

We would like to thank the following reviewers for their valuable feedback which has made Personal Best possible. We extend our thanks to the many teachers and students not mentioned here.
Brad Bawtinheimer, Manuel Hidalgo, Paulo Dantas, Diana Bermúdez, Laura Gutiérrez, Hardy Griffin, Angi Conti, Christopher Morabito, Hande Kokce, Jorge Lobato, Leonardo Mercato, Mercilinda Ortiz, Wendy López

The Publisher has made every effort to trace the owner of copyright material; however, the Publisher will correct any involuntary omission at the earliest opportunity.

Printed in Brazil by Forma Certa Grafica Digital

Lote: 778634
Cod: 290521018